THE
LIFE OF
MARY
BAKER
EDDY

MRS. EDDY'S HISTORY

I HAVE not had sufficient interest in the matter to read or to note from others' reading what the enemies of Christian Science are said to be circulating regarding my history, but my friends have read Sibyl Wilbur's book, "Life of Mary Baker Eddy," and request the privilege of buying, circulating, and recommending it to the public. I briefly declare that nothing has occurred in my life's experience which, if correctly narrated and understood, could injure me; and not a little is already reported of the good accomplished therein, the self-sacrifice, etc., that has distinguished all my working years.

I thank Miss Wilbur and the Concord Publishing Company for their unselfed labors in placing this book before the public, and hereby say that they have my permission to publish and circulate this work.

MARY BAKER EDDY

The above statement by Mrs. Eddy was published in the Christian Science Sentinel of March 12, 1910

THE LIFE OF MARY BAKER EDDY

Sibyl Wilbur

THE CHRISTIAN SCIENCE PUBLISHING SOCIETY
BOSTON, MASSACHUSETTS, U.S.A.

Authorized literature
of The First Church of Christ, Scientist

ISBN: 0-87510-285-9

Library of Congress Catalog Card Number: 39-2412

Printed in the United States of America

Introduction: Twentieth-Century Biographers Series

IN THE closing years of the twentieth century, there is a growing awareness that the hundred years since 1900 will have registered a magnitude and pace of change, in every aspect of human affairs, which probably exceeds any historic precedent. In political, social and religious institutions and attitudes, in the sciences and industry, in the arts, in how we communicate with each other, humanity has traveled light years in this century.

"Earth's actors," said the Founder of Christian Science, Mary Baker Eddy, "change earth's scenes. . . ." As we look back over the landscape of this century, some towering figures emerge into view: political leaders, scientists and inventors, authors, artists and musicians, social and religious pioneers, industrialists, and many others who helped "change earth's scenes."

Mary Baker Eddy is regarded as a major religious figure of the twentieth century and as a notable example of the emergence of women in significant leadership roles. Although her book *Science and Health with Key to the Scriptures* was published in 1875, in 1992 it was recognized by the Women's National Book Association as one of 75 major books by women whose words have changed the world.

Mrs. Eddy's works are visible today in virtually

every country of the world: in church buildings, in Christian Science Reading Rooms, in the distribution of the newspaper and religious periodicals she established and their derivative broadcast forms, in the wide circulation of her own writings, and most important, in the way hundreds of thousands of people conduct their everyday lives.

Mrs. Eddy wrote only briefly about herself, in a short volume titled *Retrospection and Introspection*. She discouraged personal adulation or attention, clearly hoping that people would find her character and purpose in her own writings rather than in the biographic record. Yet, she came to see the need for an accurate account of her life and gave specific if possibly reluctant acquiescence in the year 1910 to the publishing of the first of the biographies — Sybil Wilbur's *Mary Baker Eddy*.

As we near the close of a century which directly witnessed some of Mary Baker Eddy's major contributions, The Christian Science Publishing Society, the publishing arm of the church she established, has reexamined the church's obligations to future generations and centuries, in providing an appreciation and understanding of her remarkable career. The Publishing Society now welcomes the opportunity of publishing, and keeping in print, a major shelf of works on Mary Baker Eddy under the general series title: "Twentieth-Century Biographers Series."

Mrs. Eddy's career and works have stirred humanity in the twentieth century and will continue to do so. Perhaps an appropriate introduction for this series is captured in her statement, in the Preface to *Science and Health with Key to the Scriptures:* "The time for thinkers has come." In that spirit, this series of biographies by many different twentieth-century writers is offered to all those who, now and in the future, want to know more about this remarkable woman, her life, and her work.

*I*T is commonly said that, if he would be heard, none should write in advance of his times. That I do not believe. Only, it does not matter how few listen. I believe that we are close upon a great and deep spiritual change. I believe a new redemption is even now conceived of the Divine Spirit in the human heart, that is itself as a woman, broken in dreams and yet sustained in faith, patient, long-suffering, looking towards home. I believe that though the Reign of Peace may be yet a long way off, it is drawing near: and that Who shall save us anew shall come divinely as a Woman, to save as Christ saved, but not as He did, to bring with Her a sword.

William Sharp (Fiona MacLeod)
in *The Isle of Dreams*

PUBLISHER'S NOTE

In this as in earlier editions, textual changes have been made for the purpose of inducing greater factual accuracy. These changes are based on material pertaining to the life of Mary Baker Eddy which has come to light since the author finished her manuscript.

CONTENTS

CONTENTS

ILLUSTRATIONS

INTRODUCTION

NO mystery to-day surrounds the life story of MARY BAKER EDDY. Her birth, her ancestry for two hundred years, her education, her social development, and her individual service to the world have been scrutinized with the strong search-lights of both love and criticism. Every event of her long career has been established by unimpeachable records and testimony. It is no longer possible to invent fiction concerning the environment in which she was born and reared or the acts which made up her life.

It is possible, however, to minds careless of verity or those dominated by prejudice, to distort facts by exaggerated statement, to deduce erroneous conclusions from improper handling of data, to make wilful and far-fetched conjectures, and to suppress illuminative information in relating incidents,—information which would reveal the true inwardness of a situation otherwise left dark and sinister. Such coloring and molding of evidence is a modern method used for deducing a readable story from statistical documents.

A story told dramatically, with high lights of speculation and deep shadows of conjecture, with all the fascinating and engaging charm of the narrator's personal fancy woven into the texture, does make racy and entertaining reading. It requires a strong mind to hold fast to simple truth under such guidance. Because of the pleasure taken in a good story, whole pages of history are mistold and some of the noblest characters in the world's annals have been misrepresented.

The average modern, rationalistic and sophisticated, would far rather read Renan's "Life of Jesus," with its vivid coloring, its subtle suggestion, its bold deduction and human sympathy, than the simple gospel of St. Mark. Renan flatters his intellect and panders to his sensuality; he is made to feel himself superior in intelligence to the Lord of this earth, and his sensual nature is elevated in importance by the argument that it was the illusion of an impassioned woman which gave to the world the idea of a Deity resurrected from the grave.

What an interpretation of Jesus' agony and victory and its proclamation by the purified and sanctified Mary Magdalene,— she who gave Christendom that immortal phrase, "He is risen!" To be dominated by such interpretation is no less than a moral catastrophe occurring in the region of consciousness; for not only does Renan's "Life of Jesus" entertain, flatter, and excite the intellect as an adventure in the realm of ideas, but, as in the case of most intellectual audacities, it leaves the adventurer in disastrous confusion. Renan, indeed, professes a delicate and reverent appreciation for the divine character he so ruthlessly handles and at the close of his drama you behold him a dejected chorus with tear-bedimmed eyes, inviting you to sigh with him over the monstrous blunder of Gethsemane. But the reader finds no tears to shed. Renan has skilfully unpacked his heart of its treasure, and, by lure and wile, stolen its birthright, its title to divine heritage.

Immensely destructive is the usual commendation of this "Life." Destructive to what? Can imagination and diction destroy reality, or, rather, can they destroy that faith by which the world lives, the faith in the reality of spiritual experience?

Now the simple gospel narrative tells a straight story of Jesus' life. It is not concerned to compare the subject of its text to other men of the times in order to prove his reality. It declares his acts as they were, whether raising Jairus' daughter, walking upon the Sea of Galilee, or feeding the multitude; it reveals him scourged, spat upon, and crucified, without comment, and without comment relates his resurrection and ascension. The gospel is there for all time. It was in no haste to win attention and therefore did not need coloring or tricking out in fancy. Yes, the gospel stands after all documentary investigation, after the best modern documentary and comparative criticism can do, even after Renan and Strauss.

I have a life story to relate and I plant myself unreservedly on the methods of St. Mark. St. Mark, I believe, was a scribe who related what he had been able to gather from witnesses in a direct and unvarnished way. Now I shall endeavor to do simply that. It is not for me to explain or to expound. The facts of this life shall be left to elucidate themselves when set in an orderly and unembellished array before the world; the import must carry to that consciousness able to receive it. I shall concern myself only to report the truth.

In gathering the facts from the past I have often encountered the disappointments of imperfect memories of a small, a very small, group of men and women of advanced years who knew Mrs. Eddy in her youth; but the records in town books have yielded sufficient information to trace accurately Mrs. Eddy's residence from year to year.   These data refute certain unfounded assertions which float about as loose rumors, such as that related by an aged woman in Malden and printed in the form of an interview in the Boston *Herald*. This story was that a Mary Baker told fortunes by reading cards in a mean street in Boston before the Civil War, and had told this woman's fortune and she believed the fortune-teller to be Mrs. Eddy, the founder of Christian Science. In the late fifties Mrs. Eddy was no longer Mary Baker, but had been twice married. She was then Mrs. Patterson, an almost helpless invalid, living in North Groton, a village in northern New Hampshire. She had not visited Boston for a long period of years and did not visit it for many years to come. Another rumor there was that a certain Mrs. Glover who was a spiritualistic medium in and around Boston during the sixties, could be identified with Mary Baker Eddy as one and the same individual. It is not necessary to discover who that Mary Baker was or who that Mrs. Glover, or to establish that they were individuals in nowise related to Mrs. Eddy. It is only necessary to tell minutely the facts of Mrs. Eddy's life which are exclusive of all practices of charlatanism, and are at all times stainless and honorable.

All statements of facts made in this narrative are

founded on reliable evidence, town registers, church books, and court records. As to the memories of a few old people interviewed by the author, who associated with Mary Baker in her youth, it must be said that they were not always all that could be desired, and it is fortunate that public records can usually be depended upon to rectify careless assertion. Compared together these memories sometimes contradicted each other; referred back to themselves, they frequently shifted and showed instability; and a deplorable thing was that they betrayed evidence of having been tampered with by suggestion, the imagination having been incited by vanity or cupidity.

To remember a thing suggested, with a gift in full view, is a natural enough performance to children and to those in second childhood. But what should be said of the bribers in such a case? It is to the honor of human nature that both men and women have resisted the offer of large sums of money to remember that which would have been convenient to the theories of malicious-minded critics who preceded me in their investigations.

So if the intelligence was sometimes staggered in the search for the truth about this illustrious woman by encounter with malicious inventions, clearly discernible because of the known facts, the provable facts, which correct them, it was also frequently cheered and uplifted by touching the store of thought emanating from persons "whose spirits and cleanliness and freshness of mind and body make old age lovely and desirable." The writer has nowhere interfered with these memories, neither in interview nor in transcription; and at the risk of seeming unkind to lonely and impoverished old men and women, whom a slight kindness by way of gift might have enlivened, has refrained from any such act, lest it might be said, to the detriment of this history, that the writer, too, had set forth an invention, instead of the truth.

But it is a task which I have imposed upon myself to take the wheat of memory and leave the chaff. I have refused ignoble deductions volunteered as information. I have refrained from handling the relics of rural jealousy strong enough to endure for eighty years, asseverating what it merely conjectured almost a century ago concerning a nature it could not then and cannot now comprehend.

I ask the reader to refuse to accept as biography such gossip which the ephemeral press has detailed. For truth's sake, divest your mind of all speculation and conjecture by which the true story of this life has been so ruthlessly caricatured; divest it at least for the time, and approach without prejudice for an acquaintance with this nobly wise and inspired character. We as human beings owe something to the consciousness of the age, the great highway of souls to come after us. We should make the path straight by rejecting wilful scandal, however amusing and diverting, and by choosing to know the simple gospel truth.

THE
LIFE OF
MARY
BAKER
EDDY

CHAPTER I

ANCESTRY AND GENEALOGY

FORTY years after the close of the American Revolution Mary Baker was born in the town of Bow, New Hampshire. Her birthplace was a farmhouse in the midst of cultivated acres, situated on a crest of hills overlooking the broad valley of the Merrimac River. Bow was not a village, but a cluster of farms with a town government and four or five district schools, centers of education and rural politics. There was a meeting-house, as the homely phrase of those days described the church edifice, but many of the God-fearing of the community attended divine worship either in the adjoining town of Pembroke, across the river, or in the neighboring city of Concord, the capital of the state, from which Bow is five miles distant.

Bow was a rural settlement, but it was not remote from the stirring forces of the life of its day. The men who owned its homesteads had been born in the heat of political struggle. Their mothers' birth-pangs coincided with those of a nation. They were born individualists and democrats. New Hampshire, a mountainous state, originally covered with dense forests, had presented to its settlers a stern struggle with nature. The grandsires of the men of this day had been forest clearers, woodsmen who had hewn down a wilderness of primeval pines over two hundred feet in height. Their sons had grown tall and sinewy like the trees they felled.

1

New Hampshire lay on the Canadian frontier and the French and Indian War had swept it. Its exposed settlements were constantly menaced by the Indians, and, during the wars with England, subject to descents from Canada. In those early days the sons of New Hampshire held back the red men from the less exposed colonies, themselves coming face to face with that treacherous warfare of the forests. This life of woodsman, mountaineer, and Indian fighter had produced a generation of physical giants. Intellectually these men had been well-nigh as vigorously exercised. The colonial settlement had been fraught with bitterest disputes over grants and regrants from England, and the surveying of those woodlands was made in the heat of contention. New Hampshire sent its delegates to the first Continental Congress, and two signatures stand for this state on that charter of American liberty, the Declaration of Independence. Two delegates represented her in the Federal Congress, and, ninth of the states in ratifying the Constitution, New Hampshire in a critical hour insured the success of the Union. Two New Hampshire regiments were at the battle of Bunker Hill. The battle of Bennington, that turned the scale of the war, was won by New Hampshire and Vermont troops under General Stark, who bore a commission from New Hampshire. All through the War of Independence New Hampshire's contingent to the army was liberal. When the war closed New Hampshire men returned to the duties of clearing farms, building schoolhouses, and worshiping God. Dartmouth College was founded in 1769; and soon the little red schoolhouses marked the crossroads newly surveyed. There was a high average attendance at these district schools during the winter months and learning was prized in every home. Thus were men living, acting, and feeling in the early years of the nineteenth century in this particular community. Religion, schooling, politics, and every man his own master, the owner of his own land, made that early American life a throbbing, vital experience.

Men who counted in these communities could not be ignorant and unsocial. They were robust from contending with nature and savages, intensely patriotic and versed in statecraft, as they had but recently been evolving a constitution for the new world; religious, for they were reestablishing a church of Christ, suiting it to democracy where each man must meet God for himself; scholarly they were, too, in a large sense, for they read the best books of England and studied the journals of the day, jealously watching the Old World, that the New World of their dreams might not be found wanting in intellectual progress. These men founded colleges.

For seven generations the Bakers had been in New England. Their history is exactly the history of the typical son of New Hampshire. They had swung the ax, carried the surveyor's chain, shouldered the musket, fought off the savages, and taken part in government and the establishing of churches and schools. Mark Baker lived on his own farm, a tract of five hundred acres inherited with his brother James. His father was the largest taxpayer in the town. Mark Baker was a justice of the peace for his township, a deacon of the church, a school committeeman, and

for many years chaplain of the state militia. His
friends were the clergy, the lawyers of Concord and
surrounding towns, a governor of his state, upon
whose staff a son served. A future president of the
United States was an occasional guest at his home.
But his friends also were astute men of business, mill
owners, builders, men destined to change the character of the state from agricultural to manufacturing.

The family life at Bow was not set in a deadly
routine of depressing labor. To so conceive it is to
fail to rise to the true viewpoint which shall help us to
understand the character we are considering. There
never was a time in history when a people were more
alive and progressive than the Americans after the
War of Independence. There was no neighborhood
in America more admirably situated to reap the full
benefit of that peculiar, intense, spiritual culture than
was the town of Bow, five miles from the city of
Concord. Franklin Pierce and Daniel Webster were
reared under these identical conditions. Emerson and
Hawthorne have declared the conditions admirable
for developing genius.

Mary Baker Eddy's ancestry can be traced clearly
through seven generations to the first Baker in America,
her earliest immigrant ancestor being John Baker, who
was freeman in Charlestown, Massachusetts, in 1634.
The generations succeeding, eliminating all but the direct line, are Thomas, of Roxbury; John, of Roxbury;
a second Thomas, of Roxbury, who married Sarah
Pike; Joseph, born 1714, deacon of the Congregational
church, who held a captain's commission. He was the
surveyor of several towns in that part of New Hamp-

BENNING WENTWORTH, Esq;
Captain-General and GOVERNOUR in Chief, in and over His
MAJESTY's Province of *New-Hampshire* in NEW-ENGLAND, &c.

To *Joseph Baker Gentleman* Greeting.

BY Virtue of the Power and Authority, in and by His Majesty's Royal Commission to Me granted, to be Captain-General, &c. over this His Majesty's Province of *New-Hampshire*, aforesaid ; I do (by these Presents) reposing especial Trust and Confidence in your Loyalty, Courage and good Conduct, constitute and appoint You the said *Joseph Baker* to be *Captain* of the Foot *Company in the Place commonly called Plasury by the Name of Suncook* in *Col. Lauthens Lovewells Regiment*

You are therefore carefully and diligently to discharge the Duty of a *Captain* in leading, ordering and exercising said *Company* in Arms both inferiour Officers and Soldiers, and to keep them in good Order and Discipline ; hereby commanding them to obey you as their *Captain* and your self to observe and follow such Orders and Instructions, as you shall from Time to Time receive from Me, or the Commander in Chief for the Time being, or other your superior Officers for His Majesty's Service, according to Military Rules and Discipline, pursuant to the Trust reposed in You.

Given under my Hand and Seal at Arms, at Portsmouth, *the Thirtieth* Day of *May* in the *Thirty first* Year of the Reign of His Majesty King GEORGE the Second, Annoq; Domini, 1758

By His EXCELLENCY's
Command
Theodore Atkinson

B Wentworth

CERTIFICATE FROM GOVERNOR BENNING WENTWORTH
OF NEW HAMPSHIRE
Appointing Mrs. Eddy's Great-Grandfather Captain
of the Foot Company at Suncook, now Pembroke

America seeking religious liberty and bringing a rich
store of memories and traditions. Among them they
possessed a heavy sword encased in a brass scabbard,
with the inscription of an ancestor's name that stated
it had been bestowed by Sir William Wallace. General John McNeil of New Hampshire, who won distinction by leading a bayonet charge in the battle of
Chippewa in the War of 1812, was a cousin of Marion
Moor Baker.[1]

Leaving the Baker genealogy for Mrs. Eddy's maternal ancestry, in the same history of New Hampshire
families it is stated that Mark Baker married Abigail
Ambrose of Pembroke. She was the daughter of
Deacon Nathaniel Ambrose, a man at once pious and

---

[1] This is the McNeil connection. I shall not trace it beyond America.
Fanny McNeil, niece of Franklin Pierce, afterwards wife of Judge Potter of
Washington, was a daughter of that General John McNeil. She claimed a
cousinship with Mary Baker Eddy. This Fanny McNeil, who during Pierce's
administration frequently relieved his invalid wife of social duties as mistress
of the White House, traced as she supposed the McNeil line to which she belonged directly to Sir John McNeil of Edinburgh. She adopted the McNeil
crest for her coat of arms. Mrs. Eddy visited her in Washington in 1882.
Together they made a journey to the grave of General McNeil. They thoroughly discussed the McNeil family history, the bravery of its fighting heroes,
the deep religious conviction of its covenanting faith. Mrs. Eddy recalled
her grandmother's influence upon her whole life, an influence which shall
presently be indicated. She therefore adopted with her cousin, Fanny Mc-
Neil, the McNeil crest and coat of arms. She adopted it for sentiment and
affection. Its motto could not have better expressed the traits of character
transmitted through a long line to her. It is: *Vincere aut Mori*. The crest
was carved in the mahogany of the lintel above the inner vestibule entrance
of her beautiful home on Commonwealth Avenue, Boston, where she resided
before her retirement to Pleasant View. She also used the crest as a seal
and expressed her pleasure in the sentiment of the Scotch strain by having
the coat of arms embroidered on white silk and hung in her library.

But a sudden denial to her rights so to enjoy this connection with the
Scotch McNeils came through a Scottish descendant of the McNeils living in
Aberdeen. Whereupon Mrs. Eddy had a thorough investigation of her genealogy made and, being unable to establish the accuracy of Fanny McNeil's
genealogical claims, upon which she had hitherto rested, she requested that
all biographers refrain from connecting her with the Right Honorable Sir
John McNeil, G. C. B., of Edinburgh, sometime ambassador to Persia. It is
therefore sufficient to state that Mary Baker Eddy's great-grandparents were
kin to the McNeils; that General John McNeil, the American hero, was her
grandmother's cousin.

shire which was claimed by Massachusetts,
the rest, of Pembroke, where he afterward
He married, 1739, Hannah Lovewell, only
of Captain John Lovewell. Hannah was h
was heir to one third the estate of Captain
and inherited with her brothers the lands a
her distinguished father in Pembroke.

Captain Joseph Baker had a son Joseph,
who married Marion Moor,[1] daughter of
William Moor of Lovell's Expedition, a de
the Scotch Covenanters. They settled in I
youngest son was Mark Baker, born 1785
of Mary Baker. So the generations run
Mark, Joseph, Joseph, Thomas, John, Th
— taking the record back almost to Plym

An examination of the genealogy of
the Bakers reveals that the influx was of
through the maternal strains. The Pikes
land have an honorable and interestin
Hannah Lovewell, great-grandmother of
and born just one century before her,
courageous heart of her soldier father.
Lovewell lost his life in a severe fight wi
at Pigwacket, now Fryeburg, Maine, an
desperate that it is recorded in colonial
known as Lovewell's Fight. This Lo
was an ensign in Cromwell's army an
great age of one hundred and twenty
Lovewell was one of the bravest women

Marion Moor, the paternal grand
Baker, was a descendant of the McNe
Her forbears, both McNeils and N

[1] In some records: Maryann or Mary

public-spirited. He gave so much time and money for the "Ambrose" Congregational church in Pembroke that it became known by his name. Mrs. Eddy's mother and the grandmother of Hoke Smith, ex-governor of Georgia, and later, United States Senator from Georgia, were sisters. Governor Smith's father wrote the following letter at the time of a public discussion of Mrs. Eddy's family, a discussion which lacked a proper comprehension of the family's standing in its community and its honorable connections. Mr. Smith sent the letter to the Committee on Publication of The Mother Church, which allows this reprint:

582 West Peachtree Street, ATLANTA, GA., Dec. 28, 1906

I have known the Rev. Mary Baker Eddy from childhood. She is my first cousin. Her mother was my mother's younger sister. She [Mary Baker Eddy] was always a beloved visitor in our home. We corresponded for several years while I was in college; the correspondence ended with my regret. I have always admired my cousin's sincerity and devotion to good works. Her brother Albert was one of the ablest lawyers of New Hampshire; but Mary was deemed the most scholarly member of her family. She has always held a sacred place in my heart. It gives me great pleasure to find that God is always protecting her.

H. H. SMITH

CHAPTER II

CHILDHOOD DAYS

IF in describing the conditions of life which bred New Hampshire giants, with its granite in their will and its hemlock in their soul's fiber, one should neglect to indicate the beauty of summer days or the clear, cold magnificence of winter months in that mountainous upland, one would err in stating but half-truths of the environing influences, even though his efforts were but timid strokes.

The allurement which drew settlers into this region in the early days was doubtless the glorified face of Nature. Here was no prairie, easily tilled; here were no gold mines, promising sudden wealth. But there was a constant uplift for the heart, vaguely felt more often than it was understood. There is an enchantment in the New Hampshire panorama, the series of great pictures which unroll in one continuous stretch of glorious scenery, — an enchantment so pervading that it is never forgotten. A logger on the mountain-side to-day looks down with indifference upon a transient tourist. The logger's cup of content is full if he can make a bare living in the forest.

Summer spreads for the son of New Hampshire a shimmering wonder of green and gold with silver rivers winding placidly, fed by those headlong torrents farther up in the rocky hills, where the burning breasts of the mountains are lifted from their headless shoulders. There, too, like Victory's, is seen the stride of their sheer descents, throwing back the clouds for draperies. This is summer, — summer of ripening grain fields, summer of odorous, melodious south winds, balsam-scented and hemlock-tuned.

Autumn's brilliant moment of splendor passes and the traveler flees before the sere and drear November, gray, brown, and sodden with fog and freezing tears. The mountaineer stays and cuts his logs. Now the great nature painting of all the seasons is preparing. The frost has bitten, the snow has fallen, and once more the sun shines forth. Behold the blue peaks, lifted above the green of the hemlock and the pine, and the dazzling sweep of virgin snow. The air is stimulating and purifying. Over this land bends a sky which gathers its true sons to her heart, whose stars are eloquent, whose storms are majestic, whose day-dawns are passionately tender.

The farmer and the mountaineer of to-day feel the divine salute of Nature as did the early settlers of the state. They are sustained in their life of toil by the same enchantment. But one circumstance of life, one sacred influence they have lost, homely but potent. That is the fireplace of their ancestors. In the living-room of the early farmhouses huge logs were burned, and this resinous fire, like a pure spiritual force subduing nature to the will of man, yielded a glory to the homely walls, lighted up the faces of the family circle, drawing each member into a hallowed area, making a sanctified center of their existence.

So it should be realized it was the union of beauty and severity that gave to the New Hampshire character at its best the giant soul, — giant for wrestling toil, giant for deep and long-enduring pain, giant in its capacity for thinking and loving.

Mark Baker's farm in Bow lay on the uplands. It was cleared and cultivated by his father and older brothers before him. The farmhouse was situated on the summit of a hill from which, in gradual undulations, the land sloped to the Merrimac River. The view included three townships and was broad and picturesque rather than grand. Mountains there are in the distance; but this region of the state is scarcely in the foot-hills, though its rugged uplift gives promise of the vast range on the far horizon.

The farmhouse faced the east. It was unpainted in those days and consisted of a two-story-and-a-half main building with a sloping-roofed ell. In the main building was the living-room with its great fireplace and the best chamber adjoining. Above these were two chambers and the garret. In the rear were kitchen and butteries with chambers above. The stables were on the west, so that a long feeding-shed connecting them with the house-shed at right angles made a wind-break against the north wind for the dooryard. This was a sunny spot for the farm fowls, and a place also where logs were trimmed, horses groomed, and wagons loaded for the market.

A sunny garden surrounded the front door in which in summer were lilacs and roses and old-fashioned marigolds. To the east was the orchard enclosed by a stone wall three feet broad, part of which is still intact, though necessarily it has been rebuilt

MRS. EDDY'S BIRTHPLACE, BOW, NEW HAMPSHIRE

As it looked when she was a child. From a chalk drawing by Rufus Baker, steel engraved

and repaired innumerable times. The breadth of the walls tells the story of the labor involved in clearing the farm not only of timber but of rocks. Across the road were pastures and grain-fields, while to the north and beyond the orchard and stables were woodlands.

That the house was well constructed and comfortable was attested by its century-old frame which stood swept by storm and brooded over by sunshine on the untenanted lands still belonging to Baker descendants until 1910. The sheds were torn away and only the shell remained. It was removed to a place by itself on the edge of the pasture land, and one old apple-tree bloomed each spring at the chamber window where Mary Baker first saw the light and throughout the period of her earthly existence. The author ate of its fruit while Mrs. Eddy yet resided at Pleasant View.

The day of her birth was July 16, 1821. Mary was the youngest child. Her brothers were Samuel, Albert, and George; her sisters, Abigail and Martha. The children were not far apart in years. Albert was eleven, and Abigail less than six when Mary was born. Albert and Abigail, of them all, were especially tender to the baby sister, and in the years to come exercised greater care for her, — the brother in her education, and the sister during her invalid widowhood.

A beloved member of the household when Mary was born was the venerable grandmother Baker who received this babe into her arms with a special solicitation to God, and bestowed upon the child the name Mary. Accordingly her mother named her Mary Morse Baker. Grandmother Baker's chair stood by the

fireplace. She overlooked the farmyard and its busy
occupations when she glanced up from her knitting;
or, sending her glances out through the front door,
open on a heated summer day, she saw the bees drows-
ing in the flowers, the bending grain beyond where
the south winds made billows of light and shade. A
precious care was in her charge. Ever and anon she
touched with her foot the rocker of the cradle or bent
to scan the features of the babe sleeping there, and so
through the heat of August and the cool September
she was the good angel watching and guarding.

The household tasks were not light for the mother
of early New England days; she could not brood over
a cradle. Mrs. Baker was industrious and placid of
spirit, and the placidity meant much for the spirit of
her home. She could brew and bake and care for her
dairy, scour and sew and weave and dye — all women
did this in those days — and it is reported of Mrs.
Baker that she was "capable." But Mrs. Baker found
time for the unusual, for visiting the sick and administering to the needy; for entertaining her friends and
maintaining the social life; for overseeing her children's education and holding the family to high spiritual ideals. It is not sufficient to say of her that she
was a capable, conscientious New England woman;
this she was, but more. And she has left behind her
memories that attest it.

Mrs. Baker was one of those rare mothers of that
period who found time for reading; and when guests
filled her house, — relatives, clergymen, or men of
affairs, — her judgments and observations were sought
and her influence in conversation was reported inspir-

ing and uplifting. She was no Penelope, silent at her own fireside while the guests alone enjoyed social discourse. From touching mind and heart with these guests while serving them with hospitable attentions, she deduced ideas for the benefit of her children, ideas which she applied to each according to his temperament. After her death the clergyman, the Rev. Richard S. Rust, D. D., "who," Mrs. Eddy has said, "knew my sainted mother in all the walks of life," [1] wrote of her as one who possessed a presence which made itself felt like gentle dew and cheerful light. He said she possessed a strong intellect, a sympathizing heart, and a placid spirit, and as a mother was untiring in her efforts to secure the happiness of her family.

But the hands of this mother who labored untiringly were filled with duties in a home made prosperous through personal toil. It was an early American farm and the farm life hummed industriously from early morn until starlight, forwarded by the energy and will of both parents. Visible through the small-paned windows was the farm's center of activity where the father and brothers went to and fro, now to the fields and now to the town, removing logs and rock, tending sheep and cattle, handling grain and fruits. Within the kitchen, mother and daughters worked not less continuously, laundry and dairy, needle and loom, claiming the attention in rhythmic succession. And of all these workers one knows the mother was earliest astir and latest to rest.

And so Mary Baker grew through infancy at her grandmother's knee and imbibed her grandmother's

1 "Retrospection and Introspection," p. 5.

stories and songs; her grandmother's recollections
and store of spiritual wisdom were poured into the
hungering mind agape like a young robin's mouth.
And what stories these were and how they thrilled
the awakening imagination! for this grandmother,
descended from the Scotch Covenanters, could tell
dramatic tales of a land torn by religious dissensions
for nearly a century.

We can imagine the little Mary on a certain day
taken by her grandmother to visit the garret. Up
the steep stairs they climb together, the baby hand
confidingly in the brown and wrinkled one. Up
here under the low-slanting roof, amidst odors of
lavender, catnip, and sage, in a dusty gray twilight, weird because of the stray sunbeams that pierce
it, grandmother takes from the depths of an old
chest the sword of a far-away Scottish ancestor, the
blade rusting in its brass scabbard. The child is
allowed to handle it, tries to draw the blade, and
with great eyes hears its history. Then as she still
tugs at it, grandmother kneeling back on her heels
sings in quavering accents, "Scots who hae wi' Wallace bled."

"How long ago was it that Sir William Wallace
drove the English out of the highlands and back to
their own lands?"

"Five hundred years ago. Yes, for five hundred
years that sword has been handed down from kinsman to kinsman. My father's father's fathers were
Highlanders, wore the kilt and trampled the purple
heather and played the bagpipes that summoned
the clans."

"But why did your hero ancestors come to this land, grandmother?"

"We came away for religious liberty, child, that we might worship God according to our conscience."

"But I should not have run away. And I should have worshiped God according to my conscience. And they could have taken their swords and killed me."

"Ay, they did that, my bairn; the blood was spilled of many a God-fearing man. Your ancestors wrote their names on the covenant in blood, and that meant they would keep the covenant with their life-blood. Ay, dearie, dearie; it was a long and bitter and terrible strife, but religion was more to our ancestors than their lives."

"What is religion?" asks the child, dropping the sword and resting her hands on her grandmother's shoulders.

"Religion is to know and worship God."

And there in the twilight of the garret the child fell a-wondering, doubtless making then and there her covenant, while the grandmother returned to rummaging in the old chest which had crossed the ocean. Now the grandmother took from the chest some old newspapers, yellow with age, together with certain old manuscripts. She carried these down to the living-room and there on occasions read from them various stories to the little girl.

These stories were of Washington, of Valley Forge, of the surrender of Lord Cornwallis, of the farewell of the commander-in-chief to his troops, and of the death and burial of the first American president. The stories made a deep impression on the child's mind and she put many questions to her father concerning these events, causing the theme of the family conversation around the fireside to be set to a patriotic key.

"I remember," says Mrs. Eddy in "Retrospection and Introspection," [1] written at least sixty years after these times, "reading, in my childhood, certain manuscripts containing Scriptural sonnets, besides other verses and enigmas which my grandmother said were written by my great-grandmother. . . . My childhood was also gladdened by one of my Grandmother Baker's books, printed in olden type and replete with the phraseology current in the seventeenth and eighteenth centuries. Among grandmother's treasures were some newspapers, yellow with age. Some of these, however, were not very ancient, nor had they crossed the ocean; for they were American newspapers, one of which contained a full account of the death and burial of George Washington."

The grandmother cherished the idea that Hannah More was a relative in some way to her mother. She talked of the pious authoress and of the fact that her mother had written the manuscripts she displayed. The family rejected the idea of relationship with the English authoress, but Mary, listening to these discussions of literary talents inherent in the blood of her forebears, early resolved to grow up wise enough to write a book. There is no doubt that the great resolutions of her life, already infused with tenacious qualities of loving and willing, were made under the inspiration of the religious grandmother.

[1] "Retrospection and Introspection," pp. 1, 2.

From the reading of these old books and papers the child acquired a grave and dignified way of speaking. Mary's sayings were quoted frequently, in a different spirit, by different members of the family. The grandmother would repeat them dotingly, the father, with grim humor to his guests, and her gifted brother, teasingly and lovingly. He was at this time preparing for college.

Mark Baker was too busy a man for much leisure with his family, but he was interested in the welfare of all his children. Mary, the youngest daughter of the flock, delicate in health from her birth, was not easily understood by this man of iron will. She perplexed him with her sage sayings and grave doings. The strange stories told about this little one by the grandmother and mother made him wonder sometimes with deep concern.

The story that most perplexed him was that of Mary's "Voices." When but eight years old Mary frequently came to her mother, asking her earnestly what she wanted of her. "Nothing, child," her mother would reply.

"But, mother, who *did* call me?" she would beseech. "I heard some one call 'Mary' three times!" [1]

This assertion that some one was calling her was continually made by the child for nearly a year, until her parents grew anxious for her health. "Take the books away from her," said her father; "her brain is too big for her body."

Accordingly she was sent to romp in the fields, to gather berries and wild flowers along the walls, to sing

[1] "Retrospection and Introspection," p. 8.

among the bees. She must not hear so many exciting
tales, or be allowed to brood in fancy. As the summer turned into fall she must needs be more indoors,
but her brother Albert found her on a drear November evening huddled close to the pasture wall, singing
softly. The noisy pigs were squealing in the sty and
the child had stolen out from the warm fireside to sing
to them, thinking they needed comfort before they
would go to sleep. Carrying her in on his shoulder,
her brother deposited her in her grandmother's arms,
telling merrily of the quaint lullaby.

"But," said the child excitedly, "they are crying
and it must be because it's cold and dark out there."

"God cares for all His creatures, my bairn," said
the grandmother, soothing and caressing the chilled
little maiden.

The voices had not ceased to call the little girl,
but Mary had ceased to respond to them. Mrs. Eddy
has told of these persistent callings which were heard
by her for some twelve months, and in her autobiography says:

One day, when my cousin, Mehitable Huntoon, was
visiting us, and I sat in a little chair by her side, in the
same room with grandmother,—the call again came, so
loud that Mehitable heard it, though I had ceased to notice
it. Greatly surprised, my cousin turned to me and said,
"Your mother is calling you!" . . . I then left the room,
went to my mother, and once more asked her if she had
summoned me? She answered as always before. Then I
earnestly declared my cousin had heard the voice, and said
that mother wanted me. Accordingly she returned with me
to grandmother's room, and led my cousin into an adjoining apartment. The door was ajar, and I listened with

bated breath. Mother told Mehitable all about this mysterious voice, and asked if she really did hear Mary's name pronounced in audible tones. My cousin answered quickly, and emphasized her affirmation. That night, before going to rest, my mother read to me the Scriptural narrative of little Samuel, and bade me, when the voice called again, to reply as he did, "Speak, Lord; for Thy servant heareth." The voice came; but I was afraid, and did not answer. Afterward I wept, and prayed that God would forgive me, resolving to do, next time, as my mother had bidden me. When the call came again I did answer, in the words of Samuel, but never again to the material senses was that mysterious call repeated. [1]

What wisdom and love in this spiritual-minded mother, causing her to guide her child into the full benefit of her first deep religious experience! She did not contradict, rebuke, or deride; but guided gently part of the way, then left the child to go up alone to that mount of sacred experience which no two human beings, however tender their relation, can ascend together.

[1] "Retrospection and Introspection," pp. 8, 9.

CHAPTER III

EDUCATION AND DEVELOPMENT

THOUGH we instinctively give heredity and natural environment a close scrutiny and in viewing a character are prone to believe these to be principal formative agents, we still fancy we behold how destiny strikes through circumstances and grasping a life drags it root and all from its soil and culture to replant it for its great development. We shall see how Love inspired Mary Baker and drew her tenderly out of Puritanism to fit her for leadership in a warfare against materialism.

All the Baker children went to school at the crossroads, about a mile from the farmhouse on the way to Concord. When Mary began her schooling, her oldest brother, Samuel, with New England pertinacity, had gone to Boston to learn the trade of mason, from which he steadily developed into a contractor and builder of considerable importance. He built many brick buildings and rows of houses which stood long in Boston. Her brother Albert entered Dartmouth College when Mary was nine and returned home when she was thirteen. He studied law with Franklin Pierce at Hillsborough, and later spent a year in the office of Richard Fletcher of Boston and was admitted to the bar in both Massachusetts and New Hampshire. The youngest brother was also through with the district school when Mary began her formal studies.

Abigail, Martha, and Mary trudged to school alone along the country roads, their brother George calling to fetch them home in stormy weather. It soon developed that Mary could not endure the severe routine of the district schoolroom where restless farmers' children, with noisily shuffling feet, droned through their lessons and indulged in occasional rude pranks that ended in birchings. The ungraded district schools were at that time overcrowded and nerve-straining to pupil and teacher alike.

Mary, who could not endure to hear the calves bawl or the pigs squeal in their own farmyard without an effort to comfort them, was depressed or excited by the turbulence of school life. She was therefore soon taken out of that experience and went on with her books at home. The grandmother, full of years, was less able to guide Mary now and thus she came directly under the guidance and observation of her mother and also saw her father more freely now that the boys were away. Her mother she thought a saint, her father an embodied intellect and will.

Her father would enter the house from his farm work, his mind abstracted with business purposes, and would seat himself at the old secretary to write for an hour or arrange papers from his strong box. He was called upon to do much business for his town, making out deeds and settling disputes. Up to the front door would drive two wrangling farmers with a grievance. Mary, a shy spectator, beheld her father's unvarying courtesy, his stern repression of profanity or angry speech. On one occasion when his judgment was not accepted and one of the disputants angrily protested, the child from her corner, imitating her father's dignified bearing, though in the soft voice of her mother, interpolated, "Mr. Bartlett, why do you articulate so vociferously?"

The unexpected rebuke coming from a child and in such unfamiliar words, caused a burst of laughter, followed by general good humor, and the neighbors departed in peace. "Mary settled that quarrel," said her father with his grim smile, and for years after her speech was quoted whenever a turbulent social spirit threatened the general harmony.

Often the minister from Pembroke, "Priest" Burnham, as he was called, the man who was active in founding Pembroke Academy, would drive up to the farm to discuss with Mark Baker church matters, prolonging his visit to elucidate the faulty doctrine of a rebellious parishioner. This he did, although Mark and Abigail Baker were not members of his church; then he would offer prayer, after which, before departing, he would accept with benign graciousness the hospitality Mr. Baker would offer him at the corner cupboard. Mary watched such scenes with the gravest interest and remembered them vividly in after years, not without a peculiar relish of humor. Her father was a great churchman and sometimes visited "backsliders" with this same "Priest" Burnham, to labor with them in matters of conscience, and presently she herself became the object of such solicitation.

Among the visitors that came to their home was Governor Benjamin Pierce. He had served through the Revolutionary War and the War of 1812 and attained the rank of major-general. He was twice gov-

ernor of New Hampshire. Mark Baker was chaplain
of the state militia, and a figure of some consequence
in politics. Their politics were congenial, both being
ardent Democrats and advocates of States' rights. The
old general sometimes brought with him on his drives
to Bow his granddaughter, Fanny McNeil, who was
related to the Bakers through her father, and while
Mark Baker and the governor talked politics, the
women discussed more congenial topics.

Mary liked best to listen to the weightier conversation, especially when it touched the welfare of some
one dear to her heart. Once she heard the governor
laughing merrily with her father over the way Mark
Baker had got the best of his son, Franklin, in a lawsuit involving the towns of Loudon and Bow over a
question of pauperism.

"You are not a lawyer, and yet my son says you
beat him with your arguments," said the governor.

"He bore his defeat in good spirit and offered me
his congratulations," replied her father. "He is a
magnetic young man destined for great things. It is
gratifying in these days of general bad manners to
have an opponent of such courtesy and good-will.
He swept me a bow like a soldier saluting his commander-in-chief — no less; and then shook hands
with me like a kinsman."

"And kinsmen we are in some sort, they tell me.
See here, Mr. Baker, send your son Albert to see us
when he comes home again. Get him into politics
right! he can't understand these matters too young,
and Franklin is a zealous Democrat, you know."

Somewhat later Albert made a visit to the Pierces',

and he, the undergraduate, formed a sincere and devoted attachment for the future president. Something about the young man attracted Franklin Pierce to him. He reminded him, no doubt, of that other devoted friend, Nathaniel Hawthorne, his college mate at Bowdoin. Perhaps it was young Baker's passion for abstract metaphysics.

· "When you've finished college, come to me," Franklin Pierce said in parting, "and I'll start you reading law."

The next time Mark Baker was in Concord the governor entertained him at dinner. Governor Pierce, the politician, was pleased at the prospect of a close alliance with an old family of such wide ramifications as the Bakers of Bow and Pembroke with their numerous voters, and in significance of his satisfaction offered Mr. Baker a gold-headed walking-stick as he was leaving. Mr. Baker declined it, saying he never used a cane. His pride was as unbending as his rugged figure, which he carried erect to his grave.

The love between Albert Baker and his youngest sister was most tender, and she beheld these arrangements for his future with an interest beyond her years. She had seen him leave for college with a pang of desolation, and now with what impatience she watched with face pressed against the pane for his first return home!

When he finally came he caught her up, the frail little girl of nine, and set her once more on his shoulder to queen it through the house.

"Mother," he said, "Mary is as beautiful as an angel."

"Well, my son," said the good mother, "she is as gentle and sweet-tempered as one."

"Now, little sister, tell me about the books," was his first question, when he had kissed her cheeks and stood her before him at the old secretary. "Have they let you have the books again?"

Vibrating with the bliss of having again with her this beloved brother, she leaned upon his breast and looked up into his face with eyes like dewy violets. She clasped and unclasped her hands around his neck and nestled to his heart. The excess of her emotional nature disquieted him vaguely. Here was no farm girl's prosaic temperament.

"Now tell your brother," said he, holding her gently, for he felt again what he had forgotten, how fragile and gentle she was, how like a flower that might be crushed. It was a moment of rare intimacy, such as seldom occurs between members of the same family, except with highly organized natures. It was moreover a moment which yielded important results in her after life.

Standing before him, she explained all her heart with shy candor; how it was that she loved him so because he was brave and honorable and a scholar; how she recognized his bravery because he had persisted in his determination to go to college; and his honor, because he had never cried out against the hardship of labor that went hand in hand with his studies.

"And I want very much to be a scholar, too," she said.

"A scholar; and why, little sister?"

"Because when I grow up I shall write a book; and I must be wise to do it. I must be as great a scholar as you or Mr. Franklin Pierce. Already I have read Young's 'Night Thoughts,' and I understand it."

"Well, sister," said Albert Baker seriously, "we will have this for a secret and I will teach you. You are still a very little girl, you know; but study your grammar and my Latin grammar. Next summer when I'm home I will teach you to read Latin. Does that make you happy?"

Ah, the deep embrace when Mary flung herself into her brother's arms! Albert Baker was true to his word. He taught his sister during all his vacations. Mrs. Eddy has said that at ten she was as familiar with Lindley Murray as with the Westminster Catechism, the short version of which she had studied with her sisters every Sunday. During the four years of her brother's undergraduate work she read with him moral science, natural philosophy, and gained some knowledge of Latin, Greek, and Hebrew. He was an able teacher and she an apt pupil. A friend wrote of him after his death that he was "fond of investigating abstruse metaphysical principles and schooled himself by intense and incessant study." Mary corresponded with her brother and also with her cousin who was at college. Among acquaintances she was regarded as a young prodigy of learning whose writing fell naturally into poetry and whose thought was forever brooding on spiritual matters.

In spite of this unorthodox education, Mary Baker's spiritual experiences continued to be grave and unusual, as had been her "Voices." She was what her family thought morbidly devout, reading her Bible with absorbed interest, making its characters the familiar friends of her mind. When she discovered that Daniel prayed three times daily, she formed the habit of doing so likewise. A curious fact is that she kept a record of these prayers in order to examine herself from time to time to learn if she had improved in grace. This was kept up through a number of years and was doubtless her first effort at composition. Her phrases were formed on the style of the psalmist and the prophets. So, when with his cousin, Albert commented on the unusual diction of Mary's letters, he declared he could only account for it by the habit she had of constantly reading her Bible and writing and rewriting prayers in emulation of David.

Her religious experience reached a grave crisis when she was twelve years of age, though she did not unite with the church until five years later at Sanbornton Bridge. While still in Bow, writing and studying, her father's relentless theology was alarmed at her frequent expression of confidence in God's love. He held to a hard and bitter doctrine of predestination and believed that a horrible decree of endless punishment awaited sinners on a final judgment day.

Whether it was logic and moral science taught her by her brother, or the trusting love instilled by her mother who had guided her to yield herself to the voice of God within her, Mary resisted her father on the matter of "unconditional election." Beautiful in her serenity and immovable in her faith, the daughter sat before the stern father of the iron will. His sires had signed a covenant in blood and would he not wrestle with this child who dared the wrath of God?

And well he did wrestle and the home was filled with his torrents of emotion. But though Mary might have quoted to him her own baby speech, she was too respectful and his "vociferations" went unrebuked. It is a remarkable thing to note, the conscience of a child in defense of its faith. Can any one suppose it an easy thing to resist a father so convicted with belief in dogma, a father, too, whom all their world honored and heeded? We may be sure it was not easy; that, indeed, to do so tortured this little child's heart. But Mark Baker was acting according to his conscience, and the child knew it and respected him. She did not view this struggle of consciences as a quarrel, and repudiated all her life the idea that she ever quarreled with her father.

The notion went abroad, however, that Mark Baker and his daughter Mary were at variance over religion. The silly gossip of their world reported that she would not study her catechism. They said that Mary had a high temper for all her learning, she of whom her mother had said, "When do you ever see Mary angry?" They even said that Mr. Baker had reported in his anguish to his clergyman, "If Mary Magdalene had seven devils, our Mary has ten." The struggle, it may be seen, was no casual argument, but a deep wrestle of souls. At last the child succumbed to an illness and the family doctor was summoned. When Mark Baker drove to fetch him his religious intemperance must have given way to paternal affection and fear. He is said to have stood up in his wagon and lashed his horse, crying out to a neighbor who accosted him that Mary was dying.

The physician declared Mary stricken with fever. He left medicines, recommending her to her mother's most watchful care and admonishing her father to desist from discussions. Mrs. Eddy has said of what followed:

> My mother, as she bathed my burning temples, bade me lean on God's love, which would give me rest, if I went to Him in prayer, as I was wont to do, seeking His guidance. I prayed; and a soft glow of ineffable joy came over me. The fever was gone, and I rose and dressed myself, in a normal condition of health. Mother saw this, and was glad. The physician marvelled; and the "horrible decree" of predestination — as John Calvin rightly called his own tenet — forever lost its power over me.[1]

It is true that Mary Baker made a religious profession at this time. She was examined at the age of twelve by the pastor, who eagerly put to her the usual "doleful questions," declaring that he must be assured that she had been truly regenerated. With the eyes of the church members upon her and her own father's haggard face visible from his place in their family pew, she answered without a tremor:

"I can only say in the words of the psalmist, 'Search me, O God, and know my heart: try me, and know my thoughts: and see if there be any wicked way in me, and lead me in the way everlasting.'"

Her childish but resolute figure, and the grave words so earnestly spoken, brought about a reaction in her favor and the oldest church members wept.

[1] "Retrospection and Introspection," p. 13.

Her pastor relented toward her and the ordeal was over. However, it was not until the age of seventeen that she united with the Congregational Church.

Theological arguments with her father recurring at this time threatened another nervous illness, and the watchful love of her mother saw fit to send her on a visit to a friend in the suburbs of Boston under the care of her brother Samuel. These friends received her with kindness and sought to draw her thoughts away from serious questions with bright entertainment and pleasant diversion. That they did not entirely succeed is shown in some of her verses written at this time in which, while she shows a rapturous love of nature, she declares that all this is the poet's world-wish and only a shadow hastening away. She asserts, however, that hope lifts the thought to "soar above matter, to fasten on God,"[1] which at this very early age presaged her future religious revelation in no uncertain outline.

With the passing of his mother in January, 1835, Mark was free to leave the old homestead and its poor farmland for a better location. Philip, his brother, already had moved to the promising village of Sanbornton Bridge, afterwards named Tilton. This mill town, eighteen miles north of Concord, had better schools than Bow, and as Mark desired greater educational advantages for his daughters he searched there and bought a farm a mile to the north of the town. Before purchasing the new property he already had found a buyer for the farm at Bow so final preparations for the move to the "Bridge" were in order.

The Baker home life now became more social and

[1] "Poems," p. 64.

less patriarchal. Mary was fifteen, her sisters, Martha and Abigail, seventeen and twenty. All three sisters were notable for their beauty and good breeding. The mother's agreeable temperament, together with her hospitable nature no less than Mr. Baker's great interest in public affairs, drew many guests to this house in which the family lived for seven years. Mr. Baker became prominent in the church with which he and his wife very soon united. He conducted the "third meeting" and George Baker led the village choir. Two years later George joined Alexander Tilton's mill and rose to become a mill agent and later a partner of the owner, who before that time had married his sister Abigail.

Mary Baker was fortunate to have Miss Sarah J. Bodwell as her teacher at the district school her first year in Sanbornton Bridge. In 1841 Sanbornton Academy at the "Bridge" was joined by a private school opened by a fine educator, Professor Dyer H. Sanborn. After a year Professor Sanborn became preceptor of the academy. At this time Mary Baker attended the academy. Professor Sanborn was well known as the author of "Sanborn's Grammar." A man of literary taste, he was a frequent guest in Mark Baker's home.

The Rev. Enoch Corser, pastor of the Tilton church for all the period of their residence at the farm, was also a frequent and honored guest of the Bakers. He was a man of liberal culture as may be imagined from the fact that he privately tutored his son Bartlett, sending him to college prepared to eliminate the first two years of Greek, Latin, and mathematics. This was Mary Baker's pastor who re-

ceived her into communion. His son has declared his
father's disposition toward her to be one of highest
esteem, deep admiration, and warm interest. This
pastor regarded Mary as his special pupil and the
brightest he ever had.

An intellectual comradeship grew up between
Mary and her pastor, who, as his son declared, pre-
ferred to talk with her to any one of his acquaintance.
They discussed subjects too deep to be attractive to
other members of the family, which the family freely
and good-humoredly admitted. Walking up and
down in the garden, this fine, old-school clergyman
and the young poetess, as she was coming to be called,
threshed out the old philosophic speculations without
rancor or irritation.

He was a fine-looking old Calvinist, with leonine
head covered with a mane of silver, and shaggy brows
beneath which rolled eyes of eloquence and compassion. His mouth was wide but firm, suggesting
both humor and melancholy. His shoulders had the
scholar's droop. One can picture them of a fine summer evening, the slender girl and the old scholar, on
their usual promenade in the garden. She must have
declared to him something from her philosophy, —
perhaps that one drop of divine love melted his eternal hells. As she looked up at her pastor, her great
blue eyes poured sunshine upon him and she smiled
with such radiance that he was struck dumb in the
midst of his defense of Hades. They would be by the
willows which long remained a vital relic of the old
place, and below them rolled the valley with the village nestling there in the summer twilight.

"Mary, your poetry goes beyond my theology," cried her pastor; "why should I preach to you!"

As they turned they encountered his son Bartlett and Abigail; for Bartlett was a suitor for Abigail's hand and she once pinned a rose on his coat in this garden. It is possible that both men were uplifted as they walked down the hill from the Baker home, and that it was then the father, halting his son with a hand on his shoulder, declared to him what he at some time certainly said: "Bright, good, and pure, aye brilliant! I never before had a pupil with such depth and independence of thought. She has some great future, mark that. She is an intellectual and spiritual genius."

The young man may not have marked it then, absorbed in his thoughts of the other sister. But he lived to remember it and to pay tribute to that genius by recalling his father's words. Bartlett was an educator for some time, following his father's scholarly bent. He never married, and with two maiden sisters lived for years at Boscawen, a village between Tilton and Concord made famous by Daniel Webster. He was a country gentleman of literary tastes and hospitable habits. Abigail, after rejecting him, married Alexander Tilton, a wealthy mill owner, and became the great lady of the town. Martha, after teaching for a time in the academy, married a prison officer, Luther C. Pilsbury.

While Mary was attending the academy an incident occurred which was long related by old residents of Tilton. A lunatic, escaped from the asylum at Concord, invaded the school yard, brandishing a club and terrifying the students who ran shrieking into the house. Mary Baker advanced toward him, and the pupils, peering through the windows, saw him wield the club above her head. Their blood tingled with horror for they expected her to be struck down before their eyes. Not so. She walked straight up to the man and took his disengaged hand. The club descended harmlessly to his side. At her request he walked with her to the gate and so, docilely, away. On the following Sunday he reappeared and quietly entered the church. He walked to the Baker pew and stood beside Mary during the hymn singing. Afterwards he allowed himself to be taken in charge without resistance.

Mary Baker must have been a gladsome sight in that grim old meeting-house. She has been described as slender and graceful, with a shower of chestnut curls, delicate, refined features, and great blue eyes that on occasion of unwonted interest became almost black. She wore a fashionable mantle over her silk gown and the bonnet of the period which came around her face, relieved with a delicate ruching of white. Her curls escaped from the bonnet and shaded cheeks which were so glowing they rivaled the rose. She taught the infants' class in the Sunday-school, and an elderly lady in Boston who was in that class related to the author:

"She always wore clothes we admired. We liked her gloves and fine cambric handkerchief. She was, as I have come to understand, exquisite, and we loved her particularly for her daintiness, her high-bred manners, her way of smiling at us, and her sweet, musical voice." Indeed, in those days her name might have been sung for that of Annie Laurie in the old ballad, so beautifully did her girlhood culminate.

THE CONGREGATIONAL CHURCH, TILTON, NEW HAMPSHIRE
Mrs. Eddy was a member of this church for many years
and taught a class in the Sunday school

Within two years two events transpired which broke forever the old home circle, and changed Mary from girlhood to womanhood. In 1841 Albert Baker was scheduled for nomination to Congress in a district where his party would ensure election. Before that came to pass he died at the age of thirty-one. His death was regarded as a calamity by his party, and his family felt it as a blow to their greatest ambition. Of Mary's grief it is sufficient to say that this brother was, after her mother, the dearest of her kindred. She had developed as a flower in his heart. It was well for her that another love came to break a too long-continued sorrow.

George Washington Glover, formerly of Concord, had been associated with Samuel Baker in Boston and with him learned the first step in his business, that of a contractor and builder. He was now established at Charleston, South Carolina. On a visit to his parents in Concord he came to the "Bridge" and fell deeply in love with Samuel Baker's young sister. He was an impetuous wooer and won Mary Baker's heart.

CHAPTER IV

CHANGE AND BEREAVEMENT

MARY BAKER and George Washington Glover were married two weeks before the Christmas of 1843 at the farmhouse near Tilton by the Rev. Corban Curtice, her pastor. There was a wedding party and all the notables of the neighborhood and guests from Concord and even Boston attended. Roaring fires greeted the arriving sleighing parties and there were feasting and merriment. Mark Baker saw all his children around him at this wedding, save the lamented Albert, and felt that all were well launched in life. Samuel was there from Boston, with his wife, Eliza Glover Baker, a sister to the groom. Abigail, who had been married six years, was present with her husband, Alexander Tilton. Martha with her husband, Luther Pilsbury of Concord, and George Baker, still unmarried, were there.

Surrounded by five children, four of whom were well married, Mark Baker was justified in believing that his name and blood would go down to posterity enriched, strengthened, honored. There was to be, however, no permanent issue, save through the medium of that frailest and youngest, the flower-like girl who, in her bridal garments, clung to his arm as they walked down the stairs of the old-fashioned house. She alone, holding her father back at the parlor door for one parting embrace and long look in his eyes,

36

was to insure him descendants, though not bearing the family name.

Her father might well have looked at her with paternal pride on her wedding-day. He had dowered her with beauty, educated her with care, gathered her safely into the church, clothed her delicately and without parsimony. As finely and nobly bred was she as any bride who ever left her father's home in all New England. Yet could this father have looked into the future he would have foreseen that his daughter Mary would yet reject his religious dogmas, his political ideas, his wealth and family pride, — that she would one day depart from them all with a more significant departure than this of going forth as a bride.

The couple headed South after visiting Concord and Bow. George Glover had a promising business in Charleston, South Carolina. During the four years he lived there, from 1839 to 1844, he made thirteen conveyances of property and two were made to him. These acts involved several thousand dollars, as the registry of deeds of that city discloses. He owned a few slaves and employed a number of men in his building ventures. One of the first things Mrs. Glover endeavored to influence her young husband to do was to free his slaves.

With change of environment the whole question of slavery became a real and terrible one to her, and no longer merely a political issue as it was considered by the Bakers, the Tiltons, the Pierces, in New Hampshire. A young colored woman who worked in a boarding-house of the city (as was related by a Boston woman sojourning there) had stolen a shawl, and though she gave it up, she was taken to the sugar house and whipped. Her screams were audible on the road. George Glover could not drive out with his wife on a pleasant evening through the magnolia-lined avenues of the "Queen City of the South" and be certain that she would not see or hear some such evidence of the inhuman side of slavery. It was thus that the issue was made real to her.

The question of freeing his slaves was frequently debated between them, Mr. Glover explaining to his wife that it had been made illegal to do so in South Carolina by a statute passed in 1820, and only by special act of the legislature could slaves be made absolutely free. Her answer to this was that she had learned of some instances where masters allowed their slaves to depart of their own free will. Then her husband argued to her that it would be a loss of property for him to free his slaves as he had accepted them in payment of debts, and very likely would have to do so again. But Mrs. Glover was insistent that to own a human being was to live in a state of sin. Glover was young, prosperous, had large contracts ahead of him, and so thought seriously of yielding to her persuasions. Events soon took the necessity of decision out of his hands and left it to his wife, who decided with characteristic moral acumen.

It was June of the summer following their marriage. Mr. Glover had a contract for supplying building material for a cathedral to be erected in Haiti and on this business went to Wilmington, North Carolina. Because of her unique position in her new social surroundings, not only as an advocate of abolition in conversation, but one who had dared to write on the subject for the local papers, he took his young wife with him. He feared, indeed, to leave her behind, for she was in delicate health and impressionable to the excitement of high argument.

In Wilmington they found yellow fever raging and the city in a panic. Mr. Glover endeavored to forward his business for a speedy departure; but he was himself suddenly stricken with the fever and survived but nine days. During his illness his young wife was assisted by his brother Masons in the perilous task of nursing him. Mr. Glover was a member of Saint Andrew's Lodge, No. 10, and of Union Chapter, No. 3, of Royal Arch Masons, and his need in this hour brought a quick response from members of the order. In his delirium he constantly talked of his wife, of his hopes through her, and of his business plans which he now saw blasted. When he knew he was dying, he begged his brother Masons to see his wife safe to her father's home in the North. His request was carried out faithfully.

George Glover was interred with Masonic rites in the Episcopal cemetery of Wilmington. His business associates and members of the lodge followed his body to the grave and then strove to do all that was possible for his widow's comfort. For a month Mrs. Glover was entertained in the home of these cordial Southerners, made more than friends by the calamity of the hour. They did all that kinsmen could have done. They converted his business interests into as large a sum of money as possible and an escort was selected to accompany her to her home. She had already communicated with her family, and her brother George met them in New York City.

Mrs. Glover had brought with her a considerable sum of money, but her husband's business, as may be readily understood from the nature of it, fell to pieces at his death. Now it was that she permitted his slaves to go free, unwilling to accept for herself the price of a human life. No record exists of this transaction because of the statutes on emancipation which existed in South Carolina until the proclamation of President Lincoln. Mr. Baker, though a Democrat, and opposed to the policies of the abolitionists, was no lover of slavery and he upheld his daughter in this sacrifice of property.

Mrs. Glover was received with tenderness by her parents and given her girlhood room again, a spacious and comfortable chamber in which she had so lately donned her wedding veil. It was August, and she had escaped from the tropic heat of the South to her native mountain air. She breathed deep drafts at her window, looking out over the familiar valley. But there was in her eyes a look of loneliness, a look of fear, and they were often wide and startled, as those of one who sees a vision.

In September she gave birth to a son whom she named after his father. Mrs. Glover's life for a time was despaired of. She was far too ill to nurse her child and Mark Baker carried the infant to the home of Amos Morrison, a locomotive builder, whose wife had given birth to twins a few days before George Glover was born. Of these one had died, leaving the mother with a little girl, Asenath. This mother took Mary's child to her breast with her own and both thrived.

Mahala Sanborn, daughter of a blacksmith, was engaged to nurse Mrs. Glover, but her father would sit for long hours by his daughter's bed, often taking her in his arms and rocking her gently like a child. The roads were strewn with tan-bark and straw, and the house was hushed as if death had invaded it. When the long struggle for life ended in a feeble victory and the babe was brought home again, the young mother was very happy. Her widowed heart found comfort in maternal expression. He was a vigorous, robust infant, and to her had the eyes and smile of his father. But it seemed she was too tender and too devoted, too weak physically to exercise a mother's care, and when she had overtaxed herself her parents would send little George home with Mahala Sanborn, or it may be they merely permitted the spinster nurse to take him, indulging her fondness. This was not well, as later events proved.

A significant fact in relation to the child's infancy is found in the birth of another grandson to Mark Baker a few months later. Abigail Tilton's first child was born in June of the following year and she named it Albert, in memory of the lamented brother. This boy was very handsome as was also a daughter, Evelyn, born a few years later. Both were delicate, nervous children, while George Glover was quite the reverse. Sturdy, hearty, and romping, this child of Mary's made the house ring with his demands. When Abigail was there with her baby, to the smithy little George must go to stay with Mahala, and to the smithy he went with the Tiltons' coachman, and there his spirits were not constrained, nor was his childish nature subdued to its proper walk in life. Thus without her consent, at the very outset, was the mother's influence over her child lost.

George Baker was still living at home and Abigail came out to the farm nearly every day. George and Mr. Tilton were rapidly making a fortune. They had been manufacturing cassimeres and tweeds for eight years and were about to install new machinery, lease a new mill, and otherwise branch out. They were persuading Mark Baker to build a handsome house in town, near to the Tiltons, a house in colonial style, of very comfortable proportions. He was placing his savings in other investments than crops through his son's and son-in-law's advice, such as workmen's houses for rents, and railroad stocks. He was more and more interested in politics, and much pleased when George Baker was made a colonel on the governor's staff. His townsmen now called him Squire, in recognition of his growing wealth and influence.

As in the case with most prosperous persons, the sense of executive power tended to make Abigail wish to regulate the lives of those dear to her. She was a bit impatient of that quiet unfoldment of destiny which was now dealing with her sister Mary. She could not help discussing her future. She would have liked some definite arrangement for her, especially about her child.

But Mary was performing a sacred duty under her unseeing eyes. While the family talked of Tilton's tweed, the new Darling mill, workmen's cottages, and the spur of railroad that would facilitate

HOME OF MARK BAKER, TILTON, NEW HAMPSHIRE

Where Mrs. Eddy lived as a young widow with her father after her mother's death.
Erected in 1848, it has been removed from its original environment

the shipping, — affairs of such importance in the advancement of the family that their discussion came into the family circle, — Mary's discerning eyes were watching her mother, for her mother was dying. The daughter was receiving the content of the mother's stored-up spiritual treasury and was assisting at the loosening of the earth fetters.

Mrs. Baker did not enjoy the new home in town. She was not well enough to bear the transplanting from her rural life. In November, 1849, she died, and her death caused some important changes in the life which flowed around her youngest child. George Baker married Martha Drew Rand a few months before his mother's death and went to Baltimore to establish himself in mills in that city. About a year later, in December of 1850, Mark Baker married Mrs. Elizabeth Patterson Duncan, a well-to-do widow, whose brother was an influential man of affairs in New York and a lieutenant-governor of that state. These events occurred five years after Mrs. Glover returned to her father's house a widow.

Now Mrs. Glover had not been idle all these years. Although in delicate health, she had employed her pen in writing and at the request of the Hon. Isaac Hill prepared political articles[1] for the New Hampshire *Patriot*, published at Concord. She wrote on various subjects, but especially on slavery from her experiences in the South. Her political views were somewhat different from her father's and their views were to diverge more and more as the Civil War drew nigh. She also taught as a substitute instructor in the New Hampshire Conference Seminary, in which

[1] Her political articles were necessarily anonymous. See p. 50.

her old teacher, Dyer Sanborn, was now a professor.
The Rev. Richard S. Rust, principal of the seminary,
was so pleased with her work that he recommended to
her that she open an infants' school.

Mrs. Glover did this as an educational experiment. Her school was an early attempt to introduce
kindergarten methods. It met with much criticism,
as did all such experiments in the early days in New
England. So the experiment was one of brief duration. The substitution of love for harshness as a
means of discipline, interest for compulsion as a
method of imparting knowledge, was held up to derision by the hard-headed element of the community.
And hard-headedness had a very great advantage in
New England in those days. Hard-headedness was
the critic of things in general. It was inclined to consider culture in a woman mincing affectation, very
readily agreeing that she gave herself airs, and to be
"stuck up" in a New England village, as Margaret
Deland says, was next to being a heretic. It was not
very easy, with such biting winds of criticism blowing,
for an idealist to keep the lilies growing in the garden
of the heart. It is not difficult to perceive why Mrs.
Glover soon closed her infants' school.

A very few months of living alone with her father
and little son had passed when the talk of the family
circle broached the idea of a new mistress for Mr.
Baker's house. Those who knew Mary Baker best at
this time declare she was the soul of gentleness,
patience, and humility. She had no resistance to offer
to plans which were likely vitally to affect her. Pas-
sive and gentle, she heard the family planning and ar-

ranging. But suddenly she caught the trend of a new argument and then she did offer resistance. Mahala Sanborn, the spinster nurse, was to marry Russell Cheney of North Groton, about forty miles away in the mountains. And Mahala, who was attached to little George, wanted to take the child with her to her new home.

"What, take my little son!" the mother cried. "Abigail, you wouldn't think of it! Father, do you hear? Why, I couldn't see him for months. It would break my heart. Indeed, indeed it would!"

Nevertheless, the child was let go. One has no doubt it was done for kindness, as the stern New Englander of those days understood kindness; no doubt it was believed to be necessary and right and just. With a new mistress in the home, Mary had gone to live with Abigail, but there was no welcome for young George. Now he was almost seven and Abigail's son almost six. No doubt it was necessary to make due provision for every one's peace and happiness, for every one's but the weakest.

Mary did not give up until the very last hour. She knelt by his bed all night before they took her child and prayed for a vision of relief, for a way to be shown that she might not have to yield to the demand to let him go. But in the end she helped to dress him and pack his little things, weeping over each garment she folded away. She took his arms from around her neck and smiled through her tears when she gave him into the arms of Mahala Sanborn.

Four bereavements within a few short years separated Mary Baker from brother, mother, husband,

and son. What wonder that at this period she sank into invalidism and that in later years when reverting to this time she wrote:

It is well to know, dear reader, that our material, mortal history is but the record of dreams. . . . The heavenly intent of earth's shadows is to chasten the affections, to rebuke human consciousness and turn it gladly from a material, false sense of life and happiness, to spiritual joy and true estimate of being.[1]

[1] "Retrospection and Introspection," p. 21.

CHAPTER V

FORMATIVE PROCESSES

AS when in a patriotic symphony one hears a prolonged orchestration of a nation's woe, its anguish crying in the strings, its resentments explosive
in the brasses, its struggles hinted in the vague ruffle
of drums, there begins to be apprehended a note of
hope, which swells and grows until the horn takes it
up with confidence and sings and soars above the har-
monic conflict a pæan of faith; so in preparing to sing
its theme a great life is submerged in its community,
through periods of prolonged and poignant delay,
when affairs obtrude, other voices and other wills are
clamorous, and its clear call of faith is drowned for
the time, heard only as elfin notes on the inner ear of
him who is to play the great strain.

For three years Mary lived with her sister Abigail,
though she spent some time at her father's home,
where she accepted the new régime unflinchingly
and even lovingly, recognizing freely the good qualities and capacities of her stepmother. She occupied herself with writing when strong enough, and
likewise when strong enough assisted her sister in
her social life and entertaining which brought influential personages to their board. Mr. Tilton was
now a railroad director and foresaw a future for the
little city.

The status of the Tilton and Baker families in the
community of central New Hampshire has been indicated. The town in which they lived was not far from
Hillsborough, Franklin Pierce's home, or Boscawen,
the early home of Webster. The Bakers and the Tiltons were Democrats, their political predilection was
in the marrow of their bones. It has been indicated
that influential personages gathered at their homes,
and their friendships with leading politicians were
strong. It follows that discussion of public affairs as
well as of religion and business ventures found place
in their daily intercourse, influencing members of the
families in their relations toward each other.

This is the period of 1850 to 1853, when public
events were rapidly changing the colonial spirit of all
Americans. The passage of the Compromise of 1850,
devised by Clay, which included the Fugitive Slave
Act, was the beginning of a bitter strife in politics.
The debates which now waged in Congress were perhaps the most strenuous mental and moral wrestlings
that the republic of the United States has known.
This wrestling of mind and soul was to end only in the
mighty physical conflict which Americans call the
Civil War. In 1850 Webster was working with herculean efforts to preserve the Union against the attacks of the extreme pro-slavery men on the one hand
and of the abolitionists on the other.

The Southern states hotly resented the agitation
of the question of the morality and wisdom of slavery,
while the North seemed to experience a shuddering
horror over the Fugitive Slave Law, evading its rul-
ings wherever possible with the passage of personal

liberty laws. These laws were intended to protect free negroes falsely alleged to be fugitive slaves and threatened with reenslavement. Such a fate menaced many negroes who had been set free. This was true of the negroes Mary Baker Glover had freed. In the first place with freedom granted, the negro had had to leave the South to preserve it; now even in the North he might lose it if an unscrupulous trader claimed him.

In June, 1852, Franklin Pierce of New Hampshire was nominated for President at Baltimore by the Democratic National Convention which endorsed the Compromise of 1850 and the Fugitive Slave Law, and denounced slavery agitation. The Free Soil Democrats, a month later, nominated John P. Hale of New Hampshire for President. Daniel Webster, also a native of New Hampshire, would doubtless have been the Whig candidate but for his age and his un-compromising attitude in support of the Fugitive Slave Law. His death occurred in October of that year. New Hampshire was probably never more mentally excited and morally perturbed in its history.

At this time Nathaniel Hawthorne wrote his life of Pierce, a delightful biographic sketch. Pierce had married Jane Appleton, the daughter of the president of Bowdoin College, Hawthorne's alma mater. Had Albert Baker been alive he, too, must have supported Pierce with pen and oratory. Families were greatly influenced in their political thought by their old-time friendships. Pierce was not only personally a man of rare fascination and magical charm, but he possessed the strength conferred by family tradition throughout New England.

Mary Baker was an unusually intellectual woman; where did she stand in this hour? Conceive her position. She who might have effectively wielded her pen in this cause must allow it to lie idle. She must behold another woman do that which, with her family behind her, as the Beechers were behind Harriet Beecher Stowe, she, too, might have done. She was like a soldier paroled on honor whose sword is restless in its scabbard. Moreover, she was deprived of independence by these circumstances, for, throttled on the subject for which she felt the greatest interest, she could not write on sugary nothings as many another genius, struggling against its environment, has discovered. Furthermore, she was ill a great portion of the time, and as it has been shown that bereavement contributed to that physical condition, it must also be shown that mental isolation, caused by her independent political views, added to it. Her father, who had contended so bitterly with her on religion, would in this hour have contended with equal strenuosity over politics had she asserted her opinions. Her sister Abigail was likewise set against her in political views.

It is still remembered in that community how the Tiltons held an informal social gathering and everybody of consequence in the town attended. It appears to have been a semi-political reception, and on this occasion the Baker sisters disagreed before their guests. Mrs. Glover had come into the parlors to assist her sister. She was a notable figure, because of her grace and beauty, though wasted in health, and her large eyes burned as she listened to the expres-

sions of political opinion around her, called forth by
the presidential campaign.

"And what does Mrs. Glover have to say to all
this?" said a gentleman who had observed her re-
pressed emotion while listening and taking no part in
the conversation. All eyes turned toward her. Those
who had not dared to venture an adverse opinion in
the great house of the town hushed the lighter-minded
around them. It was a moment of suspense such as
only occasionally thrills a social gathering.

"I say," said Mrs. Glover, "that the South as well
as the North suffers from the continuance of slavery
and its spread to other states; that the election of
Franklin Pierce will but involve us in larger disputes;
that emancipation is written on the wall."

The gathering had received its thrill which went
down the backs of the several guests like baptismal
currents of lightning.

"Mary," cried her sister, "do you dare to say that
in my house?"

"I dare to speak what I believe in any house,"
responded Mrs. Glover quietly.

The report of that speech went abroad. Mrs.
Glover was remembered for it long by political
thinkers of New Hampshire. They said Mrs. Eddy
was an extremely intellectual woman at thirty, and
that she had remarkable insight in affairs. They also
said that her pride was as unbending as her father's.
Now Abigail, too, had made a speech, not easily forgotten or overlooked by a Baker.

Keeping in mind these political agitations which
stirred the country, and further grasping the hour by

remembering that it was now railroads were being built across the continent, shipping was being improved by the introduction of steam, gold had just been discovered in California, improved machinery was being placed on the farms and in the mills, it will be seen why, with rapid changes in conditions of living, it was not strange, as a recent writer[1] has said, that there should be a corresponding change in the minds of men and that their ideas should become unsettled and that transcendentalism in religion, literature, and politics should begin to flourish. Methods of education improved, newspapers were published in every town, the lyceum system of lectures became popular. Literature in America developed a new school of which the lights in New England were Emerson, Longfellow, Whittier, Lowell, Hawthorne, Holmes.

In such an era Spiritualism had its birth, and mesmerism and animal magnetism were being widely discussed. But if a Poyen lectured through New England on these subjects, he had an Emerson on his heels with saner topics. Yet it must be taken into account that in the early fifties the conversation at social gatherings was everywhere in America charged with the subject of Spiritualism. In 1848 the Fox sisters of Rochester had startled the world with the story of their "rappings." That the "undiscovered country" should be rapping to our world attention seemed almost more wonderful than if Mars should be found to-day to be signaling our planet.

London was no less excited over this topic than New York or Boston. Mediums developed on all

[1] Encyclopædia Britannica: *United States.*

sides. They saw "the vanished hand" and heard "the voice that is still." In London they handled red-hot coals and unfastened cords and bonds, they caused musical instruments to be played by unseen touch and the ringing of bells to sound upon the air. Poyen and Andrew Jackson Davis published books on mesmerism or animal magnetism. The cure of disease by clairvoyant diagnosis and mesmeric healing was quite commonly given credence. Were such ideas reconcilable with religion? They speculated on it under the very altar, though New England was not peculiar in this respect. However, it is a just assertion that not to have heard such discussions or not to have been interested in them was not to have lived at all in the atmosphere of the time.

Mary Baker did live in that atmosphere, fully and deeply. Just as she lived in the consciousness of political struggle, just as she drank in the new literary influences of that glorious school of New England writers, she was aware of that oscillation in religious notions. Every circumstance of her education and breeding had given her the habit of dealing with life in a large way. She who dared to set aside her father's and sister's political opinions to maintain her own convictions most certainly had ideas concerning Spiritualism. But to connect her life seriously at any period with Spiritualism is to make use of unwarrantable conjecture. Was this the woman to go into trances for the benefit of the superstitious country folk? Would such as these have had access to the great house, to the secluded chamber, to the invalid absorbed in her books? Even Dr. Ladd, the family physician, who was interested in mesmeric experiments, was restrained from practising on Mary Baker by the dignity of her position.

The time came when Mary Baker had thought her way through this maze of intellectual vaporing and then there came from her pen a refutation of these wonder-workings. The common people were those she then sought on the basis of an independent life of voluntary poverty. She sought working men and women, not to play upon their superstition, but to clear their vision. She associated with Spiritualists for years, more or less; she must associate with them as she must with Universalists and Unitarians. She did not avoid them or their discussions, as will be shown in later chapters. At times she was even present at séances. Her dealing with the entire subject was consistent, and her deep sounding of its contentions was as much a part of her development as the consideration of Calvinism in her earlier years.

While living with her sister Abigail, Mary was often confined to her bed for long periods. She was afflicted with a spinal weakness which caused spasmodic seizures, followed by prostration which amounted to a complete nervous collapse. In her moments of utter weakness her father would take her in his arms and soothe her as though she were again his bairn. All differences of faith and opinion were forgotten in the purely human love which was very strong in this family. Abigail sought in divers ways to make her sister more comfortable. She had a divan fitted with rockers to give Mary a change from long hours in bed, and when the invalid would be able to

HOME OF ABIGAIL TILTON, TILTON, NEW HAMPSHIRE
Where Mrs. Eddy lived with her sister before her second marriage
Removed from its original environment

go about again they would carry her down to the carriage and the two sisters would drive slowly through the village streets and country highways.

In 1853, after nine years of widowhood, a complete change was brought about in her life and in all the circumstances of it through a second marriage. Mrs. Eddy has said this marriage was unfortunate and has left it without further word of protest. It was unfortunate, yet jeweled adversity. It occupied many years in the heart of her life, and subjected her to a measure of isolation and social obscurity. But it carried her away from worldly stimulation to a prolonged retreat in the mountains where significant experiences dealt with her heart. From 1850 until 1875 was largely a period of meditation for her. She passed a great part of this time in small towns far from the madding strife of cities. She experienced much suffering physically and went through mental agony few natures are called upon to endure. She did not succumb to the assaults of pain or grief, but emerged with a work which seems destined to change greatly the world's religious thought.

Dr. Daniel Patterson, a dentist, a relative of Mark Baker's second wife, came to their home on a visit. He was a big, handsome, healthy man with great animal spirits and excessive confidence in himself. He had some knowledge of homeopathy and used the prescribed remedies for his dental patients in his journeys through the country. Mrs. Glover's invalidism interested him. He expounded it to the family. She was too delicate, he declared, for harsh remedies and would be particularly susceptible to high medical attenuations, the catch phrase of the new medical school of the hour. A crisis occurring in her illness, he experimented and brought her through successfully. On a day in due season, Dr. Patterson confided to Mrs. Tilton that he loved her sister, that he believed her to be suffering as much from the separation from her child as from organic functional disorder. He wanted to marry her, reunite her with her child, give her her own home, and make her a well woman through the care he would bestow.

It is not likely that Mrs. Tilton reflected sufficiently to detect an ambitious project, or that she saw more than an honest love offering devoted care. She consulted her father, who discussed the matter with the dentist. Mark Baker must have been doubtful of this fluent-speaking, full-bearded, broad-shouldered optimist in broadcloth. Dr. Patterson was always something of a dandy, and even in the mountains wore broadcloth and fine linen, kid gloves and boots, topping all with a silk hat. His raiment was a considerable part of his personality. Mr. Baker must have taken a more accurate measure of this man than did Mrs. Tilton, but he knew it was true that Mary never ceased to grieve for her child, — her child who was not welcome either in the home of his second wife or in the Tilton home. A marriage that would restore that child to Mary might rouse her to health and happiness. Moreover, the dentist was a kinsman of his wife.

The marriage was accordingly arranged, and took place at the Baker home. Mrs. Glover, who was at first surprised at the proposal and unsure as to the marriage, has explained why she consented to it and how disastrously it terminated for her in two succinct sentences. She says: "My dominant thought in marrying again was to get back my child, but after our marriage his stepfather was not willing he should have a home with me." [1]

Dr. Patterson first took his wife to Franklin, a near-by factory town, where they lived for two years. He employed a housekeeper but put his wife off with regard to her child. She must wait until her health improved. He was much abroad traveling from village to village. He called frequently upon his influential relatives in Tilton, and sometimes leaned a bit heavily upon their good-will. Not very prosperous, he was always confident that just around the corner was the best success in the world. When left to herself, Mrs. Patterson, as we must now call Mary Baker, read deeply in her books. She had brought to Franklin furnishings to make her small home comfortable, a few pieces of mahogany willed to her by her mother, long mirrors in gilt frames, her own excellent collection of books. A few family friends came from time to time and certain of the townspeople called. Among them, Mr. Warren Daniels, a wealthy and retired mill owner living in Franklin, said that Mrs. Patterson's reputation for intellect and beauty had preceded her, but that in Franklin she led a retired life, was the most reserved of women, and one whom all men must respect and honor.

1 "Retrospection and Introspection," p. 20.

In 1855 Mrs. Patterson persuaded her husband to move to North Groton, a village north of the Winnepesaukee region, near the entrance of the Franconia range of the White Mountains. In this village her son was living with the Cheneys. Perhaps Dr. Patterson was more easily persuaded to make the change since Martha, her sister, owned a little property in that town which he hoped to buy on easy terms. North Groton is a farming center, little changed by passing years. It boasts a general store and post-office, a blacksmith shop, district school, and Union church. Situated some miles back from the railroad, its elevation is about one thousand feet above sea-level. The journey thither is by conveyance, up through the foot-hills along a valley pass, following a turbulent trout-stream which leaps and falls over the rocks, singing a wild little song of its own. Two mountains loom blue and magnificent away to the north. On the lesser hills along the way the loggers are at work.

The new home was a little unpainted cottage off the main road. It was beside the stream in which was a mill-dam. John Kidder, a machinist and cabinet-maker, was their neighbor, and had an interest in the sawmill attached to the Patterson property. Other neighbors there were not far away. It was not a lonely or desolate spot. The town had a small library; to the church came different denominational preachers; the school had eighty-four pupils and was taught by a man who later held a position in the faculty of a Massachusetts college. Many physicians, lawyers, and clergymen now scattered over the United States came from this mountain village. Clergymen especially seemed to develop here, twenty having gone out into the world from this mountain nest in the past fifty years.

The Patterson home in exterior was not unlike its neighbors, but within it was different. Mrs. Patterson carried with her an atmosphere which was reflected in her surroundings. She was bedridden most of the time they lived here, yet her active mind secured perfect order, exquisite cleanliness, a shining radiance of books, prints, polished mahogany, and a cherished few gleaming bits of silver service and brass candlesticks. At first they had no help and Daniel Patterson cared for her himself when she was very ill. Later she took in a blind girl who came to her door seeking employment. This girl was with her for one or two years and in later life paid a beautiful tribute to Mrs. Eddy's kindness. She spoke of her as low-voiced and gentle, but at the same time insistent on perfect housekeeping.

She not only befriended the blind girl, but was kind to her sister, who said, "I thought it the most beautiful home in the world. I was a child of ten and used to visit my sister Myra. I remember well how Mrs. Patterson would call me to her room, lay down her book, and place her thin white hand on my head or stroke my cheek. She wished to comfort me, for I had lately lost a good father."

Of Mrs. Eddy's extreme invalidism at this time there is no doubt. "I had the honor to take care of Mrs. Eddy once," said a very old woman of Groton. "She was all alone in her home and I heard her bell ringing. I went in and found her lying rigid with foam on her lips. I brought her around with cold water. She motioned to her medicine chest, and I gave her what she wanted. Then I sat with her till she got better."

She was indeed far from well, but Mrs. Patterson had come to North Groton to be with her boy. Her desire amounted to a passionate hunger of maternity, and he, when he had seen his mother again, was as eager to be with her. But now a peculiar jealousy interfered between mother and son. He would come to his mother in spite of the injunctions of his foster parents and his stepfather, and once broke through the window to get into her room. Dr. Patterson would find him there with his books, leaning upon his mother's couch, while she examined his progress in studies, a poor progress indeed as she found. The blind servant stated that these visits aroused Dr. Patterson to declare a peremptory prohibition of the lad from the house, which was not entirely successful. He reported to the Tiltons that the boy could not be kept away and that he exhausted his mother. That report brought Abigail Tilton to North Groton, and the Cheneys shortly after fulfilled an ambition long cherished by going West. In her autobiography Mrs. Eddy writes of her son:

A plot was consummated for keeping us apart. The family to whose care he was committed very soon removed to what was then regarded as the Far West. After his removal a letter was read to my little son, informing him that his mother was dead and buried. Without my knowledge a guardian was appointed him, and I was then informed that my son was lost. Every means within my power was employed to find him, but without success. We never met again until he had reached the age of thirty-four.[1]

Young Glover ran away from the Cheneys after they had been in Minnesota a few years, and as a young lad enlisted in the Union army for the Civil War. He made a good record as a soldier, was wounded at Shiloh, and after the war became a United States marshal, and led the life of a prospector in the western states. Mrs. Eddy had a temporary knowledge of him. He wrote her from the front during the war, and that her love for him was not uprooted by continual separation was shown in her excitement and joy at hearing from him. She called in her friends to read his letter, and wept over it and kissed its pages. But her son passed again into obscurity, bent on the pursuit of a freedom which he first learned to love at the Sanborn smithy, and which life in the wild West of those days seemed to foster as second-nature. Thus he grew up beyond the sphere of his mother's influence and his life became fixed in a path diverse to hers. Destiny inscrutable seemed fixed in its decree that she should live childless and alone.

When they took her boy from her arms the second time, Mrs. Patterson seemed about to sink into utter despair. A very old man, of more than ninety years, devout and saintlike, used to visit her. He came nearly every day to read the Bible and pray. One day when old Father Merrill came to her home he saw Mrs. Patterson dressed and walking to meet him with a smile and outstretched hands of welcome. He

1 "Retrospection and Introspection," p. 20.

leaped with delight, clapping his hands and crying out, "Praise God, He's answered our prayer." Earnestly they discussed it together. Was her improved condition an answer to prayer? Mrs. Patterson believed that a blameless life should be healthy, but the old man thought God sometimes sent sickness for spiritual good. She did not cross this old man with argument, but she had begun to work on the idea that would haunt her for years until perfected, the nature of divine healing.

Their neighbors, the Kidders, were also friendly visitors. Mrs. Kidder was a Spiritualist and spent hours urging its claims on Mrs. Patterson. At this time Mrs. Patterson took an interest in the welfare and education of the Kidders' son, Daniel, a lad of seventeen. She spent much time tutoring him. He was an ambitious lad and later had a successful career in mechanics and railroad construction. He remembered with gratitude the help Mrs. Patterson gave him with his studies, especially those in rudimentary mathematics and physics.

Dr. Patterson had kept up his itineracy while at North Groton. He has a record for a sort of gallantry through the country and was once pursued to his home by an irate blacksmith whose wife was too attractive to the doctor. The less of this recounted is the better, save only that his weakness as a husband be shown. His fortunes did not thrive. Although he mortgaged Mrs. Patterson's furniture and articles of jewelry, he could not meet his payments on the little property. A certain farmer went to Tilton and took up the mortgage on the house, and then demanded

possession of the mill. Dr. Patterson defied him with
high words, and the villagers said they had a personal
encounter. When Dr. Patterson saw the legal paper
he prepared to remove, not only from the mill but
from North Groton.

Mrs. Tilton came over to remove her sister in a
carriage. Together they drove down the mountain
road, which was rocky, steep, and winding. They must
perforce have driven at a walk both because of the
nature of the road and because of the weakness of
Mrs. Patterson from long invalidism. The village
church bell was tolling. Dr. Patterson's enemy having
got into the church was thus signally expressing to
the rural community his complete triumph. He not
only possessed the home, but the furniture and the
books of Mrs. Patterson, and her gold chain he bestowed upon his daughter. In this dark hour Mrs.
Tilton held her sister in her arms and strove to ease
the jolting of the carriage and to comfort her distress.
Sometimes she left the carriage and walked with the
blind girl, for the stout farm-girl though blind persisted in walking behind the carriage all the way
to Rumney, a distance of six miles. She could not
ride in the carriage and listen to the sobs of her mistress. Abigail Tilton herself walked much of the way.
She who managed with such executive skill in many
affairs had managed but indifferently in arranging
this marriage.

CHAPTER VI

ILLUMINATION AND BACKWARD TURNING

IN threading the labyrinth of a mind to find its start-ing-point upon a new phase of existence, it is frequently most difficult to lay hold of the silken clue which guided it to the gateway out of a maze of turn-ings. Every life has its moments of revelation when it would seem proper to start away upon the higher adventures of the soul; but seldom does a human be-ing go forward without hesitation, leaving the past with its thousand detaining hands by an irrevocable decision. Having received the vision, beheld the clear trail of a path up the mountain, the pilgrim soul, with mystifying impulses which it cannot itself under-stand, obeying instincts which lie too deep for scru-tiny, will almost invariably turn backward on the road of experience to reembrace its worn-out illusions and weep at its old tombs. Finding the old life and its associations as disappointing and unprofitable as ever, it will agonize once more over its mistakes, and put-ting them off again one by one, will back away toward its future, with face set miserably upon the past. Not until the past smites him will the pilgrim, with a sud-den realization of himself, turn right about and rush for his mountain. Now he must search again for the path. His search may be weary and performed in humility, but the path once found will never again be forsaken for that pathless wilderness where each human being experiences doubts and despairs.

Removing from North Groton, Dr. Patterson engaged board for himself and his wife at the home of Mr. and Mrs. John Herbert at Rumney Station. The house was a substantial frame dwelling of the colonial type with comfortable chambers looking out upon broad lawns. The family life at first appeared to be as broadly harmonious as the fashion of its dwelling. Mrs. Patterson's invalidism, however, soon aroused comment among the frequenters of the home. As the frail, delicate woman had been criticized by the thoughtless folks of North Groton who in their rugged health believed the handsome doctor to be a martyr to the whims of an exacting invalid, so in Rumney she was criticized by the gossiping ladies of the boarding-house. If Dr. Patterson, obedient to his better instincts of courtesy, picked up his wife's handkerchief or readjusted her shawl, they were jealously observant, or if in hearty buoyancy he displayed the tenderness of strength toward weakness and lifted Mrs. Patterson in his arms to carry her up-stairs, they sat silently disapproving. For such misinterpretation of her invalidism and lack of appreciation of her character she was misunderstood in that neighborhood for half a century. Often a nervous sufferer, she soon felt the wisdom of retiring from this atmosphere and persuaded the doctor, who contemplated locating in Rumney, to procure a cottage in Rumney village about a mile back in the hills. This cottage occupied an eminence near the edge of the town and commanded an agreeable view. It was more attractive than the North Groton home and her blind servant was still with her and gave her devoted care.

The blind girl, Myra Smith, has described in detail Mrs. Patterson's persevering efforts to recover her health at North Groton and Rumney, and her account is interesting because of the light it throws on that period of Mrs. Eddy's life, and especially because of the edification it may be to other invalids. She has related that Mrs. Patterson faithfully observed the laws of hygiene. Every morning, even in the depth of winter when the weather was severely cold in that mountainous climate, Mrs. Patterson was lifted from her bed into a chair, wrapped in blankets. Her chair was then drawn out upon the veranda, where she remained as long as she could sit up, drinking in deep breaths of pure air and feasting her eyes upon the beauty of the hills.

Her room meanwhile was thrown wide open to admit a free current of air and streams of sunshine. Her bed was redressed for the day and when the apartment was restored to a proper temperature the invalid returned to it. She was then bathed, rubbed in alcohol, reclothed, and again lifted into her bed. She had a mattress that could be elevated at the head and many of her hours were passed in the half-reclining attitude in which it was possible for her to read, write, or even receive callers when not suffering too great pain. She ate sparingly and according to a strict diet, imposing upon herself a severe regimen of which water, coarse bread, and natural fruits were the principal articles of nourishment.

Besides attention to hygienic regulation of bathing, eating, and going into the fresh air, Mrs. Patterson received homeopathic treatment from Dr. Patterson, and she herself read books on homeopathy. But for all this, the spinal weakness was not overcome and the nervous seizures continued to occur with increasing violence. However, the brighter views and more cheerful home in Rumney brought some improvement in her health, and Mrs. Patterson even began writing poetry again.

The following year the Civil War broke out and early in 1862 Dr. Patterson left his wife alone to travel South. His journey was made primarily to carry out a commission for Governor Berry of New Hampshire, who had a fund to be distributed to loyal Southerners. This commission enabled him to push a project of his own, for he had been excited by the news of the fall of Sumter, when South Carolina, having seceded, had fired the first shot in the American Civil War, and it was Dr. Patterson's hope to secure an appointment on the medical staff of the army. But going out to visit the scene of the battle of Bull Run, he strayed too far into the Confederate lines and was made a prisoner, presumably as a spy. He was taken to Libby, the Southern war prison, but after six weeks was transferred to the Salisbury prison, where he experienced bitter privations as others in like condition both North and South. Mrs. Patterson learned of his predicament through friends of the family in Washington, and by a letter from her husband. She could do nothing to aid him though her sympathy for him was keen as expressed in letters written at this time in the effort to stir her relatives to activity in his behalf, for in spite of his many shortcomings, in all personal relations he had invariably been kind to her and she had for Dr. Patterson a true wife's devotion. Before his departure she had heard from her son for the first time since he had been taken from North Groton. He had enlisted and gone to the front. How intolerable it seemed to her to lie sick and inert in that lonely cottage, with her husband and son caught in the maelstrom of her country's agony, — how desolate and dreary her days may be imagined. Alone in this remote mountain village, with little company, she suffered a relapse, and was once more thrown back upon herself, and forced by desolation and pain to seek God for comfort and grace to endure her lot while the world was unfolding famous pages of history.

The world, in the persons of the great folk of the vicinity, came occasionally. Years later her maid recounted the airs, the rustling garments, and the consequential stir created by the calls of certain great dames who kept up the punctilious formality, if not neighborly charity, of remembering what was due Mrs. Patterson, born Baker, also sister of the wealthy Mrs. Tilton. But these intrusions of the world were few and far between.

Meantime Mrs. Patterson read her Bible day by day. At this time she more earnestly than ever pondered the cures of the early church. She has written in Science and Health[1] how "in childhood, she often listened with joy to these words, falling from the lips of her saintly mother, 'God is able to raise you up from sickness.'" She also declares how she dwelt upon the meaning of this passage of Scripture which her mother so often quoted, "And these signs shall

[1] "Science and Health with Key to the Scriptures," p. 359.

follow them that believe; . . . they shall lay hands on the sick, and they shall recover." Some of her early experiences now came back to her. She recalled how through her mother's advice to rest in God's love she had been able to recover from the fever brought on by religious argument with her father and pastor. She also recalled how she had subdued the insane man in Tilton when she was a schoolgirl and brought him into a state of calmness and tranquillity when every one else had fled from him in terror. She remembered her exalted religious state at the period of both these cures and endeavored to determine whether such cures depended upon extreme intensity of faith or whether a calm sense of assurance might not as surely be the "prayer of faith." While studying and meditating on these apparent miracles of faith in her own experience and striving to connect them with the manner and method of the New Testament cures, a singular event befell which gives verity to Mrs. Eddy's assertion that for years before the discovery of Christian Science she had been searching for mental causation for disease and a spiritual method of cure.

Aside from the calls of her aristocratic neighbors, she was not entirely forgotten by the village. The children, picking berries along the road, would often stop to talk to "the good sick lady" and often repeated at home or in the houses where they sold their berries what she said to them, how her blue eyes shone upon them, and how her thin hands touched their little brown ones with thrilling sympathy.

So by the love of the children a gentle rumor of saintliness was spread through that region, and if

Mary Baker thought upon the saintliness of her mother, some dwellers of the countryside came to think of Mrs. Patterson as a saint and to go to her for advice and comfort. Among those who sought her aid was a mother carrying her infant, a child whose eyes were badly diseased. The mother was a simple working woman, so simple that she could still believe there was a relation between piety and power. She wept as she laid her babe on Mrs. Patterson's knees and implored her to ask God to cure its blindness.

Mrs. Patterson was touched by the woman's faith and the child's apparent need. She took the babe in her arms and looked into its eyes. She saw they were in such a state of inflammation that neither the pupil nor the iris was discernible. She reflected that Jesus had said, "Suffer the little children to come unto me, and forbid them not." "Who," she asked herself, "has forbidden this little one, who is leading it into the way of blindness?" Mrs. Eddy has stated that she lifted her thought to God and returned the child to its mother, assuring her that God is able to keep His children. The mother looked at the child's eyes and they were healed. This apparently miraculous happening struck awe to Mary Baker as well as to the mother.

Here was a clear manifestation of God's eternal laws of health made to the mind and consciousness of Mary Baker. She had invoked God's mercy and power and the response had come almost instantly. She believed and yet was bewildered. Here was vision, apocalypse. God had healed the child and despite that fact she herself was still enchained with pain. She had

understood for the child, but could not, as yet, understand for herself. She had momentarily struck the
harmonious chord, and a spontaneous healing had resulted. She saw there was a path out of her wilderness, but its beginning for her own feet was not clear.
The detaining hands of the past and experiences she
was about to go through were to impede her progress
toward the clear understanding of truth.

During the previous autumn Dr. Patterson had
been much interested in circulars describing the healing powers of one Phineas P. Quimby of Portland,
Maine. This Quimby had a peculiar reputation. To
some minds he was a charlatan, nothing more, a man
who had learned some tricks of mesmerism by which
he amazed the hearts of the ignorant. To other minds
he was a humane, self-sacrificing man of rare endow-
ments who through abstruse study had become acquainted with secret laws of nature by which he was
able to restore the sick to health. From time to time
the newspapers printed accounts of him, now ridicul-
ing him and now extolling him.

Dr. Patterson had been inclined to take a favor-
able view of him and defend him against derision.
Being himself unable to cure his wife as he had confidently expected to do, he felt much interest in the
accounts of Quimby's cures. It did not matter if
Quimby were a mesmerist, or a Spiritualist, or if he
transmitted magnetic currents. The thing was he
cured. People went to him and got well. It was very
much in this matter with Dr. Patterson as in all the
affairs of life, a case of "lo here! or, lo there!"

So the doctor had written Quimby in the fall of

1861, telling him that his wife had been for many years an invalid from a spinal disease, and that, having heard of his wonderful cures, he desired to have him visit her; or if Quimby intended to journey to Concord, he would carry his wife to him. Quimby replied that he had no intention of making a trip to Concord, that he had all the business he could attend to in Portland, but that he had no doubt whatever he could effect Mrs. Patterson's cure if she would come to him.

Dr. Patterson, however, had, as has been related, projects of his own which more and more took possession of him as he read the news of Lincoln's inauguration and the call for troops to defend the Union. He was full of his proposed trip to Washington, and the preliminary visit which must be made to Concord. These plans required all the funds and energy he had to bestow.

Mrs. Patterson read the Quimby letter with its closing assurance many times. She asked herself often if it were not possible that this man withheld his real experiences from his public circular because of their sacredness, if it were not likely that by piety and prayer, rather than by mesmerism, he had learned the power of healing. This was a perfectly consistent speculation, for from her childhood, from the days of her studying with her brother and later with her pastor, she had been taught to look for a law of cause and effect. Now here was a man healing, she reflected, and there must be a law to govern his cases. Moreover, it was natural to her to take the religious view, that this law was only understood through revelation, and to credit Quimby with having received the revelation. She was a sincere Christian and believed healing without medicine must be done by God.

Still it was the law she sought for. It was not enough for her that here and there a miracle of piety could be performed by those who gave their lives up to prayer. She had come to understand that, where the Hebrew prophets had occasionally and sporadically made God's will prevail in a so-called miracle, Jesus of Nazareth had never failed in invoking health and sustenance. He had cured the most desperate diseases with the same readiness as the mildest; he had blessed the few loaves, and abundance had been found to feed the multitude. Yet here she, Mary Baker, lay on a bed of pain and in sore need of means. Did God withhold from her His bounty because she was a sinner? Like Job, she knew in her heart this was not true. Then where was the fault and what was the law?

Mary Baker had performed certain cures from which she argued as from the sure ground of experience, but these healings were incidental and accidental and she scarcely knew how they had occurred except that she knew they had happened when her thoughts were associated with God. She pondered after this fashion: Laws of God are immutable and universal. Then because His laws are so fixed and so infinitely operative, man by studying them has built up the sciences, as mathematics and mechanics. But in physics he is still crying out for the philosopher's stone and in medicine for the elixir of life. "I know there is cause and effect in the spiritual world as in the natural!" she would exclaim to herself. "I know there is a science of health, a science of life, a divine science, a science of God."

But it did not enter Mary Baker's mind in that hour that by this assertion she had declared herself the discoverer of a great truth, that by this affirmation of faith she had pledged herself to find the way and prove what she had declared. She was to herself only a woman in extremity, hungering for truth. In Portland, Maine, was a man whom she now began to endow with her own faith. If she could get to him, she would question him and find out if he had come close to God's heart. If he had, how humbly she would beg him to teach her and guide her and how joyfully would she follow! In May of 1862 she wrote a letter to Dr. Quimby, a letter which doubtless surprised that gentleman. She stated her confidence in his possession of a philosophy and that she wished to come to him to study and be healed.

She now began to make preparation to visit Quimby. She requested her sister to come to her aid and her sister responded. She rose from her sick bed and started on the journey though she accomplished it by a somewhat circuitous route. Mrs. Patterson's personal things were carefully packed up and sent to Tilton and she returned with Abigail to her home — having parted from her faithful servant some time ago. On the way to Tilton she explained to her sister her wish to visit Phineas P. Quimby, but Abigail demurred. She said Quimby was a mesmerist and Spiritualist, a quack scientist who had traveled around New England with a youth giving exhibitions in hypnotism.

"Why, Mary," she said, "how can you desire to visit such a charlatan, — you with your mind, your talents, your religion, you who have always resisted these doctrines of animal magnetism and the professions of Spiritualism?"

"I certainly do not want mesmerism or Spiritualism," said Mary, "but I somehow believe that I must see what this man has or has not. I am impelled with an unquenchable thirst for God that will not let me rest. Abigail, there is a science beyond all sciences we have ever studied. It is Christ's Science. There is a fundamental doctrine, a God's truth that will restore me to health, and if me, then countless thousands. Has this man Quimby discovered the great truth or is he a blunderer, perhaps a charlatan as you say? I must know."

"Mary, dear," said her sister, "you are excitable and intense. You have lived so long alone in the hills reading and thinking, you are morbid. You should not have been left to yourself so long."

"Then you must go with me to Portland to make up for neglecting me. You will go, won't you, Abigail?"

"Indeed I will not," cried the energetic Mrs. Tilton. "You shall go to Dr. Vail's water-cure at Hill, which is a respectable sanitarium. I will hire you a nurse and rent you a cottage there. We shall see what a physician and hospital care can do for you."

"But have I not faithfully taken medicine and lived according to hygienic rule for years?" asked Mary. Then turning suddenly to her sister, she asked, "Abigail, do you doubt the power of God?"

"I do not, but I believe God helps those who help themselves."

"So He does, sister, when they come into harmony with His law; that I know," answered Mary quietly.

Abigail Tilton's words had a way of driving home and sticking there, like arrows shot into a target. She was a woman of common sense and she proposed to exercise common sense now for her sister. She would hear nothing of Quimby. When Mrs. Tilton had employed a young woman, named Susan Rand, to go to Hill with Mrs. Patterson, had engaged a conveyance to carry her there comfortably, and had instructed the driver to be most careful with his charge, then she supplied her sister with funds sufficient for her stay, felt that she had performed her duty, and washed her hands of the event.

Mrs. Patterson arrived at the sanitarium exhausted with the journey. The driver lifted her out of the carriage rudely and set her upon her feet upon the ground. Mrs. Patterson turned and sped up the steps like a deer, collapsing in the waiting room of the hospital. The utter misery of that collapse was like death settling down upon her. Thus far she had come in her belief that God was going to help her and to help her now. But here God seemed to be forsaking her. She could only reiterate to herself in gasping weakness, "I know God can and will cure me, if only I could understand His way." But she was in the midst of the doctors again who believed in quite different agencies. She must now submit to the water-cure, the fad of the period.

They carried her to one of the little cottages and

instructed her attendant in the system of nursing prevailing at the water-cure. For several weeks the treatment was continued with little result. Mrs. Tilton's common sense was failing its purpose once more. Then Mary Baker asserted her family spirit. She had wanted to go to Portland to see Quimby, and she determined she would go without further discussion. She wrote him in August that she would try to come to him, though she could sit up but for a few minutes at a time, and she asked him if he thought she would be able to reach him without sinking from the effects of the journey. Quimby replied so encouragingly that she completed her arrangements.

Mrs. Patterson arrived at the International Hotel, Portland, in October, 1862. Here in this hotel Dr. Quimby, doctor by courtesy only, had his offices. In his reception-room his patients gathered and sat by the hour, talking and visiting, discussing the doctor's sayings and their own illnesses. And in this reception room on the morning in October when Mrs. Patterson arrived, were a number of patients together with his son George, a young man scarcely turned twenty-one, who then acted as his father's secretary.

Mrs. Patterson was assisted up the stairs to this room and her extreme feebleness was marked by all. Dr. Quimby came from his inner office to receive the new patient and she beheld for the first time the man she believed a great physician. He was of small physique, with white hair and beard, level brows, and shrewd, penetrating eyes. He was healthy, dominant, energetic. He had the eye of the born hypnotizer, the man who can persuade other wills to obey his own,

especially the wills of the sick and mentally dis-
ordered. But his face was kindly and his expression
sincere.

Mary Baker was at that time a frail shadow of a
woman, an abstracted student, given to much thinking and prayer. With great blue eyes, deep sunk, yet
arched above with beautiful brows, she looked into
the friendly face bent above her and she looked with
the deep intense gaze of the seer.

CHAPTER VII

THE APOTHEOSIS OF A HYPNOTIST

IN order to understand what sort of meeting it was which took place between the emaciated sufferer and invalid, Mary Baker, and the mesmeric healer, Phineas Quimby, at the International Hotel in Portland, Maine, in October, 1862, it is necessary to survey briefly the latter's life and work up to this period.

Quimby was the son of a poor blacksmith and was apprenticed as a lad to a clock-maker. He had no schooling and grew up illiterate but industrious and honest. He made with his own hands hundreds of clocks; and, having his interest thus awakened in mechanics, tinkered with small inventions; and is said to have perfected a number of tools, especially a hand-saw. Part of the time he earned his living making daguerreotypes.

Thus he lived until he was thirty-six years old, a nervous, shrewd little man with a piercing black eye and determined mouth. He was argumentative and somewhat combative, inquiring, inventive, and doggedly determined. These traits were partially due to lack of education; to him an axiom was not a self-evident proposition; he refused to accept anything as a truth unless he could experiment with it and prove it for himself. He was not religious, but a man of good morals and of a kindly nature, always ready to help his neighbor.

In 1838 Charles Poyen, the French hypnotist, visited Belfast, Maine, Quimby's home town, where he gave a course of lectures on mesmerism with illustrative experiments. At his first exhibition in the town hall his efforts were something of a failure, and he declared that some one in the audience perverted the hypnotic influence. He invited whoever it was to remain and meet him after the others had gone. The man who remained was "Park" Quimby, as the townspeople called him. Poyen talked with him and assured him that he had extraordinary hypnotic powers which, if developed, would make him an adept in mesmerism. Quimby was gratified and absorbingly interested. He at once began to experiment on his friends and acquaintances, and whenever he found a willing subject tried to put him into a mesmeric sleep. As he was very often successful in these efforts, people began to talk about him and if any one in the town did an eccentric thing, or had a mishap, the gossips said with waggish appreciation, "Park Quimby has mesmerized him."

His townsmen came to believe Quimby could compel a man to come in from the street by fixing his eye on him; and nothing more greatly entertained the villagers than to assist at such an exhibition at the corner store. Quimby's method of hypnotizing at this time was to fix his eyes in a concentrated gaze upon his subject. If he wished thoroughly to mesmerize the subject, that is, to put him to sleep, he would make passes across the subject's forehead, continuing his strokes down the shoulders and the length of the arms, shaking his hands after every pass. His subjects professed to thrill and tingle as though electric currents had passed through them, and some of them would perform Quimby's hypnotic commands, however absurd they might be. Quimby soon found an unusually good subject in a youth named Lucius Burkmar. As his experiments with this young man absorbed his interest and attracted considerable attention, he abandoned his workshop and devoted himself to mesmerism.

In his clock-tinkering days in Belfast, Park Quimby had been regarded as eccentric, and his home town now thought him quite mad in his new role. A few persons took him seriously and sought to have him cure minor illnesses, but more often he was derided, and sometimes even condemned as an infidel. Not appreciated at home, he left Belfast, taking Burkmar with him, and together they gave exhibitions in other towns where he was not so well known to his audiences and could command greater respect for his hypnotic feats. These are said often to have been so startling as to frighten susceptible persons, arousing in them suspicion of witchcraft and magic. More than once on his travels he stirred up a mob from which he and Burkmar had to escape by taking to their heels.

Wonder-working soon proving not entirely agreeable as a method of earning a living, Quimby returned to Belfast and settled down in his workshop again until another mesmerist visited the town in the person of John Bovee Dods. Dods was the author of a book which was published in 1850. It contained ideas he had taught for twenty years and was entitled "The Philosophy of Electrical Psychology." He gave public lectures in Belfast, exchanged ideas with Quimby,

and took into his employ Quimby's subject, the lad
Burkmar. When Quimby again employed Burkmar
he found that Dods had been using him to read clairvoyantly the minds of patients and influencing him to
prescribe remedies which Dods manufactured.

Quimby thought that overreaching, and when
Burkmar diagnosed cases for him, he influenced him
to prescribe simple herbs. These remedies appeared
to effect cures as well as the higher-priced ones and
Quimby began to believe that it was not the medicine
that was doing the curing but the patient's confidence
in the doctor or medium. This was a decided step in a
progression of reasoning which, had he possessed the
mental equipment, might have carried him into the
realm of psychological discovery. He was working
honestly and cautiously, however, and so accomplished a modicum of success as a magnetic healer.
He first abandoned medicines and second, dismissing
the subject he had so long relied upon, began to sit
directly with his patients, for he had discovered his
own clairvoyant ability to read his patient's thoughts
or induce him to tell "all his sensations." His cures
were in part accomplished by directing the patient's
thought to another part of the body from that supposed to be affected. Thus a boil on the back of
the neck became a toothache at his suggestion. He
rubbed the heads of his patients and otherwise manipulated their bodies, believing in his personal magnetism as the important part of the curative agency.

In relieving the sick of their pains he found that
he took their conditions upon himself, and he often
related how he had to go into his garden and hoe vig-

orously, or to his woodpile and saw wood most industriously, to get rid of rheumatic pains or agues, and
to reestablish his own equilibrium and recharge himself with electric currents; for Quimby was never all
his life rid of the theories of Dods relating to the
transmission of human electricity. Quimby is said to
have cured cases of chronic disease of long standing
and to have secured a worthier reputation than when
working wonders with Lucius Burkmar. He now began
to travel about New England again and issued circulars advertising himself far and wide as a healer with
a new theory. Avidity for the mysterious in the rural
mind carried these circulars to the remotest hamlets.
A curious account of his statements as to himself and
his methods appeared in the Bangor *Jeffersonian* in
1857. It was headed, "A New Doctrine of Health and
Disease," and it said in part:

A gentleman of Belfast, Dr. Phineas P. Quimby, who
was remarkably successful as an experimenter in mesmerism some sixteen years ago, and has continued his investigations in psychology, has discovered and in his daily
practise carries out, a new principle in the treatment of
disease.

His theory is that the mind gives immediate form to
the animal spirit and that the animal spirit gives form to
the body as soon as the less plastic elements of the body are
able to assume that form. Therefore, his first course in the
treatment of a patient is to sit down beside him and put
himself *en rapport* with him, which he does without producing the mesmeric sleep.

He says that in every disease the animal spirit, or spiritual form, is somewhat disconnected from the body, that
it imparts to him all its grief and the cause of it, which
may have been mental trouble or shock to the body, as

over-fatigue, excessive cold or heat, etc. This impresses
the mind with anxiety and the mind reacting upon the body
produces disease. With this spirit form Dr. Quimby con-
verses and endeavors to win it away from its grief, and
when he has succeeded in doing so, it disappears and re-
unites with the body. Thus is commenced the first step
toward recovery. This union frequently lasts but a short
time when the spirit again appears, exhibiting some new
phase of its trouble. With this he again persuades and con-
tends until he overcomes it, when it disappears as before.
Thus two shades of trouble have disappeared from the
mind and consequently from the animal spirit, and the
body already has commenced its efforts to come into a
state in accordance with them.

In 1859 Quimby went to Portland, Maine, and remained there until the summer of 1865. During this
period he had many patients and performed a number
of cures. His hypnotic practise now seems to have
changed its form to a large extent, notwithstanding he
manipulated his patients always and this seems to have
been the feature upon which he laid the greatest stress.
But he now embellished these magnetic treatments
with conversation, endeavoring to account for the origin of disease in opinions and notions, oscillating between weirdly speculative and practical points of view
and nowhere confining himself to stringent definition.
It was expedient to survey Quimby's life up to
this point and it is now necessary to arrive at a clear
conception of what sort of thinker he was. Unless we
are quite clear here, we shall stray into a quagmire
and find ourselves believing that all that follows in the
life of Mary Baker Eddy was the result of her meeting
with this man. This argument is advanced only by

those who have a vague and confused idea of Quimby. Its claims are these: that Quimby cured Mary Baker of her invalidism, that he gave her the germ ideas of her philosophy, that he presented her with manuscripts which she afterwards claimed as her own, that he focussed her mind, that he was the impetus of all her subsequent momentum. Were these contentions just, none but a perfidious ingrate would deny them. But not to deny them, circumstantially and in totality, is to leave open the gate to the quagmire that Christian Science is mesmerism religionized. For to interpret Mary Baker Eddy and Christian Science by Quimbyism is to lose sight forever of the unique and powerful significance of her life.

Summarizing Quimby, therefore, it may be stated that though he was no scientist, he was trained by over twenty years' experience in practising mesmerism and without knowing it was really a remarkable hypnotist. It would have been very extraordinary if from his quarter of a century's experience in mesmerism, clairvoyance, and magnetism he had not reduced his observations to some sort of philosophy however crude and empirical. Though he liked to call it his wisdom, what he actually attained was a jumble of reasoning which even he did not understand. He combated with vigor and manliness sickly ideas in the minds of his patients, but his healthy physical presence, not philosophy, did the work. Saturated with Poyen's theories of mesmerism and Dods's doctrines of electrical currents, he was forever trying to convey something of himself to his patients, some subtle fluid or invisible essence. He never eliminated his personality.

Quimby was not even a religious man. He habitually and stoutly denied the Messianic mission of Jesus, declaring that Jesus was a healer and never intended to establish a religion. His notion of the Creator was confused with ideas of nature, and he is said to have called God the great mesmerizer or magnet. Possessing neither education nor the least training in philosophic thinking, and having no real religious faith, this man was ill-equipped for stating a philosophy. Moreover, his belief in his personal magnetism blocked the way for forming a sound philosophic doctrine, even if his lack of cultivation had been modified by reading and scholarly association.

Quimby has been delineated that he may have his due,— Quimby the illiterate mesmerist, Quimby the blundering and stumbling reasoner, Quimby the kindly, sympathetic healer, above all, Quimby the unconscious hypnotizer. Ignorance will cover all his errors, good intentions all his accomplishments. He would never have claimed to have originated anything had he known all there was to be known of Mesmer. Quimbyism was but an excrescence on the natural growth of mental suggestion from Mesmer to the Nancy school. Quimbyism is not embryonic Christian Science; it is merely mesmerism gone astray.

When Mary Baker entered Mr. Quimby's office he sat down beside her, as was his custom with his patients, to get into the sympathetic and clairvoyant relation with her nature which he called rapport. Gazing fixedly into her eyes, he told her, as he had told others, that she was held in bondage by the opinions of her family and physicians, that her animal

spirit was reflecting its grief upon her body and calling it spinal disease. He then wet his hands in a basin
of water and violently rubbed her head, declaring that
in this manner he imparted healthy electricity. Gradually he wrought the spell of hypnotism, and under
that suggestion she let go the burden of pain, accepting for the time this counterfeit of spiritual method.
The relief was no doubt tremendous. Her gratitude
certainly was unbounded. She felt free from the ex-
cruciating pain of years. Quimby himself was amazed
at her sudden healing; no less was he amazed at the
interpretation she immediately placed upon it, that it
had been accomplished by Quimby's mediatorship between herself and God.

She had come to Quimby prepared to find him a
saint who healed by virtue of his religious wisdom,
and as soon as she met him she completed her mental picture, endowing him with her own faith. Thus
the hypnotist had actually nothing to do with it. Her
faith returned upon her, flooding her with radiance,
healing her of her pain. The modest mesmerist was
astonished at her faith. It covered him with confusion
to have her religious emotion, engendered by years of
suffering, ascribe to him a spiritual method which he
knew he did not possess. Mary Baker did possess it
unconsciously and healed herself with truth.

Mrs. Patterson's case struck Quimby as one of his
most remarkable cures. He watched with interest for
her return on the following day and his gratification
was equal to her gratitude when he found that she
was apparently in the same radiant condition of well-
being as when she stood erect the day before and said

she was well. However, he again administered his
mesmeric treatment, stroking her head, shoulders,
and back, until she declared she felt as if standing on
an electric battery.

"It is not magnetism that does this work, doctor,"
she declared. "You have no need to touch me, nor
disorder my hair with your mesmeric passes."

"What then do you think does the healing?" he
asked.

"Your knowledge of God's law, your understanding of the truth which Christ brought into the world
and which had been lost for ages."

Quimby sat abashed. He was not religious, wor-
shipful, or reverent, but he caught at the wonder of
this idea, the glory of it, and vaguely conceived the
renown of it. He stumbled, however, in his first
step to the pedestal of a greatness which he knew
was not his.

"I see what you mean," he said musingly, "that
Christ has come into the world again; but in that case
I must be John and you Jesus."

Delicate religious apprehension and clear mental
acumen developed by years of prayer, study, and discussion had fitted Mary Baker's mind to meet such a
statement. She took instant umbrage at the startling
irreverence.

"That is blasphemy," she declared quietly, and
Quimby's eyes, already half whimsical over his tentative remark, dropped before hers. He became instantly serious, and said:

"I didn't mean it so; I don't understand the way
you explain your cure. No one before ever believed

it was divine truth that operated through me. They have said I healed through some mysterious force in myself. I have told them it was healthy electrical currents together with my 'Wisdom' that I imparted which effected the cure. But the faith in Christ which you declare enables me to heal I have not. It makes me think it is your faith in Christ that heals you, and all I can do is to acknowledge it. If the spirit of Christ is with you and I acknowledge it, then I bear the relation to you of John to Jesus."

As is very well known to-day the subject under hypnosis reveals the inner recesses of his mind and gives up to the hypnotizer the thoughts of years. Mrs. Patterson remained for three weeks in Portland and was daily at Mr. Quimby's office. Quimby always spoke of her as a remarkable woman and would daily question her as to her understanding of her cure. She continually invested his mind with her own ideas. He was eager to take advantage of her superior mental qualifications to add something to his "Wisdom," and he would converse with her by the hour for that purpose. Unconsciously she was learning a deep lesson for the world, namely, what is hypnotism and its effects.

"You say there is a principle which governs the healing," he would remark. "Now what do you think that principle is?"

"I think it is God," she would reply. "You should understand, Dr. Quimby, much better than I that this is not your magnetism or your wisdom but God's truth. I try to understand my cure every day, but I am still confused. You should make clear statements concerning your understanding of this truth for your patients' sake, not in scribbled notes, but in a developed argument summed up in a treatise. There must be a truth underlying your healing. Do you analyze your processes?"

"I do not understand entirely what I do," the doctor would say; "so how can I make the patient understand?"

"But there can be no science of health until the laws can be stated," Mary Baker would reply. "If this is a philosophy it can be reduced to philosophic arguments. This is a very spiritual doctrine, the eternal years of God are with it, and it must be stated so that it will stand firm as the Rock of Ages."

Such portentous appreciation greatly excited the ambition of Quimby. He desired to measure up to this conception of himself and his work. He would retire to his study after treating to attempt to reduce a history of his cures to a science. He gathered from Mrs. Patterson's conversation that he should write something, and perhaps with a quite innocent idea of copying a model he asked her to write something out first. For this purpose he gave her some notes he had made, commenting on the symptoms of recent patients. She took these to her boarding-house and occupied several days striving to piece them into an essay.

Her efforts were not a brilliant success. His penciled thoughts continually contradicted themselves and not only themselves, they directly contradicted her conception of her own cure or any other she had known of. When Mrs. Patterson talked with Quimby, he did not contradict her; on the contrary, he quickly adopted both her language and ideas; but such words as science, principle, truth, inserted at random in his subsequent notes, found no place in his jumble of theories and produced an extraordinary result. As an example of this result, the following quotation is said to be from Quimby's pencil:

I will now try to establish this science or rock, and upon it I will build the science of life. My foundation is animal matter or life. This set in action by wisdom produces thought. Thoughts, like grains of sand, are held together by their own sympathy, wisdom or attraction. Now man is composed of these particles of matter, or thought, combined and arranged by wisdom. As thought is always changing, so man is always throwing off particles of thought and receiving others. Thus man is a progressive idea; yet he is the same man, although he is changing all the time for better or for worse. As his senses are in his wisdom, and his wisdom is attached to his idea or body, his change of mind is under one of the two directions either of this world of opinions or of God or Science, and his happiness or misery is the result of his wisdom.

Though Mary Baker's own pure stream of religious thought wrought such confusion to Quimby's materialistic theories as to make his utterances sound like philosophy gone mad, her cure, whether a temporary one wrought under hypnotism, or a permanent one achieved through a momentary realization of God, was secure. She consistently maintained that God was the "wisdom" Quimby brought to his patients. Quimby never told her so, and the hypnotist to-day would say that Quimby may have allowed her to hypnotize herself with that thought. However that may be, by seeing God as the principle of her cure, she stood safe on her own foundation, laid in the years of orthodox religious experience, though she was not to understand this until Quimby the hypnotizer lay in his grave.

Quimby really seemed to desire to adopt the idea of bringing God to his patients and would declare with all the wisdom he had that God was the great mesmerizer. Continuing to mesmerize his patients, he began to occupy the position of a lesser god in the minds of many who gathered round him. They quickly took up this idea of God as the great mesmerizer, and Quimby in a sense became His representative. When Quimby, "condensing his identity," would visit them in waking hours of the night, or when they had returned to their homes, it was to them the shadow of the Almighty. This produced hypnotism more absolute than anything Quimby had hitherto dreamed of. It quite appreciably increased his success as a healer. Though he acquired the idea of God as the healer from Mary Baker, he reversed it and made of the Supreme Being a necromancer.

CHAPTER VIII

THE MYSTERY OF THE QUIMBY MANUSCRIPTS

THROUGH the writings of Mary Baker on what she thought Quimby believed, "Quimbyism" and Quimby manuscripts came to have a factitious existence. Her writings were given into Quimby's keeping and were doubtless copied by other patients; her explanations of his cures were often accepted instead of Quimby's, even Quimby himself accepting them in part, flattered at the interpretation put upon him and his work. A curious commingling of mesmerism and religious faith resulted from the association of these distinctly differing minds, and the manuscripts handed from one to another perpetuated this confusion.

Mary Baker dwelt long under the influence of Quimby's mesmeric belief and it came to have a great, though not supreme, significance in her later teaching, the significance of a counterfeit of the truth she was later to discover and proclaim. From 1862 to 1866 were for her so many years in the wilderness, after which came that search for the mountain which was to be her Horeb, and which had first been shown her by illumination when in Rumney she healed the child of blindness. A sublime faith held her firmly through this period of confusion as it did through subsequent travail of spirit, but the confusion temporarily wrought in her induced her to give honor where honor was not due.

In later years, roused by the assault of critics hostile to her restatements of Jesus' teachings, Mrs. Eddy wrote fearlessly of her confused condition at this period. She related how for years she struggled with the effects of Dr. Quimby's practise, acknowledging that she had written and talked of him with ignorant enthusiasm until she realized the harmful influence of teaching such "a false human concept." She said:

It has always been my misfortune to think people better and bigger than they really are. My mistake is, to endow another person with my ideal, and then make him think it his own. . . . I would touch tenderly his [Quimby's] memory, speak reverently of his humane purpose, and name only his virtues, did not this man Dresser [Julius Dresser] drive me, for conscience-sake, to sketch the facts. . . . I was ignorant of the basis of Animal Magnetism twenty years ago, but know now that it would disgrace and invalidate any mode of medicine. . . . The animal poison imparted through mortal mind, by false or incorrect mental physicians, is more destructive to health and morals than are the mineral and vegetable poisons prescribed by the matter-physicians. . . . I denounced it [Quimby's method], after a few of my first students rubbed the heads of their patients, and the immorality of one student opened my eyes to the horrors possible in Animal Magnetism. . . . I discovered the Science of Mindhealing, and that was enough. It was the way Christ had pointed out: and that fact glorified it. My discovery promises nothing but blessings to every inhabitant of the globe.[1]

The confusion of her ideas with Quimby's in her early writings, which were widely copied and circulated, gave rise to the Quimby manuscript tradition. This tradition grew into a controversy which deserves

[1] *The Christian Science Journal*, June, 1887.

some explication, lest, in treating it as negligible, a fabulous fame of incongruous origin shall be perpetuated. The existence of writings of any consequence which are *veritable* Quimby manuscripts would be negligible were it not for the possible confusion of them with Mary Baker's writings. Veritable Quimby manuscripts are absolutely hypothetical, as hypothetical as was the inheritance of Mme. Thérèse Humbert of Paris. It will be remembered that credit for an enormous sum was secured for a period of over twenty years by the Humbert family on a basis of nothing. Nay, not upon nothing. Mme. Humbert had a *copy* of a will, and she had an affidavit from a notary that securities representing the property she claimed to be heir to were sealed in a strong box and held for her in the safe of a bank. When the court finally ordered this strong box opened, it was found that there were not securities for twenty millions, but there were one thousand dollars, a few copper coins, and a brass button. Eleven millions had been advanced on this absurd basis.

The Quimby claim is a purely intellectual one and the credit secured has been an extravagant belief, a belief which provokes unjust and invidious suspicion as to the origin of the fundamental principles of Christian Science. To show how baseless is this suspicion, it is necessary to examine the Quimby claim.

Some twenty years after Quimby's death (which resulted from a tumor of the stomach in 1866), when Christian Science had been placed on a firm foundation, it began to be contended by Quimby's son and a former patient of Quimby that he had left manuscripts

on a number of subjects, setting forth a system of philosophy. Jealously guarding the proof of his claim,
the son, by indirect assertion, implied as his reason
for not publishing the alleged manuscripts that their
authorship would be claimed by the author of Science
and Health if he published them during her lifetime.

This is a rather strange suggestion, but it sets
forth the shadow of a fear justified by circumstances.
It has been shown that Mrs. Patterson in 1862 wrote
certain manuscripts for Quimby and gave them to
him. She repeated this generous, if unprofitable, act
in the early part of 1864, when she spent two or three
months in an uninterrupted effort to fathom and elucidate "Quimbyism." It seems almost incredible that
a woman of her intellectual and spiritual development should have devoted so long a period to the
struggle of formulating a philosophy out of the cha-
otic but dogmatic utterances of this self-taught mesmerist. But there was a deep-lying reason for this
long struggle, which was bound to end in dire failure,
and the reason both for the struggle and for the failure could only be made known to her by the extraordinary and impressive circumstance of an original
discovery.

As the deviation of the needle from the true North
caused mariners to investigate for centuries the cause
of deflection until the eminent scientist, Lord Kelvin,
successfully insulated the compass; so, though she
subsequently discovered the principle of Mind-healing, it was not until Mary Baker learned what "Quimbyism" really was, namely magnetism, that she came
to understand why she so long strove in vain to have

Quimby unfold to her that which was not his to give, why she so long sought for principle where there was no principle. Quimby was navigating without a compass, and his zigzag course could only fetch home by accident.

But Quimby believed in his own course as the true one. While he acknowledged to other patients that he was delighted with Mrs. Patterson's enthusiasm and asserted that her perception of truth was keener than that of any other of his patients, it is not in evidence that he ever gave her credit for a scope which exceeded his, save in religious apprehension, which to him was not authoritative. He received from Mrs. Patterson manuscripts to which she unselfishly and unguardedly signed his name. These manuscripts in Mrs. Eddy's handwriting, interlined with Quimby's emendations, may still be in existence.

Lest the implied reason for not publishing the alleged Quimby manuscripts — the fear that their authorship would be disputed — should be retroactive, there is still another reason advanced. This reason, too, is given only by implication, but it is worthier of commendation than the former. The second reason is the illiteracy of Phineas Quimby, for which he was in no wise to blame, but which, as has been shown, prevented his accomplishing anything in the way of literature.[1]

---

[1] The author made the journey in the depth of winter to the little city of Belfast, Maine, off the main line of travel and somewhat difficult of access, to see, as I supposed, the Quimby manuscripts. Arriving there the custodian of the manuscripts, George A. Quimby, said to me:

"If all the people who have come to see me in the past twenty years about these manuscripts of my father were fishes and were laid head and tail together they would stretch from here to Montana. If all the letters that have

"My father was self-educated," said Mr. Quimby, "but he had read a great deal. His head was full of speculative ideas and he was constantly writing down his thoughts. He wrote without capitalizing or punctuating. His mind was always ahead of his pen, and

been written to me on the subject were spread out they would make a plaster that would cover the country."

When I asked Mr. Quimby for permission to see these much-talked-of manuscripts, he took from a drawer in his desk a copy-book such as school children use to write essays in. It was in a good state of preservation, not yellowed by age, and was written in from cover to cover in a neat copyist's hand. There were no erasures, or interlineations, no breaks for paragraphs and very few headings. There were dates at the end of the articles, of which there appeared to be two or three different ones in the book. The dates were 1861 and 1863.

"Is this your father's handwriting?" I asked Mr. Quimby.

"It is not; that is my mother's, I believe, and here is one in the handwriting of one of the Misses Ware."

Mr. Quimby went to a great iron safe in the wall of his office and brought out six or eight more books of a similar character. I glanced through the pages and saw that all were written in this style with some variation in the handwriting and then asked:

"Are none of these in your father's handwriting?"

"No, they are all copies of copies. . . . These are the only manuscripts I have shown to any one and the only ones I will show."

"But," I objected, "there have recently been printed facsimile reproductions of your father's manuscripts over the date 1863 in which appear the words 'Christian Science.' I particularly wished to see that manuscript."

"I am showing you exactly what I showed others. That is the very page that was photographed."

"And in whose writing is this?"

"My mother's, I believe, or possibly one of the Misses Ware; . . . they are copies of things my father wrote. He used to write at odd moments on scraps of paper whatever came into his mind."

"And have you those papers now?"

"Yes, I have."

"Will you let me see a few pages of them?"

"No, I will not. No one has seen them and no one shall. . . . I tell you they have all been after them, Arens, Dresser, Minot J. Savage, Peabody, and these recent newspaper and magazine investigators. But I have never shown them. Dr. Savage wrote me that I owed it to the world to produce them."

"And did you not think so?"

"No. I have said I will never print them while that woman lives."

"Do you mean Mrs. Eddy?"

"That is just who I mean."

—*Human Life*, April, 1907.

he would not paragraph or formulate his thoughts into essays. I guess many of his words were misspelled too."

If the son cherished and guarded the papers containing his father's original notes, there must have been some more sufficient reason, which he alone knew, why he so long withheld them from publicity. He for years refused to submit them for inspection to any person competent or incompetent to judge of their value. Under the most urgent demand he failed to bring them forth into the light, to allow a friend in dire need to use them in defence in a suit at law, or to permit a distinguished scholar to prepare a brief in their interest. Literary men, lawyers, and journalists have urged their exhibition in vain. In 1887 Mrs. Eddy advertised that she would pay for their publication. But for some deep and inscrutable reason it has been impossible to unveil them.

The conclusion seems warranted that there is nothing worthy of the name of manuscripts in the Quimby safe. It may be that there are certain deposits of fragmentary pencilings of Phineas Quimby. It may be that there are certain of Mrs. Eddy's writings there. It may be that these writings are interlaced, and to produce one is to produce the other. Thus the Quimby manuscript tradition may rest, not on nothing, but, as in the Humbert will case, on something so near to nothing as to be negligible of consideration.

But though the original manuscripts, if such there be, have never seen the light, it must be understood that George A. Quimby has exhibited some writings which he calls Quimby manuscripts. These are a series of copy-books filled with writing. Originality is not claimed for these writings which are described as copies of copies of Phineas Quimby's notes, but only are they so described when exact information is required. Ordinarily they are loosely called by Mr. Quimby, "my father's manuscripts."

Authenticity is rendered doubtful for these writings, because, not only has no one ever seen the originals on which they are said to be based, but also because the world never heard of these copy-books until after Science and Health had long been published, was in its third edition, and the book and its philosophy had begun to make a stir in the world of thought. It would have to be shown clearly upon what they are based to clear them of the possibility of plagiarism. It is possible they are of an earlier date than when they first came to be spoken of; it is possible they are enlargements on conversations held with Phineas Quimby by the patients who made the transcriptions; it is possible they are emended Mary Baker writings.

But unless originals exist, how can these copy-book writings be authenticated? Yet the copy-book manuscripts with their uncertain dates, the "copies of copies," are all that is meant when critics of Christian Science refer ambiguously to Quimby's writings. These copy-books have been evasively exhibited in lieu of the original Quimby notes, and the owner of the copy-books has allowed books to be written from them on the philosophy of Quimby, has given out photographs of their pages as facsimili of Quimby's manuscripts, and has generally led the world to believe they were the writings of his father. He appears himself to be a victim of the Quimby manuscript tradition.

If the copy-book manuscripts themselves were published, illustrated with original Quimby notes, illiterate scrawls it may be, yet the genuine pencilings of Phineas Quimby, some interest might be evoked for them. But until this act of sincerity be performed, so far as the evidence goes Quimby left no writings.

CHAPTER IX

MESMERISM DOMINANT

GRATEFUL to Quimby, and believing in his ability to heal, Mrs. Patterson returned to Tilton a well woman the following January. A week after arriving in Portland she had climbed to the dome of the city hall by a stairway of one hundred and eighty-two steps to signalize what then appeared to be her complete recovery from spinal weakness. Attributing her well-being entirely to Quimby and asserting that he was not a Spiritualist or a mesmerist, she wrote two articles for the press of Portland, giving him the honor of her cure and revealing a gratitude so heartfelt and sincere that the most cynical must have admitted her generosity. In one article she said she could see dimly and only as trees walking the great principle which underlay his works.

That neither Quimby nor any of his patients could discern this principle, and that he did constantly resort to Spiritualistic clairvoyance for diagnosis and to mesmerism for healing, made no alteration in the faith of Mary Baker. She heard and saw only what was in her own mind and experience, and continued to identify publicly and privately her faith with Quimby's in the face of all the evidence to the contrary and his own occasional expostulation. The Portland public, reading her articles, fairly caught its breath and asked in amazement, "What, this Quimby compared to Christ! well, what next?" In her attitude toward Quimby she was like a daughter idealizing a father whom all the world knows to be other than she thinks him. In her unbounded gratitude for improved health she attributed to him a method and system which he did not possess.

On arriving at her sister's home she talked to the various members of her family and all their intimate friends about Quimby's power to heal, talked until she really excited in her sister Abigail a curiosity to know something of Quimby. The handsome boy, Albert, whose birth had been largely responsible for the banishment of Mary's son, George Glover, had grown up into a rather wayward young man. Abigail wanted her boy cured of his habits and she instructed Mary to write "Dr." Quimby to come to them, as he professed himself able to do, spiritually, or in his "condensed identity," or by his "omnipresence," and give Albert the benefit of his magnetic "wisdom." As nothing resulted from the writing to change Albert's habits, Mrs. Tilton determined to take him to Portland. She made the journey along with her son about a month after Mary's return, but she returned home confirmed in her own mind that Quimby was exactly what she had previously supposed him to be, an ignorant quack with a jargon of cant which made no impression upon her. She was gratified that Mary was cured, but what had cured her she failed to comprehend from her experience with Quimby. Abigail Tilton came near to the truth, however, when she told her family that it was Mary's own faith and had nothing whatsoever to do with the Portland mesmerist. As for Albert, he was not benefited, and his life ended in an early death.

Prior to Mrs. Patterson's journey to Portland to see Quimby, her husband, unknown to her, had escaped from Salisbury prison. For seven dreary weeks he worked his way to the friendly Northern lines and finally reached Tilton. On finding that his wife was in Portland he travelled on to join her in December. He was penniless, threadbare, and emaciated, a spectacle to excite commiseration. His share in the fortunes of war had been inglorious and bitter, but he had a thrilling tale to unfold and was eager to relate it. The income he might gain from lecturing would have been more than welcome at that time. While still in Portland he planned to give his first talk. Unable to draw a large audience he abandoned the attempt, although not the intention. After this experience, in January they both returned to Tilton, but Patterson did not at once resume his dental practise, nor did he seem disposed to reassume his domestic obligations. Some natural toleration was felt by all who knew him for his desire for a vacation and he was humored in an imaginary importance which impelled him to a lecture tour. So he departed on a leisurely round of visits to the various towns where he had formerly practised, speaking on his prison adventures.

Mrs. Patterson remained with her sister and took an active interest in the sewing-circles which were organized to provide garments for the soldiers and lint and bandages for the hospitals. In this work both sisters were active and much together in their old-time affectionate intimacy. With her wasting illness gone, Mrs. Patterson recovered her early comeliness, her cheeks again became rosy, her eyes sparkling, and

her spirits gay. She wrote a letter at this time to
Quimby in which she said, "I am as much an escaped
prisoner as my dear husband was."

All through the summer she remained at Tilton,
active in charitable work; but in the fall her sense of
private duty and personal obligation led her to go to
Saco, the early home of her husband. Here she
visited his brother and was for a time with her husband, whom she endeavored to persuade to return
to his practise. His wander-fever was not yet satisfied, but he agreed to make an effort to establish
himself, and for this ultimate object went to Lynn,
Massachusetts.

Disappointed in his purposeless conduct, Mrs.
Patterson felt a spiritual depression overtaking her.
It seemed likely that she was going to find it difficult
to reconcile her husband to orderly living, just when
her improved health made life seem to stretch before
her invitingly with many avenues open for usefulness.
Her perplexity was so serious that it amounted to
anxiety, and now she experienced a return of a number of minor ailments and illnesses which threatened
to culminate in a serious renewal of suffering.

Was this cure of hers, so widely proclaimed, to
lapse, and was she again to return to the old misery?
In the year which had just passed she had been more
or less absorbed in the world, traveling, and actively
working in the relief organizations. Her religious life
had not been exclusively absorbing, for she had been
conforming more to the customary ways of the world
than for many years. But if she could not take her
understanding of God's laws into every-day life and

use it to meet the shock of events, of what use was it to her or to others, how could she really claim to possess an understanding? She began to see that she had not possessed herself of clear and definite understanding, or any sound philosophy; and with the hope that she would yet acquire such an enlightenment from Quimby, she left the home of her husband's family and went again to Portland. This was in the early part of 1864.

During this sojourn in Portland Mrs. Patterson resided at a boarding-house where were also living two other of Mr. Quimby's patients, Mrs. Sarah Crosby and Miss Mary Ann Jarvis. They became acquainted and shortly a friendly intimacy was established among them all on the basis of their common interest. Mrs. Crosby had an especially vigorous personality and was later to show herself possessed of considerable business ability. At the time of her meeting Mrs. Patterson she had been broken down in health by the birth of several children and thought her vitality exhausted.

Mrs. Crosby's experience under Quimby's treatment was like Mrs. Patterson's in outward seeming. He sat opposite her and gazed fixedly into her eyes; he laid one hand on her stomach and one on her head to establish an electric current; and finally rubbed her head vigorously and told her his spirit would accompany her home. In describing him she says he was a "natural healer."

It was the custom of the patients to take their treatment in the morning and the afternoon hours were largely spent in disentangling each other's hair from the mesmerist's snarling and their ideas from his confusing statements. Mrs. Patterson did not linger long with this feminine seminar. Quimby frequently invited her to return to his office after he was through practising to continue those interviews which he had had with her on her previous visits, remembering the absorbing discussions of the topic of spiritual healing which she had introduced at the time. On these occasions she sometimes argued long and earnestly with him, endeavoring to lead him to accept her ideas and to group his thoughts into a logical syllogism. Her evenings were almost entirely spent in the attempt to harmonize his notions with her own spiritual ideas. Mrs. Crosby has said that Mrs. Patterson labored long into the night at her writings. These are some of the writings which supposedly form the basis of the copybook literature.

In the spring of 1864 Mrs. Patterson spent two months at Warren, Maine, with Miss Jarvis and her consumptive sister, striving to further the work Quimby had begun and to complete the cure of the consumptive. She had traveled home with the invalids from Portland and they clung to her for healing. She was able to help them, but at the time she was trying to believe in "Quimbyism" with all the force of her nature and she talked Quimbyism to the exclusion of all other topics. In Warren she even gave a lecture on Quimby's "science" in the town hall, defending him from deism and Spiritualism; and in an interview with the editor of the *Banner of Light*, the Spiritualistic organ, she continued this defense, much to his bewilderment. For what was she, an avowed philosophical Christian, working, this gentleman asked. How could she claim to be the pupil of a disbeliever in Christ's Christianity — a clairvoyant and a magnetic healer? If Quimby were not such, as all who knew him believed, but something else which he could not fathom, as Mrs. Patterson held, then he wished to see this "defunct Spiritualist" and look into this new doctrine. Thus, in those days, Mary Baker's divine impulse seemed to bring confusion to others.

Late in the summer she went to Albion, Maine, to visit Mrs. Crosby. Here a family of numerous members dwelt in a large roomy farmhouse and life was carried on in the patriarchal spirit of the American colonial period. Mrs. Crosby lived with her husband's family and spent much of her time in the big sunny nursery while her mother-in-law directed the work of the household. She was delighted to have Mrs. Patterson with her, and after years of experience in the world she confessed to the author in 1907 that this visit and her companionship with Mary Baker were among the most stimulating, interesting, and inspiring experiences of her life.

Her little daughter Ada became Mrs. Patterson's shadow, following her everywhere, about the house, on her walks, and bringing her hassock to sit at her feet to hear fairy stories when she was not banished to outer gloom. She was the first of three young girls who were attracted like young disciples by the wonder and enthralment of the unfolding spiritual nature which entertained them with glimpses of the land of heart's desire. Mrs. Patterson spent a great deal of her time here as elsewhere in writing, but there were long hours which she passed in conversation with Mrs. Crosby, and the latter has said no woman was ever such a friend to her, no friend had up to that time or has since done so much to help her to "get hold of herself." She has described Mrs. Patterson as possessed of a vigorous intelligence, but a gentle and refined personality, and witnesses her daughter's devotion to the womanly sweetness of her guest.

Spiritualism was a dominant interest in this family as in many New England families of the period. How Mary Baker strove to overcome the inherent superstition in Sarah Crosby, and how Sarah Crosby curiously misinterpreted the effort and continued to misinterpret through all the years to come makes the most illuminating anecdote which can be told of this visit. It portrays a source of much offense that has trailed its revenge through years, pilloried density and wounded pride crying long and loud against the sprightly wit that cornered them.

Mrs. Patterson was radically opposed to Spiritualism and Mrs. Crosby was almost as strenuously set in its defense. She would describe its phenomena as conclusive argument while Mrs. Patterson, bantering her, protested she could reproduce the so-called phenomena. Failing by raillery or argument to convince her friend, she resorted to illustration. In their conversations of a long summer's afternoon, Mrs. Patterson had occasionally reverted to the influence her lamented brother had exercised over her studies and ideals. She had described his appearance, talents, and personality with the loving strokes of reminiscence which make vivid portraiture. Mrs. Crosby was an impressionable listener. She possessed a sentimental imagination combined with practical energy, and she became enamored of the mental picture of the departed Albert Baker.

To cleanse her mind of such trumpery rouge of false sentiment and to administer a sharp corrective to her superstition, Mrs. Patterson conceived and put in practise an admirable though harmless hoax. One day, as Mrs. Crosby has described it, while they sat together at opposite sides of a table in the big nursery, Mrs. Patterson suddenly leaned back in her chair, shivered from head to foot, closed her eyes, and began to talk in a deep, sepulchral voice. The voice purported to be Albert Baker's, saying he had long been trying to get control of his sister Mary. He wished to warn Mrs. Crosby against putting entire confidence in her, for though Mary loved her friend, the voice said, life was a hard experiment for her and she might come to slight Mrs. Crosby's devotion.

As the message was uncomplimentary to herself, Mrs. Patterson expected Mrs. Crosby would shortly recognize the pretense and laugh with her over it. Not so. Mrs. Crosby became mysterious, shook her head sagely, and declared that she knew what she knew. Mrs. Patterson, with a gaiety which she rarely indulged, continued the hoax. She pretended to go into another "trance" on the following day to inform Sarah Crosby that if she would look under the cushion of a certain chair, she would find letters from Albert. Mrs. Crosby eagerly did so, and her seriousness affected Mrs. Patterson. She had not intended to really mislead her friend, but seeing that she persisted in taking the affair seriously, Mrs. Patterson wrote her some good advice, couched in language supposedly appropriate to spirit utterance, and laid it in the secret place, as good mothers reply to the letters written the fairies. These letters Mrs. Crosby has kept and has always maintained that they came from the spirit land. Though their source was in humor, their character was not facetious; they were not harsh or misleading, subtle or filled with guile; they are gentle admonishments to right living, and cheerful encouragement to believe in the sure reward.[1]

It seems unnecessary to point out that this whilom indulgence in nonsense during a rather long and tedious visit does not in any sense connect Mrs. Eddy with the belief in Spiritualism, nor does it show levity concerning sacred things. It was simply an effort to disabuse a too confiding mind of its credulity, which, failing, was turned into a harmless toleration of its limitations. Mrs. Crosby very shortly after her association with Mrs. Patterson took up the study of stenography. She had imbibed from Mary Baker's

---

1 Mrs. Crosby allowed these letters to be printed and the following extracts are taken from them: "Sarah, dear, be ye calm in reliance on self, amid all the changes of natural yearnings, of too keen a sense of earthly joys, of too great a struggle between the material and the spiritual. Be ye calm or you will rend your mortal being, and your experience which is needed for your spiritual progress lost, till taken up without the proper sphere and your spirit trials more severe. Child of earth, heir to immortality! love hath made intercession with wisdom for you—your request is answered. Love each other, your spirits are affined. My dear Sarah is innocent and will rejoice for every tear. The gates of paradise are opening at the tread of time; glory and the crown shall be the diadem of your earthly pilgrimage if you patiently persevere in virtue, justice, and love."

companionship the desire to make her life useful. She was one of the earliest female court reporters in New England. After a business career which netted her a small fortune, she settled in Waterville, Maine, where she acquired property, and in continuation of her liking for the esoteric, she became a member of the society of mystic adepts of New York or elsewhere.

CHAPTER X

THE DISCOVERY OF THE PRINCIPLE OF CHRISTIAN SCIENCE

IN the summer of 1864 Mrs. Patterson rejoined her husband in Lynn. After some desultory practise in the offices of other dentists, he had established himself in an office of his own, and the results of his application to business had made it possible for him to send for his wife.

Lynn, a manufacturing center about ten miles from Boston, was now to be her home, save for short periods, for fifteen years, and here her great discovery was made and first promulgated. Lynn is too large and important a city to be thought of as a suburb of Boston, though towns more distant from the metropolis of New England bear that relation to the larger city. Lynn is now a foremost city of Massachusetts and was then a thriving town, where the largest shoe manufacturer in the world had his establishment. It is on the seacoast, but has not a shipping port; residential streets skirt the shore; there is a broad plaza, sea-wall, and promenade along the ocean front, and a beautiful drive connects the town with quaint old Marblehead. This drive marks the beginning of what is known in New England as the North Shore, which extends all the way to Gloucester, about thirty miles, and along which stretch of ocean view are situated Manchester-by-the-Sea, Prides Crossing, and Magnolia, the summer homes of the greatest wealth of America.

Though Ocean Street, Lynn, has many handsome residences, — the people living there boasting that nothing intervenes between them and Ireland save the stormy Atlantic, — still the city is not regarded as a summer resort, nor a residential district of Boston, but, as a factory town, one of the most important shoe factory centers in the world. When the American Civil War made a great demand for shoes, the old-fashioned method of producing footwear by hand labor was not adequate to meet the demand. Men who held patents on machines for sewing sole-leather found it lucrative to rent their machines and many small factories sprang up at this time, not only in Lynn, but in other towns adjoining Boston where land rent was cheaper than in the city and where labor could be attracted. Lynn easily led in this industry. Its situation was beautiful, the climate healthful, the accessibility to Boston with its many advantages easy. This industry very early attracted women workers as well as men and whole families went into the shoe factories, for women and children could operate the machines and find employment in the many divisions of the labor which arose from the factory method. Thus the character of a large proportion of the population of Lynn is indicated, and it will be readily grasped that this was an excellent starting-point for a great religious work, even as Jesus found a seed place among the fishermen of Galilee and Paul among the tent-making Thessalonians.

The thriving town attracted professional as well as business men. A dentist should find plenty to do where so many of the population of both sexes earned good wages. Dr. Patterson after frittering his time away here for months had been to see his wife's family and doubtless had been admonished by both Mark Baker and Mrs. Alexander Tilton. The latter, believing rigidly in the conventionalities as she did, thought it not proper that Dr. Patterson should keep up his meandering and his desultory occupations. His fitful, incoherent busying of himself with first one project and then another bore no relation to the continuity of existence and compelled his wife to remain in suspended expectation, a guest of relatives and friends, awaiting his mood. Thus Abigail Tilton had taken him to task roundly, and smarting under her words, he had rented the office in Lynn and, with a revival of exuberance and excessive overconfidence, had inserted an advertisement in the local paper in which he asked those whom he had met in his brother dentists' offices to patronize him in the future and stated that he hoped to secure the patronage of "all the rest of mankind." He gradually secured a respectable practise, for he was a good dentist and might have succeeded very well had he been less idle, boisterous, and romantic. But he was a born rover, and coupled with his restlessness was a silly vanity in his powers of fascination over equally silly and romantic women. When Mrs. Patterson rejoined him after intermittent separation, it was for but a brief reunion of little less than two years' duration. It was her final effort, a serious and praiseworthy effort, to reconcile her husband to regular living and social obligations. She had no light task in holding to right conduct her handsome, wayward, unstable husband, whose nature

craved the flesh-pots, the gauds and baubles of sentimentalism, the specious glamour of notoriety, and
over whom "sweetness and light" had but little sway.

With a loyal devotion Mrs. Patterson strove to
fulfil her duty as a wife, never betraying what her
gentler nature suffered in outraged pride, wounded
sensibility, or humiliated aspiration. This man was
her husband, she threw the cloak of love over his
shortcomings and sought to interest and lead him into
the highest associations with which he could be affili-
ated. During the months which followed, as they
were not householders and she had no home duties,
she occupied herself with writing, many of her poems
and prose articles appearing in the Lynn papers. She
attended church and became acquainted with some
of the excellent old families of the city, of which
friendships some interesting associations continued
throughout a long period of her life.

Mrs. Patterson readily made friends whose attachment was strong. Her social success was easy,
and she quickly gained a place of high regard among
the most reserved. Her immediate conquest of
strangers was through her indefinable charm which
among the ruggeder qualities of both men and women
came like the gentle graciousness of a Southerner.
Society in New England cities has been remarked for
a certain brusqueness, a downrightness which often
ruffles the stranger. But though the New Englander
is used to this sort of manner, he is not insensible to
the gentler appeal and invariably falls captive to the
foreigner or Southerner who more easily practises
graciousness. Mrs. Patterson was gentle and engag-

ing, her manner in meeting a stranger winning and convincing in its frank sincerity. Her substantial qualities of natural gifts and cultivation, however, held what she so readily gained. Entering into this larger life of Lynn after a long absence from any extended social intercourse, she at first felt the instinct to enjoy its natural pleasure; but she must have been forced soon to the discovery that she could not maintain a social life suitable to her breeding, for people who received her with every evidence of pleasure were but ill-disposed toward the flamboyant dentist whom they must sooner or later encounter. It would be remarked as a disappointing and amazing bit of social data that so gifted and attractive a woman should be married to a man so ordinary, if not common. What could follow for Mrs. Patterson but a social aloofness and a tuning of her strings to suit the necessities?

Ordinary was not the word for Dr. Patterson, since common persons more often than otherwise possess the virtues. Extraordinary was the word for him, who was florid, pretentious, and bombastic. He who had so effectively disported his frock coat, silk hat, kid boots and gloves in the rural mountain districts, making artisans' and farmers' wives yearn after his departing figure, in the keener social light of Lynn appeared as rather a boorish Beau Brummel, not over-nice in the proprieties. In fact gross Impropriety was soon to stamp him unmistakably and thereafter claim him for her own.

Not for the satisfaction, therefore, of any aspiration of her own, but to interest her husband and give him a social environment in which he would not trip at every step, Mrs. Patterson joined him in uniting with the Linwood lodge of Good Templars. The "Worthy Chief" of that organization found that Mrs. Patterson wrote for the press occasionally and was gifted as a speaker and that when she could be prevailed upon to address the lodge, she was listened to with unfeigned interest. Her well-stored mind invested any subject she handled with vital interest and her pleasing address made her a most engaging speaker.

"Mrs. Patterson was unusual in almost every particular," the lodge president has said, "unusually well-bred, cultivated, and fine-looking, and of excellent taste in matters of dress and the toilet. Some people would comment unfavorably through a sense of inferiority, I firmly believe, and would call her affected, for she was unusually scrupulous in the observation of social form. She had a quiet way about her of commanding attention and in the delivery of an address was, in a strangely quiet way, impressive."

With such a member on their lists it was not long before the lodge chose her as presiding officer of the Legion of Honor, the women's branch of the association, and members have said she was in this capacity gracious and dignified, displaying a courteous charm with executive force. It is likely that in this office, obscure and unimportant as it was, Mrs. Eddy learned her first lessons in organization and leadership.

Thus the Pattersons lived an outwardly calm and decorous existence, and whatever was transpiring underneath of social waywardness on the part of the husband no outward sign was allowed to manifest itself through the wife's deportment. No breath of scandal was ever circulated as to their domestic harmony. Mrs. Patterson's writings occupied the time she spent alone. Some of her poems written at this time were outbursts of patriotic feeling. The Civil War was drawing to a close, and the woman born with the blood of heroes in her veins found expression in verse for her deep love of country and her sympathy with emancipation. Her poems were printed side by side with those of John Greenleaf Whittier, Oliver Wendell Holmes, and Phœbe Cary, and are preserved in the files of the Lynn papers. She wrote of the bells that rang out the proclamation of emancipation, of the fighting heroes at the front and those fallen in battle, of "our beloved Lincoln," who "laid his great willing heart on the altar of Justice." Thus she showed an ardent interest at all times in the affairs of her country. While her verse would not take rank with either Whittier's or Holmes's in poetic rhythm or diction, it expressed the fervor of her heart for the cause of freedom. In other instances she revealed an exquisite sensibility to the beauty of nature. Her sublime faith in God is a constant and pervading influence in all her writing, whether verse or prose.

Outwardly calm and decorous, Mrs. Patterson's interior life was far from tranquil. She had come to Lynn from a period of philosophic abstraction, had come to fulfil her obligations as a wife and this task, as has been shown, was by no means a light or simple one. But difficult, almost desperate as it was, and doomed to failure in the end, it was not the greatest or most important problem of her existence. In meeting the demands of such a task she found the ordinary exercise of long-trained domestic and social faculties available. In writing verse and news-letters she exercised developed mental powers. Her news-letters to the Lynn *Reporter* from Swampscott, the suburb in which she lived, were bright, gossipy communications in which she mentions affairs of the church, the schools, the construction of new and beautiful homes, with descriptions of the laying out of estates in agreeable schemes of landscape gardening. They indicate that she was a special writer of ability with a style peculiar to herself which characterized all her later writings. They betray a vivacity, color, fancy that give a sense of a living, glowing, radiant personality to whom life is always a wonderful revelation.

But underneath all assumption of gaiety and social charm, underneath the outward calm and sweetness of wifely devotion, there was a desolating war going on in the heart of this woman. It betrayed itself only occasionally and in half light to those who were most intimately associated with her and was the occasion of the withdrawal of some half-proffered friendships. She spoke too much of religion was the complaint of the shallow worldlings. No one of them comprehended, save one family of true friends, the depth of her struggle at this period. Something bigger, greater, more portentous, more far-reaching than domestic trials of a tragic character, than even the sense of the struggles of her country for honor and perpetuity, — and to Mary Baker these struggles were real affairs of her own living interest, — yet something more far-reaching

than home or national life was making war Titanic
in the subjective regions of her soul.

So far the effort has been to portray Mary Baker's
spiritual life side by side with the account of the incidents of her worldly experiences. She has been shown
as a docile little girl absorbed in books, a beautiful
young woman marrying and leaving home, a bereaved
widow in her parents' house comforting the declining
years of her mother, a heart-broken mother herself, a
much tried wife in a second marriage, — but through
all the various changes in her outward fortune her
spiritual life had been developing consistently. This
life, awakened in the days of her loving communion
with a devout mother, was strengthened in her conscientious struggles with a dominating Calvinistic
father; it was stimulated by the uplifting companionship with her clergyman teacher; it was confirmed in
the subsequent personal seeking for God in the clois-
tered suffering in the mountain home. Going out
from that cloister she met the first real obstacle to her
faith in the weird doctrine of Phineas Quimby. How
she strove to harmonize his strange theories with her
faith, how she labored to evolve a philosophy from his
incoherencies has been related. She had come to a
crisis when her faith would no longer endure the
association with ideas so incongruous. Her angel
fought with the intruder which, veiled in obscurities,
could not be named or recognized. The battle was
terrific and it was prolonged. It had begun in 1862
and was still going on when the year 1866 dawned.
The woman who was to promulgate a new understanding of Christianity, which would shake the world's

thought to its center, was undergoing a cataclysmic upheaval which she concealed from all the world and bore alone.

She has written of this period that the product of her own earlier thought and meditation had been vitiated with animal magnetism and human will-power, the nature of which she was as ignorant of as Eve of sin before taught by the serpent. What serpent was to teach Mary Baker the nature of magnetism? That lesson was still far off. The unveiling of the angel's face, the shining visage of Truth in her heart, was to precede the unveiled vision of error by years sufficient for her to grow to the fighting stature in the consciousness of its power.

But now she was all but dominated by the power of the darker error she has named mesmerism or magnetism, and her mental state was worse than the disease which had formerly tortured her body. While held in this state she still ascribed her cure to Quimby. His thought, his personality, was still obtruding itself between her and God. He was squarely in the light. Her religious peace, her faith, her spiritual being were threatened. Her anguish was intolerable and to no one could she turn for counsel to obtain relief.

Out of this smothered torment in which she sounded a deeper hell than Calvinists had ever imagined, she was lifted suddenly by a physical shock which set her free for her great discovery and revelation. This shock was caused by an accident which carried her to death's door and from which she recovered in what seems a miraculous manner on the third day following.

This accident has been called, with various shades of sentiment, the "fall" in Lynn. To many thousands that fall with its subsequent uplifting has been the fall of their own torment, mental and physical, and the uplifting of their lives with Mary Baker Eddy's. The incident or event, as one may look upon it according to his own experience, was recorded in the Lynn *Reporter* of Saturday morning, February 3, 1866, as follows:

Mrs. Mary Patterson of Swampscott fell upon the ice near the corner of Market and Oxford streets on Thursday evening and was severely injured. She was taken up in an insensible condition and carried into the residence of S. M. Bubier, Esq., near by, where she was kindly cared for during the night. Dr. Cushing, who was called, found her injuries to be internal and of a severe nature, inducing spasms and internal suffering. She was removed to her home in Swampscott yesterday afternoon, though in a very critical condition.

When this fall occurred Mrs. Patterson was going to some meeting of the local organization of Good Templars. A party of the lodge members was walking with her. She was in the full tide of that life which she had taken upon herself as a duty, but which lay so far apart from the path her conscience would have had her follow. In the midst of apparent light-hearted social gaiety she slipped on the ice and was thrown violently. The party stood aghast, but soon lifted her and carried her into a house, where it was seen that she was seriously injured. Then certain of them volunteered to sit by her bedside during the night. When the physician arrived he said little, but his face and manner conveyed more than his words. It was apparent to the watchers that he regarded her injuries as extremely grave and they believed him to imply that the case might terminate fatally. But divine Will had another fate in view for Mary Baker.

Forty years after this event Alvin M. Cushing, who was the physician, began to say that it was he, and not God, who cured Mrs. Patterson of her injuries after the fall. The author interviewed Dr. Cushing at Springfield, Massachusetts, in 1907. He stated that he administered a remedy which he called the third decimal attenuation of arnica which he diluted in a glass of water. He related that Mrs. Patterson was taken up unconscious and remained unconscious during the night and he believed her to be suffering from a concussion, and possibly spinal dislocation.

On the following morning, having visited her twice during the night, he found her still semi-conscious but moaning "Home, home." He therefore administered one eighth of a grain of morphine as a palliative and not a curative, and procured a long sleigh in which she was laid wrapped in fur robes and carefully driven to her suburban residence.

This physician said he afterwards prescribed a more highly attenuated remedy which he himself diluted in a glass of water and of which he gave the patient a teaspoonful. He did not know whether she took more of it or not, but when he called again she was in a perfectly normal condition of health and walked across the floor to show that she was cured. He did not remember being told anything at the time of a miraculous cure through the power of prayer. But he was, according to his own reminiscence, an unusually popular man at the time, and had sixty patients a day. He drove a dashing pair of trotters and was much in evidence on the speedway when not in the consulting room. It is possible he was told of the manner of the cure, that he did congratulate his patient and then forgot the incident. But one thing he did not forget, for he claimed to have it in his memoranda, and that is the remedy he prescribed. He doubtless wrote it down in his tablets that the third decimal attenuation of arnica had marvelous curative properties for a concussion of the brain and spinal dislocation with prolonged unconsciousness and spasmodic seizures as concurrent symptoms.

Mrs. Eddy's account of this accident differed from the physician's and she knew what healed her and how she was healed and when it occurred. She was not responsible for the calling of the physician and only took his medicine when she was roused into semiconsciousness to have it administered, of which she had no recollection. After the doctor's departure on Friday, however, she refused to take the medicine he had left, and as she has expressed it, lifted her heart to God. On the third day, which was Sunday, she sent those who were in her room away, and taking her Bible, opened it. Her eyes fell upon the account of the healing of the palsied man by Jesus.

"It was to me a revelation of Truth," she has written. "The lost chord of Truth (healing, as of old) I caught consciously from the Divine Harmony." [1] And

[1] *The Christian Science Journal*, June, 1887.

she further states: "Adoringly I discerned the Principle of his holy heroism and Christian example on the cross, when he refused to drink the 'vinegar and gall,' a preparation of poppy, or aconite, to allay the tortures of crucifixion. . . . The miracles recorded in the Bible, which had before seemed to me supernatural, grew divinely natural and apprehensible." [1]

A spiritual experience so deep was granted her that she realized eternity in a moment, infinitude in limitation, life in the presence of death. She could not utter words of prayer; her spirit realized. She knew God face to face; she came to "touch and handle things unseen." In that consciousness all pain evanesced into bliss, all discord in her physical body melted into harmony, all sorrow was translated into rapture. [2] She recognized this state as her rightful condition as a child of God. Love invaded her, Life lifted her, Truth irradiated her. God said to her, "Daughter, arise!"

Mrs. Patterson arose from her bed, dressed, and walked into the parlor where some friends were gathered waiting, thinking these would be the last moments of the sufferer who, they believed, was dying. They arose in consternation at her appearance, almost believing they beheld an apparition. She quietly reassured them and explained the manner of her recovery, calling upon them to witness it. They were the first doubters. They were there on the spot; they had withdrawn but a short time since from what they supposed was her death-bed. She stood before them fully healed of the injury. They shook their heads in amazed confusion at what they had seen and heard. Although

---

[1] "Retrospection and Introspection," p. 26.   [2] *Ibid.*, p. 24.

the clergyman and his wife rejoiced with her, they could not comprehend her statements. But for all the dissent of the opinion of friends, and later of medicine and theological dogma, Mrs. Patterson escaped, if not death, the clutches of lingering illness and suffering.

Mary Baker did more than experience a cure. She in that hour received a revelation for which she had been preparing her heart in every event of her life. She had really walked straight toward this revelation, though seemingly through a backward-turning path. The backward-turning was a part of the marvelous fitting of her nature, the enlightenment of her mind for the immense service later of delineating the counterfeit of spiritual healing and to post the warning signs against the dangers of hypnotism. She herself has written of the discovery:

In the year 1866, I discovered the Christ Science or divine laws of Life, Truth, and Love, and named my discovery Christian Science. God had been graciously preparing me during many years for the reception of this final revelation of the absolute divine Principle of scientific mental healing.[1]

When apparently near the confines of mortal existence, standing already within the shadow of the death-valley, I learned these truths in divine Science: that all real being is in God, the divine Mind, and that Life, Truth, and Love are all-powerful and ever-present; that the opposite of Truth, — called error, sin, sickness, disease, death, — is the false testimony of false material sense, of mind in matter; that this false sense evolves, in belief, a subjective state of mortal mind which this same so-called mind names *matter*, thereby shutting out the true sense of Spirit.[2]

[1] Science and Health, p. 107.   [2] *Ibid.*, p. 108.

Of the great discoveries in the world's history it may be well to consider a moment which have blessed the human race most. The discovery of gunpowder and the invention of movable types came in about the same period. The discovery of the use of ether as an anesthetic and the discovery of Mind Science also occurred in relatively the same period. Whatever appeals to the senses gains an audience with humanity more quickly than the gentler, more insistent appeal to the intelligence. Yet the former palls and dies, and the latter nourishes and lives. Hate, war, and death astound us and fill us with consternation; thought, love, and life come unawares like dawn and grow tenderly, gently into meaning, blessedness, and power. Gunpowder created a special hell, movable types the blessedness of literature. Ether anesthesia brought in its train an elaborated surgery; Mind Science has begun to abolish the necessity of surgery, healing of itself the lame, the blind, the deaf; teaching mothers to bear children without pain, children to grow normally without malformation, men and women to abandon evil habits which bring consumption, scrofula, leprosy; nations to abandon wars which slaughter and cripple and leave a heritage of poverty and disease, — slowly but surely it works its way like civilization transforming savagery and the jungle. It is as fundamentally incontrovertible as the axiom that truth is eternal, or that error dies of its own nature.

This great discovery depended largely on the fall of Mary Baker in Lynn, causing her to grapple with the violence of magnetism, rousing her from a mesmeric lethargy, and bringing to her developed spiritual nature the understanding of the principle of life. There was an interval before she could demonstrate what dawned upon her in that hour. When the apple fell for Newton and the kettle steamed for Watt, natural scientific truth dawned on them, but each must apply himself to make clear his conception through years of careful elucidation and working out to a demonstrable point his scientific statement of principle. Mrs. Eddy writes:

My discovery, that erring, mortal, misnamed *mind* produces all the organism and action of the mortal body, set my thoughts to work in new channels, and led up to my demonstration of the proposition that Mind is All and matter is naught as the leading factor in Mind-science.[1]

Indeed her thoughts were to work in new channels. She had risen as it were from death. Her friends immediately set up an argument that she was self-deluded, that she ought to be flat upon her back, that she was defying the laws of nature. This clamor of fear had a temporary effect upon her; it bewildered her into some doubt of her ability to maintain her discovery, even into some doubt as to its basis in truth. Two weeks after she had risen from her prostration she wrote a letter which was a backward glance to Quimby and Quimbyism,—and yet a letter which sounded the small notes of the clarion. The letter was written to a former patient of Quimby, for Quimby was now dead. He had died the preceding month and could not again obtrude his unformulated theories between her mind and its own spiritual apprehensions.

1 Science and Health, p. 108.

Her discovery waited for her full comprehension and acknowledgment. Yet she wrote a letter which, had it been answered differently, might have taken her back into animal magnetism and the confusion of hypnotism.

In the letter she describes her accident and says that the physician attending her had said that she had taken the last step she ever would, yet in three days she had gotten up from her bed and *would* walk. She says: "I confess I am frightened, and out of that nervous heat my friends are forming, spite of me, the terrible spinal affection from which I have suffered so long and hopelessly. Now can't you help me? I believe you can. I think I could help another in my condition."

To this request the former patient replied that he did not know how Quimby had performed his cures and doubted if any one did. He distinctly declined the task of reviving Quimbyism or attempting to stand in the shoes of the mesmerist. So there was a closed door against that refuge from her own responsibility, a refuge which had presented itself to her mind as a last temptation. Quimby was dead; Quimbyism had perished with him. No one remained of those who had gathered round him in life to perpetuate his peculiar influence. Her fall had destroyed the very work she had so long credited him with. Everything must begin anew for her; life must be made completely over. She was forced to turn to God.

Her whole environment was about to be changed, for she was to be left without family and with the barest means of subsistence. Her faith faltered, her limbs trembled, but backward she could not go. It dawned upon her more and more insistently that God had laid a work upon her. The truth of spiritual being had illumined her and to acquaint humanity with this truth became imperative.

Some years after this period, when her work had begun to make headway, the patient of Quimby to whom she had written came forward to harass her with a pamphlet in which he displayed her former eulogies of Quimby and her letter to him asking him to take up Quimby's work. She replied to this pamphleteer in the article on "Mind-Healing History" in *The Christian Science Journal*, from which a quotation is given in regard to the manuscript controversy. In it she says:

Was it "an evil hour," . . . when I exchanged poetry for Truth, grasped in some degree the understanding of Truth, and undertook at all hazards to bless them that cursed me? Was it an evil hour when I discovered Christian Science Mind-healing, and gave to the world, in my work called Science and Health, the leaves that are "for the healing of the nations"? Was it "for some strange reason" that the impulse came upon me to endure all things for Truth's sake? Does ceaseless servitude, while treading the thorny path *alone* and for others' sake, arise from "a purely selfish motive"? . . . After the death of this so-called Originator of Mind-healing, it required ten years of nameless experience for me to reach the standpoint of my first edition of Science and Health. . . . It was after the death of Mr. Quimby, and when I was apparently at the door of death, that I made this discovery, in 1866. After that, it took ten years of hard work for me to reach the standard of my first edition of Science and Health, published in 1875.[1]

1 *The Christian Science Journal*, June, 1887.

Mary Baker very shortly began to walk the "thorny path" of which she writes, began the "nameless experience" with its incidents of painful humiliation which she has never recounted or disclosed. She has covered this period with the brief statement that she retired for a time from the world to carry out the work which was before her. The first painful incident came quickly on the heels of the illness resulting from the fall. Shortly after her recovery, Mrs. Patterson's remarkable experience centered her attention fully upon the philosophy of religion. She determined that she would state the principle of health and life and that she would devote her pen to that purpose; she would no longer write for money or fame, but abandon herself utterly to this great cause.

Dr. Patterson's reaction to the resolution of his wife was characteristic. His response to her unworldliness was entirely worldly. He left Lynn mysteriously, deserting her, and not only did he leave her but he did so shamefully. He eloped with the wife of a wealthy citizen who had employed his services professionally. Sometime after the partner of his adventure came to the house where Mrs. Patterson was living and asked to see her. Mrs. Patterson received the repentant woman kindly and listened to her story. The woman said she had presumed to come to beg forgiveness and sue her for a favor because Dr. Patterson had so often spoken of his wife's religiousness. The favor she had to beg of the woman she had wronged was that she would make intercession for her with the deserted husband that she might go home. This Mrs. Patterson undertook to do and succeeded in bringing about a complete reconciliation. She even persuaded the husband to forego a plan he had for confining his wife to her apartment for a period of penance, and by such persuasion so induced this man to allow sweetness and light to prevail that his home was thereafter a happy one. This was the second time in her life that she performed the office of peacemaker for a woman who had been party to the desecration of her own home.

The summer months of 1866 were for Mary Baker a time of reconstructing and dedication of her life. Her husband had gone, gone forever. She could no longer in reason contemplate a life with him. He came back to ask forgiveness after the elopement; it was in his nature to do that, for to him there was no finality to the good-will he expected, however great his offense. But his wife did not receive him. "The same roof cannot shelter us," she said quietly. "You may come in, certainly, if you desire, but in that case I must go elsewhere." He stood fumbling with his hat upon the door-step and then placed it upon his head. "Of what use would that be, Mary?" he faltered. "No, it is I who will go."

Dr. Patterson thereafter roamed from town to town in New England, falling from the social standard of conduct on various occasions and losing social caste by degrees, until he was forbidden houses which had at first received him and, losing his practise when well begun in different towns, he at last retired to live the life of a hermit in Saco, Maine. In 1873 Mrs. Patterson secured a decree of divorce from him in the courts of Salem, Massachusetts. Directly after visiting his wife for the last time he went once more to the

Tiltons. Mark Baker was dead; he had passed away the preceding autumn. Mrs. Tilton heard the dentist's confession in silence. She had nothing to offer by way of advice for the patching up of difficulties. She saw they had reached a climax. But her practical mind made one suggestion as the *amende honorable* for the husband, that he should settle some sum, however meager, on Mary and not leave her utterly destitute. To this the doctor agreed and a sum was fixed upon to be paid twice a year. This small allowance she had received for about two years when Dr. Patterson failed to fulfill his obligations.

When the doctor had taken his departure, Abigail wrote to her sister to come home. "We will build a house for you next to our own and settle an income upon you," she said. "You shall have suitable surroundings and not be annoyed by the friction of life in another home than your own. We can be together very much, and you can pursue your writing. There is only one thing I ask of you, Mary, that you give up these ideas which have lately occupied you, that you attend our church and give over your theory of divine healing."

To this Mary Baker had but one reply, "I must do the work God has called me to." But Abigail did not believe her sister. She decided to let her alone for a time. She felt sure that the grip of poverty, the silence of her family, the desertion of her husband would operate in time to bring her back to the old relations. She wanted her sister, but not keenly enough as yet to sacrifice one iota of her pride. Her boy Albert was just twenty-one, handsome, and a bit wayward; but she meant to master that and make a successful man of him. Her daughter Evelyn was only twelve, delicate, studious, pious, the idol of her father. She had great hope of her future. So then Mary, the sister, was after all outside her immediate concern, — save only she hoped Mary did not mean to disgrace them.

Sometimes, indeed, she had inward fears lest that strange spiritual genius of Mary's really would make itself felt in the world and bring the reproach of "queerness" upon them. Up to this hour their family had been conventional New Englanders, farmers, manufacturers, wealthy, influential, and orthodox both in politics and religion. Mary had stood out for abolition when it was unpopular and fanatical to do so. Her difference had made the townspeople talk years before. She had proclaimed curious religious ideas when she was last at home, ideas that had made the ladies of the sewing circle wonder and gossip. Perhaps after all it was as well that Mary should wear out her theories among strangers. Some day she would come back to them and they would take care of her. So thought Abigail Tilton, reckoning and weighing the contents of the situation with a mind of worldly prudence.

Poor Abigail! Husband and children were to be taken from her, too. Strangers who thought mainly of her fortune were to flatter her in her declining years of dictation, until dictation was no longer a joy. And pride which had separated her from her beloved sister so long kept her from imparting her last farewell to the one whom she truly loved deepest and best.

So Mary Baker sat alone through these summer months. She had her saddest thoughts to scan at the beginning and not the close of her career, for to her this was truly the beginning. She was forty-five years old and had lived through the experiences of more than a normal life. Let no one think that even the greatest philosopher could contemplate the ruin of so many earthly hopes without heart-pangs. Her child, long ago alienated from her by wile and subterfuge, was now a man roaming through the wild life of the West; the husband who had promised so much had gone in disgrace to live out his aimless whims for many years and die alone in his hermit's hut. Her parents were both gone and her sister was obdurately set against the deep faith of her heart. Without worldly resources or even the social status of recognized widowhood, deserted by all who should have cherished her, might she not with sanction lay her head low to mourn?

Whether for many days or weeks she thought on these things, certain it is that this same year saw her gathering up the strands, strengthening her heart with courage, accepting her mission, and venturing forth steadfastly upon her destiny never again to turn back. From this year the story of Mary Baker's life deals with religion. She has given up family for voluntary poverty, society for the contemplation of a new faith. She will for a time nourish this truth, elucidate it to her own mind with her pen, to her own heart with prayer, and in a decade will begin the work of promulgation.

CHAPTER XI

THE TEST OF EXPERIENCE

FOR three years after my discovery, I sought the solution of this problem of Mind-healing, searched the Scriptures and read little else, kept aloof from society, and devoted time and energies to discovering a positive rule. The search was sweet, calm, and buoyant with hope, not selfish nor depressing. I knew the Principle of all harmonious Mind-action to be God, and that cures were produced in primitive Christian healing by holy, uplifting faith; but I must know the Science of this healing, and I won my way to absolute conclusions through divine revelation, reason, and demonstration. The revelation of Truth in the understanding came to me gradually and apparently through divine power.[1]

After a lengthy examination of my discovery and its demonstration in healing the sick, this fact became evident to me, — that Mind governs the body, not partially but wholly. I submitted my metaphysical system of treating disease to the broadest practical tests.[2]

Mrs. Patterson had boarded with her husband in several places in Lynn and Swampscott. She had made a few excellent friends who were steadfast in their interest and loyalty through the hardships which were to befall her in the next few years. Of these friends none were more devoted than the Phillipses, an excellent Quaker family. Mr. Thomas Phillips was a manufacturer of shoe-findings and lived with his family in Buffum Street.

[1] Science and Health, p. 109. [2] Ibid., p. 111.

Mary Baker was very devoted to this elderly couple whom she called by the endearing names of "Uncle Thomas" and "Aunt Hannah." Their home became a refuge to her. Apart from short stays she did not live with them, but boarded with Mr. and Mrs. George D. Clark of Summer Street. The Clarks lived in their own home, taking in boarders to increase their income. They were a kindly, social family. In their home Mrs. Patterson had solitude when she desired it, and a friendly democratic society when she felt the human yearning for sympathetic interest in other lives. For such independence and comparative comfort the charges were not heavy. Indeed she could not possibly have met them had they been so, for her purse was but scantily furnished at this time.

But to the Phillips home in Buffum Street she fled for true social and spiritual companionship. They were of that excellent breeding which comes of true piety, and they cherished this stricken woman, too proud to admit herself desolate among strangers, as a very lamb of the Lord. Their aged mother lived with them. She was a saintly Quaker, who had passed her ninetieth year, and as the years rolled by and she lived on toward the close of her century of human experience, she grew weary of earth. She would sometimes say with gentle impatience, "I fear the good Father hath forgotten me." One day she refused to rise from her bed, and said to her children, "Thee need never bring my gown again." She was determined to go, and so she slept sweetly out of this world's life.

But before that calm change came upon her, she spent many hours with Mary Baker, hours of mutual consolation and uplifting. These two women, between whom yawned a half century, loved each other tenderly, calling one another by their Christian name, which in both cases was Mary. Their intercourse was of a heavenly sweetness. They would sit side by side on a sofa with hands clasped, sometimes conversing and sometimes meditating. Mr. Phillips, returning home and finding them there, would call his wife and say, "Hannah, do you see our two saints? There they sit together, the two Marys."

In this house silent prayer was the custom before eating. Mary Baker yielded to this custom with great reverence, often saying it seemed to her like a holy communion. With Mr. Phillips she had frequent conversation about her religious views and her healing experience, delineating for him the features of her discovery, stating the principle to be divine Life operating in human consciousness. He was the first to listen to her intelligently; he was the first to see that she was depicting a new mental state that would elevate all human existence. Upon the aged grandmother her words fell like dew, graciously accepted as pious utterances, but scarcely understood. Upon other members of the family they made but slight impression and, were it not that they loved their guest, they would have been guilty of an occasional smile of incredulity.

Incredulity there must have been among them. A daughter of the house was afterward a Christian Scientist. She was not a believer in these ideas for many years — not indeed until after Mrs. Eddy had long passed out of her life with the death of her parents. She has related to the author her father's impressions of the future founder of Christian Science. In rebuking their unbelief he voiced a prophecy by saying: "Mary is a wonderful woman, Susie. You will find it out some day. I may not live to see it, but you will."

This daughter Susan married George Oliver, and in her own home often entertained Mrs. Patterson. Her husband was a business man with a growing shoe trade which actively engaged his mind. He would, however, neglect to return to his business for hours if Mary Baker happened to be at his home for luncheon.

"I cannot understand it," he would say to his wife of their guest's conversation, "but I would rather hear Mrs. Patterson talk than make a big deal in business. After listening to her arguments I feel some way as though I would be the better able to cast my net on the right side."

It was on Susan Oliver's brother Dorr, then a young man, that Mrs. Eddy made her first demonstration of Mind Science. Dorr had a bone felon which kept him awake at night and incapacitated during the day. Mrs. Patterson had not been to the Phillips house for several days, and when she did go and found Dorr in agony walking the floor, she gently and sympathetically questioned him.

"Dorr, will you let me heal that felon?"

"Yes, indeed, Mrs. Patterson, if you can do it," he replied.

"Will you promise not to do anything for it or let any one else, if I undertake to cure it?"

"Yes, I promise, and I will keep my word," said Dorr Phillips. He had heard his father and their friend discuss divine healing many times, and had a quite healthy curiosity to see what would happen if all this talk was actually tried on a wicked, tormenting, festering felon that was making him fairly roar with rage one minute and cry like a girl the next.

That night Dorr stopped at his sister Susie's house. "How is your finger?" she asked solicitously.

"Nothing the matter with my finger; it hasn't hurt all day. Mrs. Patterson is treating it."

"What is she doing to it? Let me look at it."

"No, you'll spoil the cure. I promised not to look at it or think about it, nor let any one else touch it or talk about it. And I won't."

The brother and sister looked at each other with half smiles. They were struggling with skepticism.

"Honest, Dorr, doesn't it hurt?"

"No."

"Tell me what she did."

"I don't know what she did, don't know anything about this business, but I'm going to play fair and keep my word."

Dorr actually forgot the felon and when his attention was called to the finger it was found to be well. This strange result made an impression on the family. No one quite knew what to say, and they were scarcely ready to accept the healing of a sore finger as a miracle.

"But it is not a miracle," said Mary Baker. "Nor would it be if it had been a broken wrist or a withered arm. It is natural, divinely natural. All life rightly understood is so."

Mr. Phillips said there was something in that which he could not understand, and there it rested. With peace restored to his body, Dorr Phillips decided to learn a little about divine Science.

At the Oliver home lived a rich young man from Boston who had come to Lynn to learn the shoe business. He was intense and active, eager to show his father his business sagacity. But severe application to business and excitement over his new responsibilities threw him into a fever. He was brought home from the factory and put to bed, where he promptly lapsed into delirium. The Olivers saw that he was very ill, and sent for his parents. Before they arrived Mrs. Patterson came to the house and found Susan Oliver in distress over the serious situation.

"If he should die before they come, what would I do?" she asked excitedly. "Perhaps I should call our physician. But they might not like it. He is their only child. Think of his prospects, his father's fortune — and for him to be stricken in this way!"

"He is not going to die, Susie," said Mary Baker. "Let me go in and see him."

"You may go in, if you think best; but he won't recognize you," said Mrs. Oliver.

Mary Baker went into the sick chamber and sat down at the side of the bed. The young man was tossing from side to side, throwing his arms about wildly and moaning. She took his hand, held it firmly, and spoke clearly to him, calling him by a familiar name.

"Bobbie," she said, "look at me. You know me, don't you?"

The young man ceased his monotonous moaning, his tossing on the pillows, and his ejaculations. He lay quiet and gazed steadfastly at the newcomer.

"Of course you know me, Bobbie," she persisted gently. "Tell me my name."

"Why, yes," he said with perfect sanity, "it's Mrs. Patterson." In a few minutes he said, "I believe I will go to sleep."

He did go to sleep and waked rational, and did not again have delirium. His parents came and carried the boy off to Boston for medical attention. But he escaped espionage of nurse and doctor, and of his parents also. They had taken him to the old Revere House, where they were living, and had established him comfortably in the famous Jenny Lind room. But all this solicitation could not hold him. He returned to Lynn and sent word of his state of mind and whereabouts to the distracted parents. Mrs. Patterson had made him well in spite of the physician's declaration that he was in for a run of fever. So simply was the youth's release from fever accomplished that none who knew of the case would credit her with having done anything. However, Mary Baker had in this instance once more illustrated her discovery.

Her power to heal the sick was shown once again among these friends. The Charles Winslows of Ocean Street were related to the Phillipses, and Mrs. Patterson knew them as intimately as she knew the Olivers. Mrs. Winslow had been for sixteen years in an invalid chair, and Mrs. Patterson, who occasionally spent an afternoon with her, desired to heal her.

"If you make Abbie walk," said Charles Winslow,

"I will not only believe your theory, but I will reward you liberally. I think I would give a thousand dollars to see her able to walk."

"The demonstration of the principle is enough reward," said Mrs. Patterson. "I know she can walk. You go to business and leave us alone together."

"But I want to see you perform your cure, Mary," said Charles Winslow, half mirthfully. "Indeed, I won't interfere."

"You want to see me perform a cure," cried Mary Baker, with a flash of her clear eyes. "But I am not going to do anything. Why don't you understand that God will do the work if Mrs. Winslow will let Him? Leave off making light of what is a serious matter. Your wife will walk."

And Mrs. Winslow did walk, walked along the ocean beach with Mary Baker and around her own garden in the beautiful autumn of that year. She who had not taken a step for sixteen years arose and walked, not once but many times. Though a wonderful thing had been accomplished, the woman's pride kept her from acknowledging a cure. The method seemed to her so ridiculously inadequate. To accept it was like convicting her of never having been ill. So she returned to her former beliefs.

Such were some of the first results of Mary Baker's efforts to prove that she had grasped a great truth and was not asserting an imaginary doctrine of fanciful or fanatical origin. She began to see in the wilful pride of one patient, the scornful rejection of her services by the parents of another, and the kindly indifference of still another, who guessed things just happened so when you were not watching, that this could not be her field of activity. But she had at her very door abundant opportunity among the humbler shoe-workers. The Phillipses were satisfied with their religion and culture; the Winslows were wealthy and secure in their own well-being. They meant to be her friends and told her that the world would say she was mad if she continued to preach divine healing. "It is better not to talk of it," they said. It seemed to them an unnatural doctrine, something that might become an awkward topic in their drawing-room, something that this interesting woman should be persuaded to forget.

Interesting Mary Baker was, more interesting than ever in her life, with a strange power of impressing the world with the wonder of things which was to grow more and more a part of her. A description of her appearance at this time and of her daily life is afforded through the reminiscences of George Clark, the son of the family in which she was boarding. He says she was a beautiful woman with the complexion of a young girl, her skin being fair, the color often glowing in her cheeks as she talked; her eyes were deep blue, becoming brilliant and large under emotional interest, and her hair falling in a shower of brown curls about her face.

"She usually wore black," says Mr. Clark, "but occasionally violet or pale rose in some arrangement of her dress. And I remember well a dove-colored gown trimmed with black velvet that she wore in the summer. I remember the colors because she suggested a flower-like appearance; she had a refreshing

simplicity about her which made one think of lilies.
Yes, that is the very flower, because she had distinction, too. She was a little above medium height, slender, and graceful. Usually she was reserved, though
her expression was never forbidding. But when she
talked, and she talked very well and convincingly,
she would often make a sweeping outward gesture
with her right hand, as though giving her thought
from her very heart.

"So characteristic were her gestures that I would
recognize her to-day were I only to see her outstretched hand. She sat at the head of our table, my
mother occupying the center of one side, and I, in my
father's absence, the opposite seat. From this place
at our table she easily dominated attention when she
cared to talk, and she was always listened to with
interest. Every one liked and admired her, though
sometimes her statements would cause a protracted
argument.

"We were a rather mixed household and were
fourteen at table. There were several shoe operatives
from the factories, a salesman or two, and a man who
has since become a well-known bootmaker. There
was a painter amongst us, who afterwards became a
successful artist in landscape. He was an argumentative talker, inclined to be skeptical of most things.
The wives of several of the men were also guests
at table, and conversation was usually lively, often
theological.

"My mother had been a Universalist, but she was
progressive in her views, a come-outer, as you might
say. She was much interested in Spiritualism and

used to entertain the Spiritualists. Séances were sometimes held at our house. Mrs. Patterson sometimes was present at these affairs held in our parlor, just as she took part agreeably, but not conspicuously, in any social gathering. You see she liked people, liked to meet them unaffectedly and kindly, but, mind you, always with that air of distinction, that something that made her different. I think she was hungry for hearts, if I may so express it, but she would draw them up to her level rather than go to theirs.

"On days succeeding a séance my mother would often leave the breakfast room with the ladies to talk over the doings of the night before and the nature of the 'phenomena.' My mother and Mrs. Patterson would occasionally get into a lively argument, and both expressed themselves most positively on opposite sides of the question. They never fell out about it, for they were both too well used to such divergence of view among their friends. My mother was always having to defend her views, and indeed so was Mrs. Patterson. They respected each other, I may say they had too much affection to quarrel.

"But their arguments were highly entertaining to me, and I often wondered how persons holding such opposite views could shake hands so amiably over their differences. I was a youngster and felt very important, for I was going to sea. I used to think that when I came back from seeing the world, all these religious matters would have become of no importance to me. In that I was mistaken, and I fancy now that the arguments going on there at my mother's table and of an evening when some of the party played whist and others gathered around Mrs. Patterson were the everlasting and eternal arguments of our lives, and that a prophet was among us unawares." [1]

Among the boarders in this mixed and highly democratic household were Hiram S. Crafts and his wife. The former was known as an expert heel-finisher in the shoe factory. He possessed an ordinary intelligence, a common school education, and a tendency toward transcendentalism. This tendency was as marked a characteristic in New England middle-classes during the middle years of the last century as Puritanism was in England during the reign of Charles I, two centuries before. It made Unitarianism and Universalism possible as an outgrowth of Calvinism.

It may appear extravagant to credit with notions of transcendentalism a shoe-worker of Lynn; but in great mental movements in a nation such as the American, or in a race such as the Anglo-Saxon, history has shown that the artisans, craftsmen, and farmers share in the intellectual experience of the scholars, if that experience is more than a passing ripple. This is especially true in the United States. If they are somewhat later than the scholars in arriving at their convictions, the sympathies and antipathies of the laboring class go deeper and are more compelling. Their "feeling" has to be reckoned with. Thus it will be recalled that Cromwell sought religious men for his army, knowing that unless armed with some staying convictions his common soldiers could never stand against the gentlemen and cavaliers of the forces of the king.

[1] Notes from a conversation with Mr. George Clark in July, 1907.

Transcendentalism is a big mouthful of a descriptive; but this term had scholarly origin, being Germanic, not Yankee or British. A brief history of the word may not be impertinent. The term was first applied to Kantian philosophy, which only a very exceptional shoe-worker of New England could have been expected to read. How then could a shoe-worker acquire tendencies toward such speculations? But the philosophers may wrap their notions in very unusual language and still occasionally coin words the vulgar will learn to handle. Kant used this word to denote intuitions which the descendants of Puritans had already analyzed before Emerson made the word transcendentalism familiar in New England as Carlyle did in old England. Thus it was not left for the Yankee shoe-worker to dig it out of the Critique.

A little before the Civil War broke out, in the late forties and early fifties, the lyceum system became popular in America, especially in New England. Courses of lectures were instituted in the small towns as well as in the large cities, and the latest thoughts in science, art, literature, politics, and philosophy were given to the people. How democratic these audiences were was shown in results. Now transcendentalism in both religion and politics began to flourish. The working people were ready to believe something in religion that released them from the pain and cramp of a long-preached doctrine of inherent total depravity. The "rise of man" was being substituted for the "fall of man" and the cramp in the brain and the ache in the heart were letting go their clutch.

Much earlier than this the intellectual world had revolted from the Calvinistic "plan of salvation." William Ellery Channing had done such work in Boston that Lyman Beecher left his parish in eastern Massachusetts in 1823 to go to Boston to "confront and stay the movement"; and he shortly wrote in a letter that "all the literary men of Boston, the professors of Harvard College, the judges on the bench are Unitarian." That was in 1823. The movement continued among the scholars and intellectuals until about 1836, when it reached the people and spread like contagion. Elias Hicks became the unorthodox leader of the Quakers, and Hosea Ballou was with less intellectual difficulty attacking the Calvinistic dogma with the doctrine of Universalism. This last was the really popular reaction in New England. Unitarianism was scholarly, Universalism popular. But it all amounted to a revolt against dogmatic theology. Channing denied the depravity of man to show "how capable God had made him of righteousness." He was the center of a bitter fight, but to-day he looks calmly down from his pedestal in the Public Garden of Boston, and the average passer-by may wonder why he is there. Emerson taught that the revelations God made to man were made within the soul, that the soul had infinite dignity and capacity, that transcendentalism was an experience of the immanence of God. He also had his bitter fights with the college men — all forgotten now in the universal reverence for his name. Margaret Fuller described the idea of transcendentalism as an exalting conception of the Godlike nature of the human spirit.

Now it must be remembered that this liberalizing work had been going on in New England for fifty years. Its most prominent teachers were Channing, Emerson, and Theodore Parker. There was a danger in the work, looked at religiously, for whereas the scholars might be supposed to take care of themselves philosophically, the breach made in religious customs for the common man left him nothing. In giving up creed and catechism he could scarcely be expected to come into "living touch" with the philosophy of Germany. So the spectacle is presented of Puritan churches becoming Unitarian and Universalist, and presently a large percentage of the members of these, unable to feed on elevated ethical ideas, dropping off into Spiritualism. Yet Spiritualism, so bizarre and tempting, did not generally satisfy the religious need of the descendants of the Puritans. They had been used to the teachings of stern duty, and it was in their nature to show themselves capable of spiritual effort. Though often of but ordinary intelligence, the artisans and craftsmen and agriculturalists of that period had a deep capacity for religion.

Hiram Crafts was such a man, a Yankee workman transcendentalized. He was not singular, but a type of the man who was to be reached by Christian Science in the first struggling years of its promulgation. Out of the hunger of his heart for religion, he was drawn to a more intimate conversation with Mary Baker than he could gain at table, though he sat next her on the left hand and often lingered after supper for an hour of eager questioning and attentive listening. Nor was it singular that her first convert should be made in this way. This man had no intellectual antagonisms to overcome. He was simply hungry for spiritual experience, hungry to realize that personal communion with God that the religious movement of his times had led him to crave. The hunger of this shoe-worker was such that Mary Baker saw she must provide mental food.

She began to systematize her ideas and to write out a new manuscript, not entirely different from those she had prepared for Quimby. She still believed Quimby had shared the truth of divine healing with her, but her writings were now entirely based on her own experiences. These were written that Hiram Crafts might have something to study. The writings were exceedingly simplified, they were brief summaries, a primer of the simplest statements. Hiram Crafts in describing his pupilage years afterwards said:

"Mary Baker G. Eddy, the discoverer and founder of Christian Science, was not a Spiritualist when she taught me Christian Science in the year 1866. At that time I was a Spiritualist, but her teachings changed my views on that subject and I gave up Spiritualism. She never taught me in my mental practise to hurt others, but only to heal the sick and reform the sinner. She taught me from the Scriptures and from manuscripts that she wrote as she taught me."

In answer to a story intending to reflect discredit upon his teacher, a story which charged her with living upon this poor workman and his family without payment, he further said:

"Mrs. Eddy boarded at my house when I resided in Stoughton, Massachusetts. She furnished our parlor and gave us the use of her furniture."

But this statement, while it throws a little color on the picture, is not the one to bear in mind concerning her relation to this family. Hiram Crafts was Mrs. Eddy's first pupil. She taught him to return to his Bible, to seek in primitive Christianity the religion which he had lost through liberalism, and to become a mental practitioner to the sick and the sinning. In fact she gave him a profession by which he not only was able to live a religious life, but to earn his living. For a long period he did so earn his living and made some unusual cures.

Crafts had gone to Lynn to work in the factories for the winter, but becoming absorbed with this topic of Mind Science, he decided to return to Stoughton to practise it. He invited Mrs. Patterson to go with him and his wife as he was not satisfied with what he had learned, and wanted further information, instruction, and advice in practise.

In leaving Lynn with these humble people, Mary Baker took a radical step. She had tried for months to persuade those who were more akin to her in social and intellectual heritage to accept the truth she had to impart. Of these some, as the Phillips family, loved her, but were impervious to her doctrine. The Winslows had begged her not to talk of it, the Unitarian clergyman of Lynn and his wife were friendly, but they feared for their faith when she spoke to them of God as Principle. The Ellises of Swampscott, mother and son, the latter a teacher, listened with grave inter-

est and amiable social spirit to her arguments for a
higher religion when she was a lodger at their house;
but they were not moved to accept her tenets. Her
doctrine seemed to have the effect of provoking discussion. It aroused in some minds resentment. In
some homes where she had experienced agreeable
friendships, she found it necessary to withdraw. In
these few months of 1866 this feeling had augmented
almost to persecution.

Dr. E. J. Thompson, who was at the time and long
afterward practising dentistry in Lynn, told the author
that he remembered talking to Mrs. Patterson on several occasions about her ideas of religion.

"I used to say to her," Dr. Thompson said, " 'It
may be all true, but I do not grasp it.' As long as
Mrs. Patterson, afterwards Mrs. Eddy, lived in Lynn,
she was known as an unusual woman holding peculiar
religious views. Never have I heard anything more
against her, and I used to see her every day for many
years. It was said she held peculiar views at which
many people laughed. But no one spoke against her
otherwise."

Yet it was her very life that they were against,
these friends of hers; for life meant nothing to her
without religion. She could more easily give up society, culture, books, even church, than she could give
up speaking of the understanding of God which had
come to her. So she made the decision to go into what
would have been for her at an earlier date a social
Sahara.

To the Crafts she took her personal belongings
and house furnishings and helped to make their home

more like what she was used to. Her efforts resulted in an attractive home, though one of great simplicity. It would have been impossible for her to do otherwise than make her environment at least interesting. She lived there not entirely as a guest, for she had made an agreement with Mr. Crafts to guide and tutor him. She also diligently applied herself to writing. The whole problem of the science, of the text-book, and of the practical demonstration might have been worked out here. The wandering of the next few years need not have occurred, but for those inherent traits deep in human nature which show themselves as jealousy, envy, and resentment.

Perfectly natural as an exhibition of human nature was the gradual revelation of Mrs. Crafts' state of mind. She resented playing the role of Martha in this household. To her naturally fell the marketing and housework. Her tasks were not unusual or heavier than she could well assume, but the presence of a woman in her house who was not contributing dollars and cents directly into her palm was disconcerting to her sense of thrift. Moreover, the guest was a woman conspicuously her superior, one upon whom she must occasionally wait as a serving woman. This waiting and serving was honorable and necessary, and looked upon in a very democratic sense by the household. No one dreamed of making it a badge of shame to the wife, certainly not the husband who had been accustomed to seeing his wife so occupied; certainly not Mrs. Patterson, who on occasion had performed the most menial tasks herself, as every New England girl is instructed to do when occasion requires. It had been imparted to Mary Baker as a part of the ethics of her breeding.

However, the thoughts of serving a woman who held long conversations daily with her husband and otherwise occupied herself with writing aroused in Mrs. Crafts a jealousy which was only increased as the days drifted by and the life they all lived was shown to be without blame. There was no ground for reproach, but Mrs. Crafts found a fault expressed in the statement, "She carried herself above folks." Her jealousy may be regarded as natural by many, but it was certainly unfortunate in that it presently cut off the development of her husband's work, and broke the continuity of Mary Baker's.

But Mary Baker was finding out an invaluable secret. She was learning to pursue her work unmindful of petty disturbance. She seems to have mentally registered a vow, or engraved it upon her heart, "This one thing I do." She was searching the Scripture, keeping aloof from society, and devoting time and energy to discovering a positive rule of healing. It must be remembered that she was finding the task "sweet, calm, and buoyant with hope, not selfish nor depressing." [1] She was winning her way to absolute conclusions through reason and demonstration. The revelation in her understanding was coming to her gradually. This was the test of experience.

After a winter of such work as was thought necessary to prepare Hiram Crafts to practise mental healing, the family removed to the neighboring town of Taunton. East Stoughton, where they had passed

1 Science and Health, p. 109.

the winter, is now called Avon and is sixteen miles directly south of Boston. Taunton is still farther south, thirty-two miles distant from Boston. Mr. Crafts opened an office and advertised in the local papers his readiness to deal with various mentioned diseases. He declared, however, that if patients gave him a fair trial and were not benefited he would refund their money. In three weeks he was able to print the testimonial of a woman patient who had been healed of an internal abscess. The patient tells of her own and her friends' utter astonishment that this should have been done in an incredibly short time when she had suffered for twelve years and that it should have been done without medicines or applications, but she added that she was convinced that he was a skilful physician and that his cures were not the result of accident.

Such indorsement coming from one living in his own town, whose name and address were printed in full and could be easily seen by the villagers and country folk, had a good effect in swelling the number of his visitors, and Hiram Crafts found himself in the way of doing a great deal of good, while his livelihood, which his wife had feared would be threatened by the abandonment of cobbling, seemed secured. She made it a source of complaint, however, that Mrs. Patterson did not herself practise.

Mrs. Patterson encouraged, advised, and supported her student in all he did. During the evenings she discussed the principle of healing with him. Every cure that he made, however simple, was a further demonstration of the science. She was as deeply in-

terested and as greatly rejoiced over each cure as was
the practitioner. It was a season of wonder and delight to both teacher and student, and also at times to
the faithful Martha of their household. But doubting
relatives filled Mrs. Crafts with dissatisfaction and
suspicion. To make shoes was a tangible, legitimate
method of earning a living. To practise religious
healing was, in their estimation, a pious fraud.

Conversations of this nature with her relatives
had its effect in due time. It brought about strained
relations in the household and made a new adjustment of conditions necessary. But fortunately before
this took place a certain work had been accomplished
which could not be undone. Mary Baker saw that not
only could she herself heal, but she could impart the
understanding of the *modus operandi* to another. In
this respect her work already differed from Phineas
Quimby's; she could detach it from herself, separate
it from her personality. What remained was to give
her discovery its scientific statement.

CHAPTER XII

GERMINATION AND UNFOLDMENT

THERE is no period in the life of Mary Baker so difficult to delineate as the one before us. Its outward aspect might be rapidly sketched, the incidents of the next few years might be related comprehensively in a few pages, but the significance of these years, which is of vast importance, can only be indicated with the most reverent suggestion.

Whether outlining with bold pencil strokes or working up the picture from the canvas of environment with subtlest brush touches, how can one hope to convey the idea of a life such as this, gathered out of its past, confirmed for its great future, girded with purpose and panoplied for resistance? Luminosity is attained only by the greatest skill in portraiture, and by what perspicuous, lucid, sane observations of sympathy and understanding only the masters can tell. But even such portraiture meets with success only when the eye to which it is submitted will attentively comprehend. Discernment of transmutation in character must accompany the enlightenment of events.

Mary Baker was not ready to state the science of Mind-healing directly after her discovery through her own personal healing. She was not ready after she had healed others by this discovery; nor was she ready when she had fitted her first student to heal disease.

How she was prepared for this work cannot be explained by the usual methods of the biographer, by rehearsing the facts of her residence in various places, her associates, or her occupations. A process of germination and unfoldment took place in her which must have had its apocryphal hours as well as apocalyptic moments, its seasons of doubt and fog as its times of certainty and sun. The work laid upon her was that of renaming, actually rechristening, the verities.

In her autobiography Mrs. Eddy has endeavored to explain how she approached this great work. He who runs may not read here. Loose conceptions arise from a careless use of terms, and, as in a trial where life depends on exact and technical phrasing, so in knowing the real Mary Baker Eddy one must apply himself to comprehend her terminology and how she came to adopt it in order to realize what business she was about.

"I had learned that thought must be spiritualized, in order to apprehend Spirit," she has written. "It must become honest, unselfish, and pure, in order to have the least understanding of God in divine Science. The first must become last. Our reliance upon material things must be transferred to a perception of and dependence on spiritual things. For Spirit to be supreme in demonstration, it must be supreme in our affections, and we must be clad with divine power. Purity, self-renunciation, faith, and understanding must reduce all things real to their own mental denomination, Mind, which divides, sub-divides, increases, diminishes, constitutes, and sustains, according to the law of God." [1]

1 "Retrospection and Introspection," p. 28.

Thus in her own words we have the secret of her submission to adverse circumstances and conditions with a marvelous cheerfulness. It was submission to the spiritual sense of things, docility to the tutelage of divine inspiration. She further says:

I had learned that Mind reconstructed the body, and that nothing else could. How it was done, the spiritual Science of Mind must reveal. It was a mystery to me then, but I have since understood it. All Science is a revelation. Its Principle is divine, not human, reaching higher than the stars of heaven.[1]

I have said that her task was to re-christen the verities. She says that she withdrew from society for about three years to ponder her mission, "to search the Scriptures, to find the Science of Mind that should take the things of God and show them to the creature, and reveal the great curative Principle, — Deity."[2] How did she set about this task? She says:

The Bible was my textbook. It answered my questions as to how I was healed; but the Scriptures had to me a new meaning, a new tongue. Their spiritual signification appeared; and I apprehended for the first time, in their spiritual meaning, Jesus' teaching and demonstration, and the Principle and rule of spiritual Science and metaphysical healing, — in a word, Christian Science.[3]

In a brief paragraph is related the actual, technical work of reducing her discovery "to the apprehension of the age"[4] in a new terminology, the foundation upon which all her subsequent work was built, the

---

1 "Retrospection and Introspection," p. 28.
2 *Ibid.*, p. 24.   3 *Ibid.*, p. 25.   4 *Ibid.*, p. 26.

naming of the fundamental conceptions. She says of this earliest work in the stating of her Science:

> I named it *Christian*, because it is compassionate, help-ful, and spiritual. God I called *immortal Mind.* That which sins, suffers, and dies, I named *mortal mind.* The physical senses, or sensuous nature, I called *error* and *shadow.* Soul I denominated *substance*, because Soul alone is truly substantial. God I characterized as individual en-tity, but His corporeality I denied. The real I claimed as eternal; and its antipodes, or the temporal, I described as unreal. Spirit I called the *reality;* and matter, the *unreality.*[1]

This is the actual work of several years. How it was accomplished who shall say? Who can say when it first grew clear in Mary Baker's understanding that "matter neither sees, hears, nor feels Spirit" [2] and that the five physical senses testifying that God is a physi-cal, personal Being like unto man are testifying falsely? Was it while she was at the Crafts' humble and unpretentious home, or while with the turbulent Wentworth family? Was it during the quiet hours spent with the motherly old woman in the great empty house on the banks of the Merrimac in Amesbury, or was it while leaving an inhospitable roof in a deluge of rain late on an autumn night? It is idle to inquire whether in calm or turbulence the spiritual facts grew clear. But both calm and turbulence were her lot, and sometime during these years of trial it became clear to her what her mission was and why it was that ceaseless toil and self-renunciation were laid upon her after years of physical suffering and the sunder-ing of almost every natural or human tie of affection.

[1] "Retrospection and Introspection," p. 25.   [2] *Ibid.*, p. 25.

"It is often asked," Mrs. Eddy has written, "why Christian Science was revealed to me as one intelligence, analyzing, uncovering, and annihilating the false testimony of the physical senses. Why was this conviction necessary to the right apprehension of the invincible and infinite energies of Truth and Love, as contrasted with the foibles and fables of finite mind and material existence.

"The answer is plain. St. Paul declared that the law was the schoolmaster, to bring him to Christ. Even so was I led into the mazes of divine metaphysics through the gospel of suffering, the providence of God, and the cross of Christ. No one else can drain the cup which I have drunk to the dregs as the Discoverer and teacher of Christian Science; neither can its inspiration be gained without tasting this cup." [1]

Taking up the incidents which formed the setting of this work of germination and unfoldment, we find the last tie which bound her to family and home broken. Or to speak more exactly, we find her submitting to the severing of the last tie, for Mrs. Eddy never broke one tie with her own hands, never was herself the cause of one separation from all those who went out of her life, never neglected a duty to a relative or friend, or failed to show grateful remembrance for any service performed in her behalf.

There had been backward looks, many and often, to those loved ones of her family. Sitting alone in the twilight of many a day, she had reflected long and sadly on the lights and shadows of the past, dreaming of her mother's love, dearer to her than her pen could

1 "Retrospection and Introspection," p. 30.

relate. She wrote of that mother as she oftenest remembered her, bending over her and parting the curls
to kiss her cheek. The dear love of sister and brother
found a place in her poetry and the sterner affection,
deep and tried, of her old father is often referred to.
She had thought of herself as a young bride, of the
lights of her own home, the remembered glance of
her husband's eye. Of all these memories that was
most poignantly sweet which pictured

> " . . . a glad young face,
> Upturned to his mother's in playful grace;
> And the unsealed fountains of grief and joy
> That gushed at the birth of that beautiful boy." [1]

These verses called "I'm Sitting Alone" were
written in September, 1866, shortly after Dr. Patterson's desertion and before she left Lynn with her first
student. In the summer of 1867 her memories culminated in a passion of affection. She must see some
of her family once more and look again upon the
mountains around her old home, those hills to which
she had lifted her eyes when a schoolgirl, walking in
the garden with her pastor; when a young bride leaving home; when a young mother with her babe in her
arms; and when coming back from a visit to her own
mother's grave.

Yes, Sanbornton Bridge (or Tilton) was dear to
her. Her native soil and natal horizons drew her as
they must always draw all that is human in the hearts
of the least and the greatest. Perhaps her compelling
impulse in visiting Tilton was to see her brother

1 "Poems," p. 9.

George who had returned from Baltimore and now resided there with his wife and child. He had become
blind. This great sorrow rested upon him heavily, indeed so heavily that he shortly yielded to an illness
and died. But a few months before his death she
made this visit home. How sensible she was of his
sorrow and affliction she revealed in certain other
verses in which she would have conveyed to her
brother more than sympathy, the understanding of
her own faith. But this conveyance of her faith was
not possible; he could not accept it, though her
stanzas with a depth of affection beg him to dispel the
shadow and give back from his earnest eyes the image
of the soul of Truth and Light.

On the occasion of this home-going Mary visited
her brother and her sisters Abigail and Martha. With
Abigail she talked earnestly. She was not able to
reconcile her to her views any more than she was able
to inspire her brother with her faith. There was much
of homely criticism to be endured and passed over,
much of that sort of reminding of the trivial which
makes a prophet in his own land and in his own house
unknown because the outward circumstances loom big
and the inner life is unguessed. So it was with Jesus
when in Nazareth. "Is not this the carpenter's son?"
they asked, and, "Are not his brothers and sisters here
with us?" So "he did not many mighty works there."
In her sister Martha's home Mary Baker did, however,
perform a significant healing. Martha, who it will be
remembered, married Luther Pilsbury of Concord,
was now in Tilton with her daughter Ellen, then a
young woman of twenty-one. This daughter lay crit-

ically ill of enteritis. Mary Baker went to the sick
chamber and sat with her niece for a while. The girl
lay supinely inert and helpless in bed; she is said to
have been exceedingly ill and to have had perfect
quiet ordered.

The day after her aunt's visit to her sick chamber,
they appeared together in the family living room. The
young woman was dressed and expressed a desire to
eat supper with the family. Every member of the
household protested at once on seeing her. They
were seriously alarmed. But Ellen, obeying her aunt,
refused to return to her bed and suffered no ill effects.
Ellen Pilsbury recovered completely, and within a
few days returned to Taunton with her Aunt Mary, a
distance of a hundred miles. The story of this healing
was told the author by Martha Rand Baker, widow of
George Baker, who lived long in Tilton.

It is rather singular that such an incident as this
should have had no convincing effect on Mary Baker's
family. As a matter of fact it only the more alienated
them from Mary and her religion. Even Ellen Pilsbury came in after years to repudiate the healing, and
repudiate it with resentment.

During the visit with her to Taunton this niece was
detached in her affections from her aunt. Ellen was
amazed at the simplicity and humbleness in which
she found her Aunt Mary living at the home of the
Crafts, was amazed at the social isolation, the rigorous
application to a severe regimen of work which her
aunt had imposed upon herself. Moreover, she resented a firm guidance which her aunt directed over
her. All would have been made simple, beautiful, and

acceptable had Ellen been able to imbibe the tenets of the faith which had healed her. But these she rejected. She returned to Tilton and ever after scoffed at the very mention of Christian Science. It was she who prevented her Aunt Abigail in her last sickness from sending for Mary. She would turn pale with resentment when reminded that she had herself been lifted from a critical illness by her aunt. Her antipathy amounted to a passion, and was related with wonder by old neighbors. It is but another instance of many remarkable antagonisms which Christian Science healing has given rise to through its very unanswerableness. Ellen Pilsbury appeared to resent the notion that she was made to be a living witness of its power. She acted as the final disintegrating factor in Mary Baker's home relations.

Shortly after Ellen Pilsbury returned to Tilton, Mary Baker severed her relations with the Crafts, finding that no further good could be done along the lines of procedure she had marked out with them. Mrs. Crafts was a confirmed Spiritualist, and after a very temporary lull in her resistance to Christian Science she renewed her opposition with all the energy of a narrow mind and found countless ways of expressing her resistance. Mary Baker went to Lynn for a short visit with the Winslows. She explained to them her desire for a quiet home in which she could write and work out her great problem. They suggested that she go to Amesbury and their reasons were clear. They were Quakers. In Amesbury, a quiet little town in the extreme northeast corner of Massachusetts, situated on the Merrimac River, nine miles from the sea, dwelt the great Quaker poet, Whittier. It was natural for them to suggest this as an admirable place for literary seclusion. It was a quiet, peaceful village with historic tradition. The Winslows had friends there to whom they commended Mrs. Glover, as she was now called by her own request.

But the Quakers could not take her. It will be remembered that the Winslows were disquietly affected by her ideas, even after being convinced of their healing power. They had told her if she persisted in presenting such doctrine she would be thought insane. This was also the opinion of a Unitarian clergyman and his wife. It was not in Mary Baker's heart to arouse such opposition further or to enter carelessly another environment of resistance. She now turned her footsteps to the home of an elderly Spiritualist woman of whom she had heard much. Mrs. Eddy has told the author that the cause of her frequent removals during this period from one residence to another was the revolutionary character of her teaching. She found that Spiritualists revealed a greater willingness than others to receive truth, and she wanted to teach; she was ready to teach whoever would accept her doctrine. It was to the simple-minded that she was constrained to address herself and to the simplest society. How these uneducated and simple folk were variously wrought upon to receive and reject her compels the narration of many painful episodes. Of these Mary Baker was not unduly mindful. Mrs. Eddy once pointed out to the author that the assaults of the trivial-minded counted for but little in comparison with the kind words of the nobly serious who, dif-

fering from her in belief, differed according to their
honor and nobility. Of these Bronson Alcott was one
who came to her in her darkest hour with the words,
"I have come to comfort you."

It was at the home of Mrs. Nathaniel Webster that
Mrs. Glover applied for board. Mrs. Webster lived
alone in a three-story house of some fifteen rooms at
the foot of Merrimac Street near the river. Her husband, a retired sea-captain, was at that time a superintendent of cotton mills in Manchester, N. H., and was
away from home except for an occasional Sunday's
visit. With open heart and open arms Mrs. Webster
received the religionist. She had a sympathetic and
hospitable nature, and moreover an inquiring mind.
She was agreeably impressed when Mary Baker told
her that she was engaged on a very serious work and
that her work required reflection and solitude. She explained to her that she was writing, but did not further enter upon a discussion of her ideas at the time.
They came to an agreement for modest terms and Mrs.
Webster gave her a large chamber at the southeast
corner on the second floor. Here she had sunlight and
a view of the river.

The winter and part of the following summer were
spent very quietly. These two women were placidly
content together. If "Mother" Webster was inclined
to discuss Spiritualistic "phenomena" this was not a
new experience for Mary Baker. She had listened to
these ideas before and in many instances had shown
rare toleration, even as she did in this case. In some
of their conversations Mrs. Glover endeavored to lead
Mrs. Webster into an understanding of the Science of

Mind. But the elderly woman showed but little comprehension. She so far failed to understand her as
to think that Mrs. Glover was writing a revision of the
Bible. Mrs. Webster had numerous guests of her own
faith; many invalids came to her for a resting-place.
With these Mrs. Glover sometimes mingled and performed not a few cures. These simple people came to
speak of her with awe and reverence, and the rumor
went abroad that a woman was living at Mrs. Webster's who could perform miracles. When walking
along the river banks on pleasant summer evenings
with Mother Webster, Mrs. Glover attracted the villagers' attention. Young people loitering on the
bridge would gaze at her curiously, half expecting to
see Mrs. Glover walk upon the water of the river.
Such incidents made this sojourn in Amesbury a mingled experience. Seeking absolute retirement, she
was forced to endure a somewhat unpleasant notoriety
through the volubleness of the kindly old soul with
whom she made her home.

What she was writing at this time was a commen-
tary on the Scriptures, setting forth their spiritual interpretation, the Science of the Bible, and laying the
foundation of her future book. Of these writings she
has said:

If these notes and comments, which have never been
read by any one but myself, were published, it would show
that after my discovery of the absolute Science of Mind-
healing, like all great truths, this spiritual Science developed itself to me until Science and Health was written.
These early comments are valuable to me as waymarks of
progress, which I would not have effaced.[1]

1 "Retrospection and Introspection," p. 27.

THE SQUIRE BAGLEY HOMESTEAD, AMESBURY, MASSACHUSETTS
Where Mrs. Eddy met John Greenleaf Whittier in 1870

This quiet work and spiritual unfoldment came to an abrupt halt in this home through the return to the house of her hostess's son-in-law. In sardonic reminiscence he has related that in spite of Mrs. Webster's protests he dragged Mrs. Glover's trunk out upon the front veranda, ejected her into the night and storm, and locked the door upon her. He has explained that he wished to clear Mrs. Webster's house of strangers that his vacation might be agreeable. This is a startling account of a ruffianly act which almost any man would hesitate to tell of himself, and it gives rise to the question as to what really happened there that so unmannerly a deed should be unblushingly proclaimed.

The incident apparently did occur, however. There was cause for much offense, but the cause decidedly lay not with Mrs. Glover. She left the house with the same composure that she had entered it. And she might have gone sooner had she had a place to go. Two other guests went with her, either at the son-in-law's bidding or in sympathy. The young man went his way but the woman who accompanied her took her to the home of Miss Sarah Bagley. Here arrangements were made for Mrs. Glover's provision though in less than two months she would return to Stoughton.

Miss Bagley's home, while simple and modest, was nevertheless a home of refinement, a place admirably adapted for a quiet and studious life, and many months later Mrs. Glover returned to stay seven weeks with her. The house was an old homestead built by Squire Lowell Bagley. It stood for a century, just below the hill clothed with cedar and pine on which the poet Whittier lies buried after living for fifty years in the

quiet old town. Across the way and a little farther up
the street was the home of Valentine Bagley, who had
been a sea-captain. Once in his wanderings he had
been a castaway in Arabia. Suffering tortures of thirst
in the desert, he resolved, if he reached home, to dig
a well by the wayside, that no passer-by should ever
want for water. This well was dug and Whittier, hearing the story, wrote his poem on the "Captain's
Well." Indeed, the town was full of the legends of
the past which Whittier poetized, of witches sent to
Salem to be tried and put to death, of Friends de-
ported or hounded across the boundaries. Historic
old mansions built in the seventeenth century still
stood upon the street.

When Squire Bagley died the townspeople were
much surprised that he had not left a fortune to his
daughters. He had led a retired life for a number of
years and given his daughters a good education. Miss
Sarah Bagley, however, found it necessary, when her
father's affairs were settled, to teach school for an income, and Whittier was one of her first committee-
men. With him she had very pleasant associations.
She taught for several terms and then remained at
home to be with her sister who was not strong. They
opened a small-wares shop in their home which stood
so close to the street as to make it convenient. But
in spite of these occupations which Miss Bagley found
it necessary to take upon herself, and though she did
some sewing in connection with tending her shop, it
is an injustice to her memory to speak of her as the
village dressmaker or school-teacher with a show of
condescension. She was well read and cultivated, a

friend of Whittier, and regarded by him as a gifted woman. She was able to perform the service of bringing Mary Baker Eddy and John Greenleaf Whittier together in one or two significant though unrecorded meetings.

When Mrs. Glover came into this home quietly and composedly on a stormy evening of the late summer of 1868, after the unpleasant episode at the Websters', she brought with her new life and new interests to the somewhat gray and saddened existence of the maiden daughter of the old squire whose fortunes had faded. Miss Bagley had been a Universalist and had become a Spiritualist in religious belief, but she soon became interested in Mrs. Glover's doctrine. She was an agreeable companion who needed only the living touch of sympathy and interest to waken her from the apathy into which her dreary round of duties had drawn her. Mrs. Glover taught her the elements of Christian Science, for it must be remembered that she had not yet definitively grasped this Science herself.

After Mrs. Glover left her they corresponded for nearly two years, until Mrs. Glover returned again to live with her and teach her to heal. This event changed her whole subsequent life. She laid aside her needle and closed her shop, devoting herself to practising the healing art. She earned her living for twenty years as a practitioner and laid aside sufficient to keep her in comfort for the last ten years of her life during seven of which she was afflicted with semiblindness. But Sarah Bagley was never a Christian Scientist. She did not follow her teacher out of the maze into the bright light of complete understanding.

She refused, as did another student, to lay aside mesmerism and confused her practise with such doctrines.

While living in Stoughton with the Crafts, Mrs. Glover met Mrs. Sally Wentworth, who brought her daughter Celia to her to be treated for consumption. Mrs. Glover healed her. Mrs. Wentworth invited Mrs. Glover to come and live with her, and wrote her while she was in Amesbury, repeating the request. Mrs. Glover now accepted the invitation, and was a member of the Wentworth household for eighteen months. This household was composed of father and mother, two daughters, and a son Charles. An older son, Horace, who was married, was an occasional visitor. When Mrs. Glover went to live with the Wentworths, Celia was about nineteen, Charles was younger, and Lucy about fourteen. Horace was a journeyman shoemaker, and was very much averse to religious discussions.

In complying with Mrs. Wentworth's earnest appeal that she should make her home with them and teach her Mind Science, Mary Baker did not entirely realize the conditions she was to encounter. Mrs. Wentworth was a domestic-minded woman, not over-gifted with intellectuality, but of a receptive and teachable nature. She had been a practical nurse and had gone out to the sick of the neighborhood for years. But she was a Spiritualist, and believed in rubbing the limbs of her patients to give them comfort. She had eagerly drunk in all that Mary Baker had imparted to her of Mind-healing when she met her at the Crafts', and thought she could combine this with her nursing and massage to make her a more practical healer.

MRS. EDDY
As She Looked while Living with the Wentworths
at Stoughton, Massachusetts
Where she began writing the manuscript, "The Science of Man"

From the very start Mary Baker had to disabuse her mind of such a hope. She talked to her of the fallacy of such a procedure, often illustrating by her experience with Phineas Quimby. In just what way this doctrine of rubbing and clairvoyantly reading the patients' minds was inimical to a cure in Mind Science Mary Baker did not herself at that time know. Hence she could not authoritatively direct Mrs. Wentworth in her thinking. Mrs. Wentworth was inclined to the Quimby method and Mary Baker had not found herself sufficiently to gainsay her predilection. She told Mrs. Wentworth freely all that she knew of Quimby's method, but she herself worked on her own ideas, writing for hours in her room, struggling with the conflicting theories.

Mrs. Glover had with her a manuscript which she had prepared while at Portland under the sway of Quimby's thought. Mrs. Wentworth wanted to copy this. She found in it certain comfort for her Spiritualistic leanings. Mrs. Glover did not refuse it to her, but felt so uncertain of its character that she did not want her to circulate it and made her promise to keep it only for her own perusal. Not yet certain enough to condemn it absolutely, she gravely doubted the statements which she had herself penned at an earlier date while still under Quimby's influence.

Now, as has been said, Mary Baker was engaged on a manuscript concerning the spiritual significance of the Scripture. On this she was devoting the closest thought, endeavoring to make clear the apprehensions of pure spiritual doctrine. Mrs. Wentworth, as Mrs. Webster had done, spoke of this as "Mrs. Glover's

Bible." So the family gossiped among themselves and came to speak of the manuscript Mary Baker lent Mrs. Wentworth as the "Quimby" manuscript, and the one she was at work on as "Mrs. Glover's Bible." Horace Wentworth, the shoemaker, visiting home, caught up these phrases with the readiness of a jocular and jeering temperament. He had an able second in all his jests and gibes in the person of a cousin, a gay-hearted, mirth-loving girl, given to mimicry. Between them they tormented the patient mother with a bur-lesque of her work.

Mary Baker was never a witness of these hilarious scenes. She kept rather strict hours at her desk, vary-ing her work with recreation of a suitable nature. She lived for nearly two years in this village surrounded with wooded hills. She knew well its quiet walks and inspiring vistas. In her room she wrote assiduously and spent many hours in meditation and prayer. Her relations with the three children in the home, as well as with the father and mother, were cordial and agree-able. Far from being a recluse, she welcomed the chil-dren to her room when not engaged with her writ-ing, and made their joys and sorrows her own. The daughter Lucy was particularly devoted to her.

"I loved her," Lucy Wentworth told the author, "because she made me love her. She was beautiful and had a good influence over me. I used to be with her every minute that she was not writing or otherwise engaged. And I was very jealous of her book. We talked and read together and took long walks in the country. I idolized her and really suffered when she locked her door to work and would not let me come to

her. After she had worked for hours she always relaxed and threw off her seriousness. Then she would
admit us, my brother Charles and me, and sometimes
a school friend of Charles's. The boys would romp in
her room sometimes rather boisterously, but she never
seemed to mind it. Our times together alone were
quieter. When she finally left our house it seemed to
me my heart would break.

"But a coolness grew up in the family toward our
guest. I don't know how it came about. My father
thought she absorbed my mother too much and that
she was weaning me away from them. Perhaps she
was unconsciously, for she made a great deal of me.
Yet her influence over me was always for good. We
read good books and talked of spiritual things. She
loved nature; she was cultivated and well-bred. Her
manners seemed to me so beautiful that I imitated her
in everything. I never missed any one as I missed her.
She said good-by to me with great affection, held me
in her arms and looked long into my eyes. 'You, too,
will turn against me some day, Lucy,' she said. And
if I have seemed to, did I not have reason? Why did
she never write to me? I have never heard from her,
not one word since she left our house thirty-five
years ago."

It was not in Mary Baker's nature to wean a child
from its parents. She had had her own heart-breaking
experience of this herself. Her experiences with the
Wentworths, following upon her experiences with
the Crafts, taught her to avoid in the future a too close
mingling with another family. And her conclusions
were based on just analysis of human nature. Richard

Kennedy of Boston, an early student with Mrs. Eddy, in commenting upon her relations with this family, made these observations to the author in explaining the situation there and elsewhere when Mrs. Eddy was working out her religious statement:

The Wentworths were well enough in their way, as were the Crafts with whom Mrs. Eddy lived at an earlier period, and the Websters of Amesbury. It was an unfortunate fact that Mrs. Eddy with her small income was obliged to live with people very often at this time in her life who were without education and cultivation. It was never her custom to keep apart from the family. She invariably mingled with them and through them kept in touch with the world. She had a great work to do; she was possessed by her purpose and like Paul the apostle, and many another great teacher and leader, she reiterated to herself, "This one thing I do." Of course simple-minded people who take life as it comes from day to day find any one with so fixed an object in life a rebuke to the flow of their own animal spirits. Mrs. Wentworth was what old-fashioned New Englanders call "clever," that is to say, kind-hearted. She looked well after the creature comforts of those under her roof. Lucy was a spirituelle young girl, Charles was a sensible, lively boy, but Horace was something of a scoffer, without any leanings toward religious inquiry.

Horace Wentworth, the scoffer, in later years did more than scoff at the memory of his mother's guest. He even made allegations of a grave nature against Mary Baker Eddy. He related that in leaving his father's house Mrs. Glover maliciously slashed the matting and tried to set the house afire by putting live coals on a pile of papers. He gossiped after this manner for many years, and finding that his stories went well in the village square, he eventually told them to newspaper correspondents and saw them printed in the metropolitan press. The apparent foundation for such slanderous gossip is that the children playing roughly in Mrs. Glover's room tore the matting with their heavy shoes, and some dead ashes were laid on a newspaper to be removed with the rubbish. There was no thought of serious unpleasantness when Mrs. Glover left his father's home, nor dared this son speak against his mother's teacher so long as his mother lived.

But the scoffings of the son and the mimicry and mockery of his cousin Kate did create a discord in the home which came to wear on Mrs. Glover's mind. She frequently overheard the wordy and worldly clamor in the rooms down-stairs. She heard the harsh laughter and mincing mimicry; she heard the passionate defense made of her by the young daughter Lucy; she heard Mrs. Wentworth sharply reprimanding her eldest son with the words, "If ever there was a saint on earth it is Mrs. Glover." She heard the father interfere with a tolerant plea for his boy. The house was too small for her to live in unmindful of these indiscreet wranglings.

There seemed to be a hopeless division in the family over her, her personality, her teaching, her interpretation of the Bible. This division of opinion threatened to become a serious cause of difference in an otherwise united family. Mary Baker made up her mind one evening, after reading a letter from Miss Bagley, that she would return to the quiet home of this cultivated maiden lady in Amesbury and go on with her work where she would be less disturbed **and** in no way the cause of discussion.

But it was not Mary Baker's idea of good breeding to break off long-established relations rudely or with recrimination. She recognized the limitations of this family; she knew what she had to do and that she must be about it. She acquainted Mr. and Mrs. Wentworth with her intentions and her leave-taking was made with courteous attentions on both her part and theirs. She was escorted to the train by the elder Mr. Wentworth, who carried her bag and wraps. He found her a comfortable seat in the train and shook hands with her with expressions of regret at parting. This may not be as romantic an account as that of Horace Wentworth, who, from long embellishment of his reminiscences, came to say that his family had gone from home and that Mrs. Glover, after strewing a newspaper with smoking coals, fled clandestinely. However, the sober facts are that the leave-taking was quite devoid of adventure and as decorous as usual with well-behaved personages.

Returning to Amesbury early in 1870, Mary Baker applied herself to her writing and to teaching two students. These students were Sarah Bagley and Richard Kennedy. Kennedy was a young man a little past his majority, who boarded at the Captain Webster house where Mrs. Glover had previously lived. He had a small box factory in the town, employing a few hands and earning for himself a good living.

He was alert, active, and clear-headed, and his instruction that had begun during Mrs. Glover's earlier

stay was intensified. The winter evenings were passed
in conversation on metaphysics. The Socratic method
of teaching was necessarily adopted by Mrs. Glover, as
she had as yet no text-book. These early talks were
later systematized, the dissertations were dignified into
the form of lectures. And these lectures some of her
early students declare to have been illuminating and
inspirational beyond valuing in money.

Her dissertations as well as her writings were beginning to unseal the fountains of her inspiration.
She had arrived by this winter's work at a clear standpoint. She could now definitely wrap in words the
spiritual concepts which had before been elusive and
intangible. She was beginning to lay hold of the technical processes of her work. From this standpoint she
lifted her eyes to a far horizon. The work now opened
up before her, the work of promulgation.

Before returning to Amesbury she had already
completed a work entitled "The Science of Man." This
manuscript was copyrighted but not published until
some time later. "I did not venture upon its publication until later," she says, "having learned that
the merits of Christian Science must be proven
before a work on this subject could be profitably
published." [1]

It was first issued as a pamphlet and is advertised
in the first number of *The Christian Science Journal.*
At this time it had already been incorporated as the
chapter on Recapitulation in "Science and Health
with Key to the Scriptures." It contains the fundamental principles of Christian Science and its sim-

1 "Retrospection and Introspection," p. 35.

plest comprehensive tenet, the scientific statement of being. With this manuscript completed she knew that she could teach the science and extend her work, that the time was ripe for harvest.

Through four successive years she had labored carefully, patiently, earnestly, writing and rewriting, while the truth grew in her understanding. It is no refutation of her sublime discovery in 1866 or of her divine guidance in preparing and presenting its principles that the work was a growth and did not spring full-blown into her mind. Mary Baker could never have made her discovery in 1866 had she not been prepared for it by long application to spiritual inquiry. Nor would she have written Science and Health had she not labored long and with perfect submission to imperative spiritual guidance. The preparation for the discovery is shown by the facts of her childhood and young womanhood and, as this narrative reveals, her statement of long preparation is sustained by the facts of her life. She says: "From my very childhood I was impelled, by a hunger and thirst after divine things, — a desire for something higher and better than matter, and apart from it, — to seek diligently for the knowledge of God as the one great and ever-present relief from human woe." [1]

With regard to important dates in her memory concerning the portents of what was to be revealed to her she says: "As long ago as 1844 I was convinced that mortal mind produced all disease, and that the various medical systems were in no proper sense Scientific. In 1862, when I first visited Mr.

1 "Retrospection and Introspection," p. 31.

Quimby, I was proclaiming — to druggists, spiritualists, and mesmerists — that Science must govern all healing." [1]

Her life, her acts, her conversations all sustain this statement, though *mortal mind* belongs to the terminology of later years. Before meeting Quimby the conception of that which "sins, suffers, dies" was growing in her thought, though as a vague apprehension. In North Groton she astounded the old man who visited her to pray with her by rising to meet him in no other strength than a faith groping blindly. And there, too, she healed diseased eyes of a child instantaneously, and as a further proof that she was acquiring a more definite hold of this great truth, she was herself healed by her own religiosity while under Quimby's magnetic treatment and in spite of his manipulations. No one should be confused by these facts concerning the definite discovery in 1866. Mrs. Eddy says: "The first spontaneous motion of Truth and Love, acting through Christian Science on my roused consciousness, banished at once and forever the fundamental error of faith in things material; for this trust is the unseen sin, the unknown foe, — the heart's untamed desire which breaketh the divine commandments." [2]

If she was thus prepared for her discovery, indeed re-prepared through experiencing the workings of magnetism, that her healing might be clear and definite, then we may believe she was by the same gradual process prepared for the writing of her book. Again

[1] *The Christian Science Journal,* June, 1887.
[2] "Retrospection and Introspection," p. 31.

it is best to take her own words for a description of the
attuning of her faculties. She says:

Naturally, my first jottings were but efforts to express
in feeble diction Truth's ultimate. . . . As sweet music
ripples in one's first thoughts of it like the brooklet in its
meandering midst pebbles and rocks, before the mind can
duly express it to the ear, — so the harmony of divine
Science first broke upon my sense, before gathering experience and confidence to articulate it. Its natural manifestation is beautiful and euphonious, but its written expression
increases in power and perfection under the guidance of
the great Master.[1]

1 "Retrospection and Introspection," p. 27.

PHOTOGRAPH OF MRS. EDDY
SAID TO HAVE BEEN TAKEN IN 1876
When she was teaching her classes in Mind Science
in Lynn, Massachusetts

CHAPTER XIII

MESMERISM DETHRONED

WITH the coming of spring in the year 1870 Mrs. Glover's thoughts were definitely shaped for the work before her. She had decided to return to the city of Lynn and take up the teaching of divine Science. She had the manuscript, "The Science of Man," for a basis. From a worldly standpoint her resources were meager. Her small income had been carefully husbanded, but she had in hand only a modest sum for capital with which to venture into a city and rent rooms. Her wardrobe too was scanty, carefully preserved though it had been. That she was invariably neat and attractive in appearance is in itself a statement suggestive of a miracle. That she had had shelter, food, and clothing for four years on an income of two hundred dollars per annum, and had nowhere incurred the charge of charitable entertainment, and that she had all that time worked assiduously at her intellectual and spiritual problems is one of the mysteries of the possibilities of poverty, fully as beautiful in its revelation as the glory of opulence.

Richard Kennedy, the young man who with Miss Bagley had received her instruction during the winter, had no mind to leave his teacher. He had become so imbued with enthusiasm for the Science he had been studying that he wished to practise it, and he wished to begin his practise in the larger field of Lynn. He conceived the idea of accompanying his teacher and practising under her guidance. He talked it over with Mrs. Glover many times, joining her when she took her evening walk along the river at sunset, and eagerly setting forth his plans for mutual work. It was his desire to be under Mrs. Glover's supervision, taking the burden of practise entirely on his shoulders and leaving her free to teach and write. He also believed that he could relieve her of many business cares. He had some capital, and so sensible was he of the enlightenment he had received that he was quite ready to risk his savings and to agree to share equally with Mrs. Glover any income which he might derive from the practise of Mind Science.

Mrs. Glover was not so ready to enter into this agreement with her young student. He had an unblemished reputation, had honorably conducted himself toward her with the chivalrous devotion of a son to a mother; but he was untried in the ways of life, there had been no test put upon him such as she well knew lay before him if he took up the work with her. She knew the city of Lynn, its somewhat harsh industrialism, its free intermingling of the sexes in the factory life, and the near-by temptations of Boston — all very different from the village life of Amesbury.

"Richard," she said to him, laying a hand upon his shoulder and looking searchingly into his frank, boyish face, "this is a very spiritual life that Mind Science exacts, and the world offers many alluring temptations. You know but little of them as yet. If you follow me you must cross swords with the world.

Are you spiritually-minded enough to take up my work and stand by it?"

Richard Kennedy thought he was. His eagerness and enthusiasm carried the day. Accordingly he accompanied Mrs. Glover to Lynn and they stopped at the home of Mrs. Oliver until they could make arrangements for offices and living-rooms. Mr. Kennedy soon found a desirable apartment in a three-story building at the corner of South Common and Shepard Streets, a little out of the business district and yet within easy walking distance of the main thoroughfares. This building remained for many years the humble witness of the earliest struggles toward a metaphysical college, the place where the rudiments of Mind Science were first imparted in class.

The house was then a gable-roofed frame structure, surrounded by lawns and shade trees. The open space across the way was a large park, Lynn Common, lined with stately trees. The open view, good air, and commodious interior of the house made it an attractive place. Miss Susie Magoun had but recently leased the place for a private school for young girls, and she used the first floor for this purpose and the third floor for her own sleeping apartments. She was a good business woman, but quite young and somewhat nervous about her extensive financial obligations. When young Kennedy called on her one evening early in June, she was looking over the building and beginning to feel apprehensive about her second floor and what sort of tenants she would be likely to have there. The young misses who were to come there for grammar studies and the accomplishments of music, painting, and dancing were the daughters of the wealthier families of Lynn. It was necessary that her tenants should be desirable persons.

Accordingly Miss Susie Magoun was pleased when Richard Kennedy explained that he was a physician who would practise mental healing and that he was in partnership with a lady who taught moral science and was writing a book on her system. She thought it prudent, however, to reserve her decision until she saw the lady, who might be a Spiritualist and the mental healing resolve itself into trances and séances. All this doubt was swept away in her meeting with Mrs. Glover, to whom she straightway put those doubts into questions. Mrs. Glover unreservedly told her the facts, stating that she did not hold to any such views or practises. Her quiet, well-bred manner reassured the little schoolmistress, who forthwith let her second floor of five rooms to Mrs. Glover and Mr. Kennedy for offices and sleeping rooms. She presently found her tenants so agreeable that she persuaded an old friend to come to live with her and open a dining-room for them all in the house. Thereafter the family took their meals together.

Of Mrs. Glover's religious views the schoolmistress remained unenlightened beyond these first explanations and the fact that she attended church regularly. Indeed they rented a pew together at the Unitarian church a few doors away on South Common Street. The Rev. Samuel B. Stewart was the clergyman at the time. Why Miss Magoun should have withheld herself from a knowledge of Mrs. Glover's teaching is a matter of relatively small importance, yet it has some relation to the events of the succeeding months. She was young, social, and of a lively disposition. To her Mrs. Glover seemed somber, serious, austere. On the contrary, the young doctor, as Kennedy was now called, entered more into her plans. He took part in some of her social affairs. They met upon the same plane. It was he who paid the rent; it was he who would perform an errand for her in the city; it was he who exchanged the gossip of the hour with her. Indeed Richard Kennedy was little more inclined than was their hostess to accept the austerities of Christian Science.

The rooms which Mrs. Glover had taken were fitted up very plainly, for she had well learned the severe lesson of plain living and high thinking. She formed her first class in Mind Science shortly after they were settled. Her first pupils came from the shoe shops. Patients came in response to the modest sign which was put up outside the door. Mrs. Glover advised and instructed her associate in giving treatment. Meanwhile she continued her writing in her own rooms. The treatment interested the more speculative of the patients and they sought Mrs. Glover to talk with her and learn of this new Science. Thus the first students were gathered around her.

It is not possible to draw a picture of those first classes in Mind Science that will appeal to a sense of the beautiful. The students who were drawn together were workers; their hands were stained with the leather and tools of the day's occupation; their narrow lives had been cramped mentally and physically. Their thoughts were often no more elevated than their bodies were beautiful. They could not come to Mrs. Glover in the daytime, for their days were full of toil. At night, then, these first classes met, and it was in the heat of July and August. In the barely furnished upper chamber a lamp was burning which added somewhat to the heat and threw weird shadows over the faces gathered round a plain deal table. Insects buzzed at the windows, and from the common over the way the hum of the careless and free, loosed from the shops into the park, invaded the quiet of the room. Yet that quiet was permeated by the voice of a teacher at whose words the hearts of those workmen burned within them. "The light which never was on land or sea" was made to shine there in that humble upper chamber.

I have said this picture was not beautiful, yet it appeals to the deepest and highest sense of beauty, that sense through which the heart receives impression. Mary Baker laid her finger upon the central motive of life those summer evenings on Lynn Common, and the response was a realization of divine consciousness which reached throughout the world, not immediately, but gradually, persistently as the years passed. And that moment of exquisite tenderness, evoked in the humble upper chamber, seems destined to swell into an eon, where time melts into eternity; for it was in such a moment that the understanding of divine consciousness was imparted. "God is no respecter of persons," St. Peter discovered. He had seen the despised Nazarene impart this consciousness to the fishermen on the shores of Galilee. The shoe-worker from his dingy bench, his foul-smelling glues and leathers, the whirr and clangor of machinery, saw the walls of his limitation melt, and experienced the inrush of being where the lilies of annunciation spring.

To these students Mary Baker was not somber, austere, or formidable. She was invariably interested and interesting, possessing a sympathy which went deep down to the heart of things. She rebuked sin and sickness alike and there was an invariableness about her queries and her eyes which searched their lives. Some could not endure such testing and fell away; others stood fast and experienced amazing results in their lives. There were healings of consumption, of tumor, of dropsy, and other extreme cases of disease made by these students, and such results were so amazing to the students that some of them were confounded by their very success.

One of her first students was George Tuttle, the brother of a woman whom Richard Kennedy, directed by Mrs. Glover, had healed of tuberculosis in an advanced stage. George Tuttle was a stalwart young seaman who had just returned from a cruise to Calcutta. It is said that he was asked what he thought he would get out of Mrs. Glover's class in metaphysics. He replied that he didn't think about it at all, that he joined because his sister asked him to. When he actually cured a girl of dropsy as a result of his first grappling with Mind Science, he was so surprised and frightened that he washed his hands of it forever.

It was not by overstating what Mrs. Glover had taught them, but by misstating her teaching, through misapprehension or through wilful distortion, that

some of these earlier students became ineffectual
and subsequently, through chagrin, were entirely
estranged from the cause which they had at first so
ardently espoused. One of the rebellious students
was Charles S. Stanley, brother-in-law of the seaman
Tuttle. He was a shoe-worker and a Baptist. The
healing of his wife had led him to seek admittance to
the class Mrs. Glover was conducting. After some
questioning she admitted him, only to find him
argumentative, controversial, determined to discuss
dogma from the standpoint of a Baptist rather than a
Christian. In the class of six men and women, most-
ly shoe-workers, were students of various religious
creeds; there were Methodists, Unitarians, Universalists, and others. The controversial Baptist affected
the harmony of a class where other members had risen
above creed into the consideration of pure Christianity. His arguments recurred from day to day until
Stanley broke away from Mrs. Glover's teaching without completing her course of instruction. Indeed she
dismissed him for lack of teachableness, though he
insisted he knew all there was of Mind Science. He
practised without her sanction and with indifferent
success for a time and later became a homeopathic
physician.

Wallace W. Wright, a bank accountant, came to
grief in his practise of Mind Science. He was the son
of a Universalist clergyman of Lynn, and a brother of
Carroll D. Wright, who afterward became United
States Commissioner of Labor. His relations with
Mrs. Glover were interesting because the rock upon
which he struck was not superstition, as in the case

of Tuttle, or dogma, as in the case of Stanley, but psychology. The following year in class he precipitated a discussion which finally led Mrs. Glover to draw the line sharply between mesmerism and Mind Science, to show once and for all what Quimbyism was, what mesmerism is, and to rid her students of the custom of laying hands upon their patients.

Wright had entered her class with some intellectual perturbation but left it with enthusiasm. When he had completed the course he began to practise in Lynn and later he carried his work elsewhere with success, which continued so long as he was an obedient follower. But he began to alter in his mental attitude and to question the spirituality of what he was doing. He began to believe he was practising mesmerism. Thereupon his power to cure began to wane, until he lost it utterly. He wrote of his peculiar experience to a Lynn paper which published his letter. He said:

The 9th of last June found me in Knoxville, Tennessee, as assistant to a former student. We met with good success in a majority of our cases but some of them utterly refused to yield to the treatment. Soon after settling in Knoxville I began to question the propriety of calling this treatment "Moral Science" instead of mesmerism. Away from the influence of argument which the teacher of this so-called science knows how to bring to bear upon students with such force as to outweigh any attempts they may make at the time to oppose it, I commenced to think more independently, and to argue with myself as to the truth of the positions we were called upon to take. The result of this course was to convince me that I had studied the science of mesmerism.[1]

1 Lynn *Transcript*, January 13, 1872.

Thus was summed up in a phrase the evil which had stalked like a shadow in the wake of Mary Baker's religious investigation of years. The spurious science of mesmerism, following upon the heels of Divine Science, was dogging and menacing it, threatening to worry and tear to pieces the good that was done. It explained in a word all her long struggle with Quimbyism; it explained the dereliction of those who had been earnest for a time and the interference of her students' relations which had exhibited peculiarly baleful effects on her teaching. The full significance of hypnotism and mental suggestion did not come to her at once, though with that student's explanation of his failure a vague outline of the workings of animal magnetism appeared.

The result of this letter was soon evident in Mrs. Glover's life and affairs. It was not that Wright had abandoned the cause. Wright was bound to go by his very nature; intellectual self-sufficiency and scholarly pride were certain to claim him. He had a brief controversy with five of Mrs. Glover's students through the medium of the Lynn papers in which he called upon Mrs. Glover to walk on the water, raise the dead, and live without air and nourishment. Then retiring from the controversy, he exultantly declared that Mrs. Glover and her science were dead and buried.

Mrs. Glover minded this no more than if, as she said to a woman student, he should declare he could dip the Atlantic dry. Such harassing of herself and work she had learned to expect and knew that it was not vital. As for Tuttle, the superstitious, who dropped Mind Science because it worked results which

frightened him, he was not worthy of more than a
passing smile; and Stanley, whose grievance was a
most confused demand for a personal God, anatomy,
and manuscripts, exhibiting a virulent case of acquisi-
tiveness together with the fear that he was being
duped, was annoying but negligible. It was no one of
these three students who seriously affected Mrs.
Glover's work.

The test of Mind Science came actually and vitally
in the mental attitude of Kennedy. She had accepted
him as a co-worker in hopeful anticipation. He was in
the relation to her of a chosen disciple. To him she
had expounded more deeply and intimately the physically inscrutable and intangible apprehensions of
truth than to any other student. When this vision of
the working of mesmerism came to her so clearly in
January of 1872, she would have defined it to him.
But when she came to do so, she beheld Kennedy remove himself from her tutelage. He was blind, deaf,
and immovable. He was incapable of perceiving what
she would have pointed out to him, and revealed himself as never having comprehended the nature of
Mind Science and to be actually working with the
processes of mesmerism and the hypnotic action of
mental suggestion.

That Kennedy actually could not or would not
understand that a line of cleavage separated Mind
Science from mesmerism Mary Baker now realized.
She realized it with sorrow, because of himself and
because he had practised in her name. She had taught
him Principle, but had permitted him to make use of
the method of laying his hands upon his patients.

So she had permitted Hiram Crafts, Mrs. Wentworth, and Miss Bagley. The results now shown were personal, magnetic, confusing. In Kennedy's case, it now appeared, he had surrounded himself with a bevy of patients who were not seeking Truth but Kennedy. Through such methods and practises the pure doctrine of divine healing was liable to become a byword.

Some years later a suit was brought in her name, though without her consent, against Tuttle and Stanley for the object of collecting unpaid tuition. At the trial all three of these students, Tuttle, Stanley, and Kennedy, exhibited unreservedly their utter lack of comprehension of the first postulate of Mind Science. But Kennedy in particular, out of his own mouth, proved himself incapable of grasping it. In his testimony, which was preserved in the notes of the presiding judge, he said:

I went to Lynn to practise with Mrs. Eddy. Our partnership was only in the practise, not in her teaching. I practised healing the sick by physical manipulation. The mode was operating upon the head giving vigorous rubbing. This was a part of her system that I had learned. The special thing she was to teach me was the science of healing by soul power. I have never been able to come to knowledge of that principle. She gave me a great deal of instruction of the so-called principle, but I have not been able to understand it. . . . I was there at the time Stanley was there. I made the greatest effort to practise upon her principle, and I have never had any proof that I had attained to it.[1]

This statement made in court many years later was the fact revealed in the spring of 1872. It was the

cause of the separation of Mary Baker and Richard
Kennedy. Stated as he expressed himself in court it
sounds very simple to a worldling. And as Mr. Kennedy related the cause of his separation from Mrs.
Glover to the author, it appears a reasonable and ordinary event. He said their separation was not due to
a quarrel but to a gradual divergence of views. He
continued practising physical manipulation throughout a long career. He claimed to have no knowledge
of Christian Science, having never read the text-book
and failing to comprehend the spiritual significance
of what he had been taught by word of mouth.

This divergence of view, that culminated in the
severance of their relations, was developing for several months. The schoolmistress, Miss Susie Magoun,
had married and gone to live elsewhere. A new tenant
was in the house. Mr. Kennedy's social life in Lynn
had prospered through Miss Magoun's introductions.
His youth, charm, and affable address had made him
happy in the acquisition of some influential acquaintances. And when the day came on which Mrs. Glover
and he mutually destroyed their contract he went his
way quite content. Looked at from a purely worldly
standpoint he had been honorable and had not
wronged his teacher.

But Richard Kennedy, as a student, had absorbed
a great deal of her time, and as a practitioner he had
absorbed a great deal more. This was relatively unimportant; the vital injustice was that he had misrepresented her Science to a large number of patients
and was to misrepresent her for many years. Perhaps
he had done this unconsciously, even as he was the un-

conscious agent in the precipitation of her struggle with the counterfeit of her Science. Animal magnetism had to be apprehended, defined, and stamped as the "human concept." Doubtless it was as well that the struggle should be precipitated through him as another.

The conflict of opinion between these two resulted in fixing the purpose of Mary Baker to write a textbook. She had thus far taught Mind Science by lectures and by writing out manuscripts for students. She distributed such manuscripts unsparingly. These were copies of "The Science of Man," which had been copyrighted, and also disquisitions on the Scriptures. She had encouraged her students to write their own conceptions of certain portions of the Scriptures, to stimulate them to deeper research. This practise she discontinued. She saw that they were not fitted to do such work any more than Kennedy was fitted to make his own deductions. Upon her it rested to do the work, and to guard her doctrine with the utmost zeal from contamination and adulteration.

When Mary Baker began to rid herself completely of the relics of the influence which Quimby had exerted over her mind, she ordered all her students to desist from stroking the head while treating patients mentally. She herself had never laid hands on a patient to heal him, but she had permitted her students to practise by this method. Seeing that the method was not in accordance with the Principle of divine Science, she wished all her students to discontinue its practise. Now it was that Richard Kennedy absolutely rebelled and left her; now it was that Miss Bag-

ley of Amesbury refused to be guided by her. Wallace
W. Wright had already come to grief by the use of
the method. Mary Baker denounced it once and forever. From the spring of 1872 manipulation, or physical contact of any sort, had no part in Christian
Science. And so at that early date she substantiated
the Science of Man and divine healing.

CHAPTER XIV

THE FIRST EDITION OF SCIENCE AND HEALTH

HER application to her purpose from 1872 to 1875 was more rigid, more exclusive, more laborious than it had ever been. Her experience in Stoughton and Amesbury had yielded the "Science of Man" manuscript and also certain commentaries on the Bible. Now the book which she purposed writing was to contain the complete statement of Christian Science. It was the book and nothing but the book which engrossed her. These three years saw her in public rarely, except for the walks she took by the sea, those visits to the Red Rocks where she used to linger long in meditation. Of these three years there is very little to record of her activity. But they flowered in the first edition of Science and Health. If any one reading this life thinks this great work was accomplished easily, or that when she said the book was given to her as a revelation, she meant that a personal Deity literally guided her hand across the pages, framing the words for her, let him consider the ceaseless mental toil and spiritual application stretching between the miraculous recovery in 1866 and the publication of her book in 1875.

When Mrs. Glover severed her relations with Richard Kennedy, he removed to another house. Though she retained the rooms at South Common Street, she stayed some weeks at Peabody. When in Lynn she saw a good deal of a girl named Susie Felt, a child of twelve. Mrs. Glover took her meals at the child's home and the little maid was so attached to her that she spent as much time with her as she was permitted. The child found this woman, whom her elders sometimes thought distant and somber, to be lovely, gracious, and sweet. Like Lucy Wentworth she was devoted to her. In later years she cherished a ring, a book, and a picture as mementos of those happy hours when she had the companionship of this great soul, relaxed from the toil of the day, when she would tell her the most wondrous things her ears had ever heard. Such hours were hers in the twilight alone with Mary Baker when the divine overflow suffused sweet dew that could not harm the tender violets of a child's unfolding thoughts.

But the fresh intuitions of a young girl's questions or the harmonious enfolding of the diapason of the sea, when she listened to its voice, crouched alone on the Red Rocks, were not all that reached her. The change and fluidity of life was in the waves, in the flight of the gulls, and in the drifting ships. Returning to the city from what was in those days a rough unwalled beach, she would see the lights of the Lynn factories betokening the passionate struggle of human endeavor. Had she stood erect on those rocks by the sea, erect in spirit while her body crouched for safety against its boulders, had she felt her human ego slip away from her in some supreme moment when divine sense lifted her to the consciousness of spiritual being above the waves of time? Even so, she must still return to the city, to the work in hand, and alas, to the shock of events.

Most of her students had remained loyal to her and to her teaching. Of these were George Barry, S. P. Bancroft, Dorcas Rawson, and Miranda Rice. She lived for a time with Dorcas Rawson, and she lived at several boarding-houses until she secured a home of her own. When she left South Common Street, a student, George Barry, took charge of her furnishing. She returned to live for a time with the Clarks where she had resided directly after Dr. Patterson's desertion. George Clark, who supplied the graphic picture of Mrs. Eddy in those days, was a witness for her in her divorce suit brought in Salem, Mass., in 1873. He said that Mrs. Eddy waited until nearly night for her case to be called and they thought it would not be disposed of that day. But when she was called to the witness-stand the judge asked her why her husband had deserted her. She replied, "Because he feared arrest." "Arrest for what?" asked the judge. "For adultery," Mrs. Eddy replied quietly. The judge made a brief examination of her witnesses and the decree was granted.

George Clark said that Mrs. Eddy worked very industriously at her writing while at his mother's house and he at one time carried a prospectus of her book to Adams and Company, Publishers, on Bromfield Street. Her manuscript was not accepted, but one of his own which he had taken with him at the same time was. Clark's book was a boy's story of sea-going life which the publisher felt would sell well. He rejected Mrs. Glover's book for the reason that he saw no possibilities in it for profit.

Mrs. Glover had accompanied Clark to Boston

and they returned together late in the afternoon. She made no comment on her failure, but cheerfully encouraged the young man over his own venture, saying his wholesome, breezy story would sell well and he might come to be a great author. He was much engrossed with those thoughts of greatness when they walked through the Lynn streets in the early evening nearing home. She suddenly caught him by the arm. "Stop, George," she cried. "Do you see that church? I shall have a church of my own some day."

She struck her hands together as she said this and then stood for a minute lost in thought. The young man was ashamed of his selfishness, and for a time really wished that it had been her book, and not his, which had been accepted. But her book was not ready, nor was it to be published in the ordinary way for the profit of a bookman.

In the spring of 1875 Mrs. Glover was living in a boarding-house at Number 9 Broad Street. She had moved in these three years several times. Her doctrine and her absorbed life had brought her in conflict with many minds and many persons. Discussion, controversy, and ridicule had pursued her, making application to her work doubly difficult. She had nearly completed her book, however, and what she needed was absolute peace and seclusion in order that she might put those important finishing touches to her work which would bring it together, unify it, complete it. Leaning at the window of her room, she gazed down Broad Street, thinking of the dining-room below stairs and its many discordant personalities, the latest gibes of her worldly critics, the latest smiles and glances and expressive shrugs. Was every step of the way of this book to be disputed by such hindrance and intrusion? Leaning there at the window, she breathed a silent prayer for a resting-place.

Lifting her eyes, she saw across the way a little frame house with a sign affixed stating that it was for sale. It was a two-story-and-a-half dwelling with a small lawn around it and a shade tree at the corner. It had little bow windows and tiny balconies. Contemplating it, she resolved to own it. It should be the first home of Christian Science; there she would complete her book.

This was not an impossible venture. Mrs. Glover had received for tuition some funds which she had guarded against the possibility of publishing her own book. Her life had been frugal, orderly, and well-planned. Nothing but the book had kept her from organizing large classes. With her own home, her work could now go forward with better progress. She unfolded her plan to her little group of students and certain of them undertook the business arrangements. The Essex County registry of deeds shows that on March 31, 1875, Francis E. Besse, in consideration of $5650, deeded to Mary Baker Glover the property of Number 8 Broad Street.

When Mrs. Glover moved into her new home her means were so limited she was obliged to lease the greater part of the house. She reserved for herself the front parlor on the first floor for a class-room and furnished it plainly with chairs and tables. On the attic floor she also reserved a small bedroom, lighted only by a skylight which was in the sloping roof and could

be lifted like a trap for ventilation.   In this garret
chamber she finished her manuscript of Science and
Health, practically the work of nine years.   Here she
read the proofs of the first edition and prepared the
revisions for the second and third editions.   The room
was austerely furnished with a carpet of matting, a
bed and dressing-bureau, a table and straight-backed
chair.   Its one article of luxury was an old-fashioned
hair-cloth rocker.   No one entered this room but Mary
Baker until the book was finished.   On the wall she
had hung the framed inscription, "Thou shalt have
no other gods before me."

The greater part of Mrs. Glover's new home was
given over to tenants.   Necessity compelled her to de-
pend on such sources for an income.   She was sometimes fortunate in her tenants, but occasionally otherwise.   Her own simple and well-regulated life, entirely
devoted to religion, was never the cause of comment,
except as criticism always attaches to a new religious
movement.   The history of Methodism, of Quakerism,
of Unitarianism abundantly shows this.   The daily attendance of her students, their devotion to their
teacher, and zeal for their faith created astonishment
in Lynn and so caused some gossip.   The purple-and-
gold sign, "Mary B. Glover's Christian Scientists'
Home," just above the second story windows, was the
cause of much speculation.   It became a common thing
for cripples and invalids to go to the house for treatment, and many remarkable cures which Mrs. Eddy
performed instantaneously are recorded.

During the summer the little place grew most attractive.   The affectionate zeal of her students, many

of whom she had healed from serious complaints or diseases and some of whom she had reclaimed from intemperate lives, made her gardens bloom, kept her grass-plot like velvet, and relieved the austerity of her parlor with decoration. Mrs. Glover's balconies were filled with calla lilies of which she was particularly fond, and when she stood among them tending and caring for them with the sunlight sifting through the leaves of the elm, making splashes of green and gold upon her cool white gown, she made a picture of composure and purity.

In the fall of 1874 Mrs. Glover had given the manuscript of her book into the hands of a printer. A fund was subscribed to by some of the students to insure its publication, and was repaid to them under circumstances to be related. There was some halt in its publication, even now that everything had apparently been done for its forthcoming. Mrs. Eddy has stated in her autobiography the peculiar circumstances of this delay. She had hesitated to include in the book pages on animal magnetism, and she believed it was the divine purpose that this section should be written. Months had passed since the printer received her copy. He had been paid nearly one thousand dollars but he still delayed, and all efforts to persuade him to finish the book were in vain.

Contrary to her inclinations, Mrs. Glover set to work at the painful task of delineating the counterfeit of Christian Science. She wrote out the pages that completed the chapter and with this started to Boston to confer with the stubborn printer. The printer had himself started to see her, however, to tell her that he had already prepared the copy which he had in hand and wished her to give him sufficient more to comprise a closing chapter. They met at the Lynn railway station and both were astonished. He had come to a standstill through motives and circumstances unknown to her, but had resumed his work, as his explanations showed, at the same time that she had begun writing the pages she had been reluctant to pen; and now that he was ready for more copy he met her on her way to him with the additional pages of the first edition of Science and Health.

The book came out in 1875 in an edition of one thousand. It was a stout cloth volume, containing the succinct, concise, and lucid statement of Christian Science. Though Mrs. Eddy many times revised this book, her revision was always for what she believed to be an improvement of expression. The essential statements are the same as in the original volume. Because of these subsequent labors, because she rearranged the order of the chapters, enlarged the explanation in certain passages, curtailed it in others, altered the sequence of sentences, struck out unnecessary illustration to make room for the irresistible enforcement of the declaration of her doctrine, certain critics have said that the original work has disappeared in the book that stands to-day, and a brilliant satirist, two decades later, went so far as to say that Science and Health was the product of another mind than Mary Baker Eddy's.

Because of the supreme audacity and obvious sophism of such an assertion, this first edition is indeed a "precious volume." It holds, like the Grail, that receptacle in which the wine was given to the disciples, the verities of Christian Science. Was ever a book so attacked as this? First, this famous critic declared it absurd; second, that its ideas were not original; third, that "every single detail of it was conceived and performed by another." Witness the three different standpoints of the satirical assailant. First, the book is absurd; the critic couldn't understand it; he would "rather saw wood" than to try, for he did not find the work of analyzing it easy. Second, maybe she who claimed to be author did write it, but the ideas are not original, for the great idea of this book, "the thing back of it," the critic came to see, is "wholly gracious and beautiful; the power, through loving mercifulness and compassion, to heal fleshly ills and pains and griefs."[1] And he did not see how such an idea could possibly interest the accredited author. He did not see! But mark the culminating effect of the book upon him and then come to his third standpoint.

Why should such an idea interest Mary Baker Eddy, he wondered, unless she was, as her followers believe, "patient, gentle, loving, compassionate, noble-hearted, unselfish, sinless — a profound thinker, an able writer, a divine personage, an inspired messenger."[2] And why should they not so believe? The critic went on to say: "She has delivered to them a religion which has revolutionized their lives, banished the glooms that shadowed them, and filled them and flooded them with sunshine and gladness and peace; a religion which has no hell; a religion whose heaven

1 Mark Twain, "Christian Science," p. 284.   2 *Ibid.*, p. 285.

is not put off to another time, with a break and a gulf between, but begins here and now, and melts into eternity."

"Let the reader turn to the chapter on prayer and compare that wise and sane and elevated and lucid and compact piece of work with the aforesaid preface [the preface to the third edition] and with Mrs. Eddy's poetry,"[1] said this critic.

Indeed, let him compare it with Mrs. Eddy's sublime hymn,

> "Shepherd, show me how to go
> O'er the hillside steep,
> How to gather, how to sow, —
> How to feed Thy sheep."[2]

But the critic's third standpoint was: "I think she has from the very beginning been claiming as her own another person's book, and wearing as her own property laurels rightfully belonging to that person — the *real* author of Science and Health."

Who is this real author who was first, absurd; second, unoriginal; third, an inspired messenger? The real author of every word of the first edition, and every word, phrase, paragraph, and chapter of the very last edition is the one who wrote the limping verses of girlhood, the so-called "Quimby" manuscripts with their confusion of ideas, the statement of the Science of Man, Genesis and Apocalypse, and finally Science and Health. She was the precocious and nervous girl educated for the most part at home; she was the suffering invalid whose pure religion was

---

1 Mark Twain, "Christian Science," p. 286.　　2 "Poems," p. 14.

tampered with by the mesmeric influence of a hypnotist; she was the poor and devoted Christian, healing
the sick and distributing her manuscripts to whoever would read them; she was the absorbed student
and devotee, maligned by unfaithful students.

Who else was it that the scoffing Horace Wentworth declared he did not dislike but thought ridicu-
lous when she sat in his mother's parlor and said she
had a mission from God to complete the work of Jesus
Christ on earth? Who else was it that wrote the
manuscript which Mrs. Catherine I. Clapp, the Wentworths' cousin Kate, was employed to copy and which
this amanuensis has herself said contained the first
form of the ideas subsequently given to the world in
Science and Health, certain paragraphs of which she
used to scoff at and make fun of to her intimates?
Who else was it who worked on the book Mother Webster called "Mrs. Glover's Bible" when rustics of
Amesbury gapingly watched to see her walk upon the
Merrimac River? Who else was it that prepared the
prospectus that George Clark carried to a Boston
printer and had rejected? Who else was it that wrote
the manuscripts the student Stanley contended for
and thought he was wronged because he could not
possess? Who else was it that prepared those special
pages on animal magnetism and carried it to the
printer? Who else was it wrote the "scientific statement of being"?

Neither internal evidence nor higher criticism will
divorce this work from its author, Mary Baker Eddy,
the spiritual seer of her age. The first edition of
Science and Health, which the critics of that day fell

upon with ironic glee, stands as the conceptual outline of the finished structure of to-day. It was written under the severest hardships and was revised painstakingly in the midst of the multitudinous duties of a leader. It has been plagiarized and pirated from, vilified and burlesqued, but it will stand.

CHAPTER XV

A CONFLICT OF PERSONALITIES

THE house at Broad Street was purchased by Mrs. Glover that it might become a refuge from the distraction of fleeting worldly interests encountered in boarding-houses; that it might be a haven of security insuring her against moving from place to place and the intrusion of elements of thought likely to create discord in her little flock of students; in fact it was bought for a home and designed for a center of peace. How shortly it became a storm center, a theater of intense mental disturbance, must be shown; for it was while living in this house that Mary Baker had enough of agitation, through the discord of her early students, the dereliction and menace of those she had cherished as friends and intimate aids, the failure of the second edition of her book, the harassment of a series of petty lawsuits, and ultimately, the revelation of a dastardly plot, as ingenious as it was diabolical, to make her wish to leave not only the house but Lynn, and to seek a new base of activity.

A great work of promulgation lay before the founder of Christian Science. The twilight of dawn was revealing its elements in her mind, but they did not yet stand forth distinctly. The signs of the times were as yet but vague. Looking backward, philosophic students of history declare that no such period of freedom and pure democracy was ever experienced

THE "LITTLE HOUSE IN BROAD STREET"
LYNN, MASSACHUSETTS

in the world's history as was enjoyed in the United
States from about 1870 to 1880. What was to come
after in the despotism of trusts and the menace of great
wealth in the hands of a few was not yet dreamed of.
America felt young, happy, and virtuous. A revived
industrialism, following the disastrous waste of the
Civil War, made the consciousness of the people
buoyant. No one thought of criticizing democracy.
Only that little group of transcendentalists in New
England, known as the Brook Farm colony, had ever
ventured to raise the warning cry of the danger of a
mechanical society plunging ahead to materialism.
And the seeds of that social experiment had not
yielded their harvest of socialism.

But Mary Baker had the nature of a true seer. No
more than the great Way-shower of Palestine would
she have dreamed of leading a few followers into a
community to make a stand against the trend of the
world. Like Jesus of Nazareth, she knew the truth
must be sown broadcast. But the seed must first be
grown in the little garden plot among her earliest
students. Renan has said that Jesus could not possibly have had a knowledge of Plato or of Buddha or
of Zoroaster; yet he was aware, by the subtle sympathy of humanity, of the elements of the great philosophic speculations of his age. It is possible that
even a scholar like Renan may be mistaken in his
judgment as to how the seer of God becomes possessed
of the needs of his time. Mary Baker was not a soci-
ologist, a political economist; she was not concerned
with those social passionists whose philosophy was
shaped at the universities, and who were insisting

upon the religion of democracy. But in her heart of hearts was the seed of truth which was to multiply for the health of her age.

Classes in Christian Science were formed almost immediately after Mrs. Glover was settled in her new home. In the month of April, 1875, in spite of laborious hours spent in her little study under the eaves, she conducted a class of five intensely interested students, among whom was Daniel Spofford of brief devotion. Though her charge for tuition had been advanced from $100 to $300, Mrs. Glover's income was still meager for the reason that she privately admitted the greater percentage of her students without fee, teaching them gratis that the work might the more rapidly spread. Payment was required from those who were able, and some made their payments in instalments. Time and experience proved that those who paid valued the treasure they secured, while those who did not very shortly allowed it to become valueless. The weekly wage of the toiler is of infinite sweetness to him, while a munificent allowance is an unpalatable surfeit of indulgence to an ingrate. For in human nature is the instinct to value only that which we acquire by some individual energy. The gospel is as free as the sunshine, but the yoke and the burden, the leaving of father and mother, are indications of the service required; and diffused sunshine is regained only by labor as in mining for coal and diamonds. Concerning the tuition fee for class instruction Mrs. Eddy has written in "Retrospection and Introspection":

When God impelled me to set a price on my instruction in Christian Science Mind-healing, I could think of no financial equivalent for an impartation of a knowledge of that divine power which heals; but I was led to name three hundred dollars as the price for each pupil in one course of lessons at my College, — a startling sum for tuition lasting barely three weeks. This amount greatly troubled me. I shrank from asking it, but was finally led, by a strange providence, to accept this fee. God has since shown me, in multitudinous ways, the wisdom of this decision; and I beg disinterested people to ask my loyal students if they consider three hundred dollars any real equivalent for my instruction during twelve half-days, or even in half as many lessons. Nevertheless, my list of indigent charity scholars is very large, and I have had as many as seventeen in one class.[1]

Among the students in the first class held in Broad Street was Daniel H. Spofford, a man who figured largely in the events of the next few years. He came from New Hampshire, and as a youth had lived in eastern Massachusetts, working as a chore boy on farms and later as a watchmaker's apprentice until he entered the army at the age of nineteen. He served through the Civil War and when he was mustered out returned to Lynn and entered the shoe-shops. He first met Mrs. Glover in South Common Street. He did not enter her class there, but had access to her manuscripts through his wife, a student, who copied them, or portions, for his private perusal. Leaving Lynn for a three years' sojourn in southern and western states, he carried these copies about with him, pondering and studying them. Being awakened to a faith which he

[1] "Retrospection and Introspection," p. 50.

but partially grasped, he wrote to Mrs. Eddy regarding class instruction. But writing Science and Health was her objective now, not teaching. He returned to Lynn and attempted to practise Mind-healing.

Mrs. Glover heard of this man and smiled at the excited students who reported the facts. She sent a messenger to him with a note which read: "Mr. Spofford, I tender you a cordial invitation to join my next class and receive my instruction in healing the sick without medicine, — without money and without price." So Mr. Spofford became one of those students who because of his qualities was given his instruction gratis.[1]

1 Mr. Spofford recently made an affidavit to the effect that he met Mary Baker Glover in 1870, that she taught metaphysical healing from manuscripts the authorship of which she attributed to P. P. Quimby. Yet Daniel Spofford, shortly after his graduation from her class in April, 1875, unequivocally ascribed to this same Mary Baker Glover the authorship and discovery of Christian Science and signed his name to a resolution drawn up for the purpose of creating an organization of Christian Scientists. Mr. Spofford himself produces the data which contradict his own affidavit. The author has recently visited Mr. Spofford at his present home in a country settlement between Haverhill and Amesbury. I went for the express purpose of asking him to explain the discrepancy between his statements of Mrs. Eddy's teachings, the one in his affidavit printed in *McClure's Magazine* for May, 1907, and the one in the resolution which he helped to draw up in 1875.

Mr. Spofford is to-day a man about sixty-five, slightly bent in carriage, with clear blue eyes and whitened hair. His manner is very gentle and courteous, and his personality sensitive and I should say, idealistic. Mr. Spofford made no immediate reply to my question as to the disparity. After some hesitation he turned from the question by saying, "I believe Mrs. Eddy is the sole author of Science and Health and I believe it is the greatest book in the world outside the Bible. . . . I don't wish it to be understood that I have said Christian Science was Quimbyism. I said that Mrs. Eddy taught some of the Quimby doctrine when I first knew her in 1870. Mrs. Eddy developed her own ideas and wrote her own book, Science and Health, and I was the publisher of the second edition and I know that book thoroughly. I don't confuse in my own mind the work of Quimby and of Mrs. Eddy. I don't see why the world should do so. It is clear to me that Mrs. Eddy at first taught some of the ideas of Quimby; that later she abandoned those ideas entirely for her own, incorporating her own system of religious interpretation in her book."

Mr. Spofford stated that he had been forced by persons who came into her circle to abandon Mrs. Eddy and the teaching of Christian Science. Mr. Spofford supplied the aforesaid magazine with a private letter of Mrs. Eddy

It was directly after Mr. Spofford's completion of class work that he called together a meeting of students for the purpose of arranging for renting a hall and raising a subscription toward sustaining Mrs. Glover as a teacher and instructor in weekly services. Mr. Spofford's emotional and moral nature had been deeply stirred by his class work, so truly affected that he was able to say thirty-five years after to hostile critics of Mrs. Eddy that no price could be put upon what Mrs. Glover gave her students, that the mere manuscripts which he had formerly studied were, compared to her expounding of them, as the printed page of a musical score compared to its interpretation by a master.

The meeting of students which Mr. Spofford called together appointed a committee to carry out the will of the meeting and the committee was composed of the three who supposedly stood nearest to the teacher at the time, each one of whom was to participate in one of the petty lawsuits which presently involved the community of students in strife. These students composed for the time a committee harmonious in devotion to the cause and enthusiastic for its furtherance. They drew up the following resolutions:

Whereas, in times not long past, the Science of healing, new to the age, and far in advance of all other modes, was

to himself, written before her marriage to Dr. Eddy. In that letter occurs this passage:

"No student or mortal has tried to have you leave me that I know of. Dr. Eddy has tried to have you stay. You are in a mistake; it is God and not man who has separated us and for the reason I begin to learn. Do not think of returning to me again. . . . God produces the separation and I submit to it. So must you. There is no cloud between us, but the way you set me up for a Dagon is wrong, and now I implore you to return forever from this error of personality and go alone to God as I have taught you."

— *Human Life*, July, 1907.

introduced into the city of Lynn by its discoverer, a certain lady, Mary Baker Glover,

And, whereas, many friends spread the good tidings throughout the place, and bore aloft the standard of life and truth which had declared freedom to many manacled with the bonds of disease or error,

And, whereas, by the wicked and wilful disobedience of an individual, who has no name in Love, Wisdom, or Truth, the light was obscured by clouds of misinterpretations and mists of mystery, so that God's work was hidden from the world and derided in the streets,

Now, therefore, we students and advocates of this moral science called the Science of Life, have arranged with the said Mary Baker Glover to preach to us or direct our meetings on the Sabbath of each week, and hereby covenant with one another, and by these presents do publish and proclaim that we have agreed and do each and all agree to pay weekly, for one year, beginning with the sixth day of June, A. D. 1875, to a treasurer chosen by at least seven students the amount set opposite our names, provided, nevertheless, the moneys paid by us shall be expended for no other purpose or purposes than the maintenance of said Mary Baker Glover as teacher or instructor, than the renting of a suitable hall and other necessary incidental expenses, and our signatures shall be a full and sufficient guarantee of our faithful performance of this contract.

(Signed)

ELIZABETH M. NEWHALL . . .	$1.50
DAN'L H. SPOFFORD	2.00
GEORGE H. ALLEN	2.00
DORCAS B. RAWSON	1.00
ASA T. N. MACDONALD	.50
GEORGE W. BARRY	2.00
S. P. BANCROFT	.50
MIRANDA R. RICE	.50

This was the first step toward a Christian Science church. It will be seen from the amounts pledged by the signers of the resolutions that they did not have very much to contribute and the whole sum amounted to only ten dollars per week, part of which was to go for the necessary expense of a hall. But the meetings begun in this humble way when Mrs. Eddy was in Lynn, continued only six weeks. Her student, S. P. Bancroft, conducted the singing, his wife playing the melodeon. The hall was one used by the Good Templars and was rather small. The audiences seldom exceeded twenty-five.

Besides teaching, preaching, and writing, Mrs. Glover performed many healings. She healed George Barry of consumption; she caused Mrs. Rice to have a painless delivery of a child. These two students were so devoted to her that they were continually about her house, rivaling each other in services to their teacher. Barry habitually addressed her as "Mother." He inscribed to her the lines of poetry he wrote, of which the following is an example of his state of mind, if not of any particular genius for verse making:

"O, mother mine, God grant I ne'er forget,
Whatever be my grief or what my joy,
The unmeasured, unextinguishable debt
I owe to thee, but find my sweet employ
Ever through thy remaining days to be
To thee as faithful as thou wast to me."

The young man spaded her garden, went to market for her, carried messages to and from the printer in Boston, and in many ways made himself an efficient aid. Mrs. Glover taught him patiently for he was not educated. She corrected his penmanship and orthography, and after he had shown some advancement allowed him to do some copying for her. When he presently fell in love, he brought the young woman of his choice to see Mrs. Glover. She received her not only as a friend but as a student, and gave her sanction to the marriage which presently followed. It was understood that Mrs. Glover felt as a mother toward Barry, and such a relationship with her was recognized by the other students.

Dorcas Rawson and Barry were the students who arranged for buying the Broad Street house. When the first edition of Science and Health was published they, with Elizabeth Newhall, undertook to dispose of the one thousand volumes, making short journeys into the adjoining towns and canvassing from door to door with them, talking Christian Science wherever they could get a hearing, and frequently winning disciples who later came to Mrs. Glover for instruction. George Barry considered himself chief agent for the disposal of the book. He had an interest in its sale, for he and Elizabeth Newhall had advanced the money for its publication.

As yet everything was moving harmoniously in the little home. But the advent of a new personality was to throw the band of workers into a confusion of jealousy. The new figure in the drama of the early church work was Asa Gilbert Eddy. Mr. Eddy was sent to Mrs. Glover by the Godfreys of Chelsea.

Mrs. Glover had instantly healed a finger on Mrs. Godfrey's right hand from which she was suffering greatly. Mrs. Godfrey had broken a needle in her hand and further aggravated the wound by poisoning it with colored thread. For weeks she had carried her hand in a sling, refusing to allow the finger to be amputated as a physician advised. Visiting her relatives, who were Mrs. Glover's tenants, she had been most astonishingly healed. Retiring as usual, she arose with the finger cured. Her astonishment and gratitude were such that she sent many patients to Mrs. Glover, brought her own child through a blinding snowstorm to be cured of membranous croup, sent a workman who had fallen from the roof of a house and lost the use of his arm,—and all these cases were cured by Mrs. Glover.

Now the Godfreys were acquainted with Mr. Eddy. They described him to the author as a grave, sweet-tempered man, to whom children were devoted. He was a bachelor living in East Boston, an agent for a sewing-machine concern. He was not in good health and the Godfreys, recounting to him their unusual experiences, impressed upon him the idea of visiting Mrs. Glover.

When Mr. Eddy visited Mary Baker she not only healed him, but advised him to enter a new class she was forming. She read his character and read it aright. He was a man of such gentleness and sweetness that persons knowing him but slightly were often led to think him devoid of the true force of manliness. He was, however, so those who knew him best declared, possessed of the staying quality of sterling integrity. Seldom assertive, preferring to master a situation by patiently studying it and moving conciliatingly and gently among the forces at play, he could,

when occasion demanded, act with a masterfulness
that commanded instant respect. Mrs. Glover placed
considerable responsibility in Mr. Eddy's hands very
early in their acquaintance and as soon as she did so
a conflict of personalities began which shook her circle from circumference to center.

Daniel Spofford had opened an office in Lynn directly after finishing his class instruction. His practise had been quite successful and had had two years
to grow into a flourishing condition. Mrs. Glover had
been revising her book during these two years and was
aware of the slow and unsatisfactory way in which the
first edition was being gradually disposed of. She sent
for Spofford and laid before him the needs of the
movement. The book must be sent forth to do the
work it was written to do. She needed greater business ability than George Barry possessed to accomplish this. A new edition must be watched through
the press, and ways and means of circulation thought
out. She asked Daniel Spofford to undertake this
work. Spofford assured her of his willingness but referred to his practise. What should he do with that?
Mrs. Glover told him to give it into the hands of
Mr. Eddy.

An extraordinary move in any organization causes
instant excitement in all its parts unless the whole is
so unified that it will act in perfect harmony. George
Barry, who had professed such profound love and intentions of devotion toward his teacher, now instantly
rebelled when acquainted with her desire to relieve
him of the direction of her publication. He who had
been all docility and gentleness while he felt himself

the most important personage in the field, now went into a paroxysm of rage and would not come near the Broad Street house. Spofford was in little better mood. He affected to accept the situation cheerfully, but constantly hinted that he was being driven out, that a cloud had come between him and his teacher, that certain students were trying to compel him to leave her. But, he asserted, nothing should compel him to do so. They might try to their utmost, but he would stand faithful to his post.

The talk waged back and forth among the students. Barry was angry, Spofford was offended, the women students who had made desultory efforts to sell the book felt themselves criticized in the new arrangement. Some of the patients did not like Mr. Eddy as well as they had Mr. Spofford; some liked him better. And so the jealousies waged for many months. In the midst of the struggle of personalities Mrs. Glover quietly married Asa Gilbert Eddy, and the war temporarily ceased. The marriage took place on New Year's Day, 1877. The Unitarian clergyman, the Rev. Samuel B. Stewart, whose services Mrs. Glover had formerly attended with Richard Kennedy and Miss Susie Magoun, performed the ceremony.

Sobered by this unlooked-for event, the students for a time were quieted. Barry, who all the time had expected to be solicited to return, became ominously silent. Mr. Spofford, who received back his practise when Mrs. Eddy was married, attended to his extra duties with some address but with mingled feelings. He had entertained other ideas which this event had dashed to the ground, and for a time he knew of nothing better to do than to attend to his work without complaint. Other students showed their pleasure in what they regarded as a romantic and humanizing incident by giving Mr. and Mrs. Eddy a reception about three weeks after the wedding, bringing various bridal gifts to her house and spreading a supper there. They made speeches indicative of their good feeling and generally betrayed a desire to make a friendly circle around their teacher and the man she had chosen to honor.

Mrs. Eddy replied to their good-will offering with an address which brought them out of the somewhat hectic sentimentalism which threatened to inundate her. She spoke of her marriage as a spiritual union and recalled them to their fidelity to Truth and the noble purposes they had cherished. She then took the Bible and read from it, expounding certain passages until she brought the company into its usual sense of the spiritual work she wished her students to perform. They beheld their teacher and leader, the same Mary Baker, with hands as ever outstretched to them with the spiritual gift to be transferred through them to the whole human race and to the age; with growing solemnity they saw through her eyes the far horizon and the vision of the work they had to do. Mr. Eddy at this moment became simply one of them again, a student who stood a little closer, but still a student. He, like them, must carry out her directions that the spreading of Christian Science should not languish, but to him was the special duty given of guarding her against the onslaughts of the envious and ambitious who pressed too close with their human desires.

If for a time Mrs. Eddy's influence lulled the storm, it suddenly broke forth again and now followed storm upon storm. George Barry was the first to move. He brought suit against her in the spring of 1877 to recover $2700 which he said was due him for services extending over five years. His bill of particulars stated his services very minutely. He mentions copying manuscripts, searching for a printer, moving goods from the tenement on South Common Street, disposing of some articles at auction and storing others, clearing up rooms, paying rent for same, withdrawing moneys from the Boston Savings Bank, aiding in buying the house at 8 Broad Street, aiding in selecting carpets and furniture, helping to move and putting down carpets, working in the garden. He made items of fifty cents for fetching up a pail of coal from the cellar, items for walking out with her in the evening in search of a dwelling. There was nothing that he did not mention in his bill of particulars, even to a pair of boots which he bought for himself with her money. As for the copying, he had done it so badly that his work was useless to her. Mrs. Eddy had taught him, healed him, paid many of his debts, guided him in his marriage, and directed his practise as she did that of many of her students.

When the suit was heard in court Mrs. Eddy went on the stand and explained her relations with the young man, how she had practically adopted him, and what her intentions toward him had been. Her attorney, Charles P. Thompson, argued: "It is important to look at the relations of the parties and at what their understanding was at the time of rendering and receiving services. If the understanding was that of an exchange of services without any compensation, it cannot be revoked." Barry recovered $350 instead of $2700 and afterwards repented and made a tentative effort to return to her good-will. But whether or no that was a serious intention will be presently shown.

Mrs. Eddy's next troubles were with Spofford. She was preparing the manuscript for her second edition. In the midst of this labor Mr. Spofford began to evince a renewal of his dissatisfied frame of mind. He balked at all of her advice and continually declared that the book could not be financed. While striving to make the way plain for him, her business agent, and continuing her literary labors, her doors were thronged with perplexed students who wished her help in healing patients. The students pressed upon her so with their varying needs that she was finally driven to leave her home for a time with her husband and keep her whereabouts unknown, for they interrupted her work and the book lay waiting.

She gave Mr. Spofford a Boston address and from there wrote him several letters urging him to speak to certain of the students and patients for her. Among them were two young women of Ipswich, the wife of the mayor of Newburyport, and a manufacturer of Boston, all of whom had pressed her for attention and healing. She wished them to be instructed in the necessity of doing their own mental work and thus to cease interfering with the more important work which lay upon her. Concerning these matters she wrote him: "If the students still continue to think of me and to call on me I shall at last defend myself and this will be to cut them off from me utterly in a spiritual sense by a bridge they cannot pass over. . . . I will let you hear from me as soon as I can return to prosecute my work on the Book. . . . I am going far away and shall remain until you will do your part and give me some better prospect." [1]

And again she wrote him: "If you conclude not to carry the work forward on the terms named, it will have to go out of edition as I can do no more for it, and I believe this hour is to try my students who think they have the cause at heart and see if it be so. . . . The conditions I have named to you I think are just. . . . Now, dear student, you can work as your teacher has done before you, unselfishly, as you wish to, and gain the reward of such labor. Meantime, you can be fitting yourself for a higher plane of action and its reward." [2]

Mr. Spofford's reply to this earnest solicitation that he should apply himself to pushing the book came in July of that year. He closed out the stock of Science and Health which he received from George Barry and Elizabeth Newhall, and paid over the money from the sale of these books, something over $600, to these two students. They had supplied the capital for the first edition in consideration of gratitude to their teacher. They now received all the profits that had accrued, as Mrs. Eddy had no agreement with them for a royalty. There was a loss all around by this premature act. Mr. Spofford claimed $500 against the edition for personal expenses, which he could not by such hasty and ill-advised methods realize. The students themselves lost by the transaction. The publication of the book was temporarily interrupted and the author left without means to finance the second edition which was still in press. There were five hundred copies of the Ark, or second edition printed in two volumes. All of Volume I had subsequently to be destroyed owing to controversy. The edition was well-nigh a failure.

Now it is not necessary to inquire rigidly into the mental state of Daniel Spofford at that time to understand what had happened. He complained later that Mrs. Eddy did not understand the situation; he said that she was a woman and surrounded by many advisers, and would suggest that her life was in small like a queen's court where suspicion and jealousies are rife and that one could not act for her firmly and steadfastly and bring about satisfactory results. Doubtless he had some business trials, doubtless there were many difficulties in financing a book of this character, and doubtless there was unwarrantable interference from the various students who wanted the text-book, wanted to see it circulated speedily and widely. But a man of ability should have silenced the intruders, should have worked patiently and purposefully, and should not have wound up so important a business as had been intrusted to him by rash precipitation.

Mrs. Eddy was justly indignant at his gross mismanagement of her affairs and his extraordinary method of accounting. He left her stranded without the means to forward a second edition. This might have been remedied had he withdrawn. But he did not withdraw. He called on her, not to explain his trials and the disadvantages under which he labored, but to tell her that he intended to remove from her all means for carrying on her work, "for," said he, "you have proven yourself incapable as a leader, and I propose to carry on this work myself and alone."

Thus Spofford did not go quietly and leave Mrs. Eddy to gather up the strands that were broken. He began to practise and to teach in opposition to her and to call upon her students with the object of deflecting them from her to himself as he had threatened he would do.

How did Mrs. Eddy meet these trials? It has been stated that she authorized and inspired at her house on Broad Street meetings of devoted students who concentrated their thoughts upon individuals, — presumably Kennedy, Spofford, and Barry, — that a formula of mental suggestion was used against them.

Perhaps the charge that Mrs. Eddy so instructed her students to gather in a body and work mentally to do injury to others may be considered as an example illustrating her statement, "As of old, evil still charges the spiritual idea with error's own nature and methods."[1] Christian Scientists who were in the movement in its first decade have stated that there is absolutely nothing hidden or occult in the teaching of Christian Science and that they have never known of a concerted effort of thought being made to bring about any result against an individual. There is, in fact, no *secret doctrine*. But they have said that Mrs. Eddy steadfastly from the beginning of her teaching

[1] Science and Health, p. 564.

to the close instructed her students never to seek to
injure another mentally.

Mrs. Eddy says in "Miscellaneous Writings," [1] "I
have no skill in occultism; and I could not if I would,
and would not if I could, harm any one through the
mental method of Mind-healing, or in any manner."
Indeed, Mrs. Eddy would have had to go back on
everything she had ever taught or written of the working of divine Love in the consciousness of the individual had she suggested that destructive thought be
used against those who were opposing her work. The
idea is utterly inharmonious with the fundamental
tenets of her faith.

However, it is not possible to state whether that
early group of pioneer students did or did not meet to
concentrate their thoughts against individuals with
the idea of destroying their harmful influence. Certainly they did not have Mrs. Eddy's inspiration for
such an endeavor, and in doing so must have departed
from her teachings. But Mrs. Eddy had propounded
not only the doctrine of divine Mind governing all
reality, she had indicated the rival force of illusion in
the theory of mesmerism or animal magnetism and in
the second edition of her book, the so-called Volume
II, she had further indicated the working of this hypnotic force. She had come to see that manipulation
is not the only method of hypnotism, but that the
mind acts independently of matter for evil as well as
for good. Now the little handful of struggling neo-
phytes had not learned how to meet this evil and were
doubtless more or less frightened at the notion of it.

1 "Miscellaneous Writings," p. 351.

Some of the students saw in the dereliction of Daniel Spofford the operation of malicious animal magnetism,[1] and became much alarmed. Miss Lucretia Brown of Ipswich particularly declared that Mr. Spofford was causing her to suffer a relapse into ill health by calling upon her and suggesting that she was not in health. Miss Dorcas Rawson, who was one of the earliest students, was Miss Brown's teacher and healer. She reported Miss Brown's condition to Mrs. Eddy and the fact that Daniel Spofford had called upon Miss Brown. Miss Rawson suggested that he be restrained from malicious interference with her work. Miss Brown also urged it, as she declared she suffered much from his interference.

[1] Malicious Animal Magnetism is a term used in Christian Science, and perhaps it may be proper to define its significance, since it has been largely misapprehended in the public press of late. The word magnetism was first applied to a peculiar attraction of iron ore, so named because it was discovered in the city of Magnesia. Later the word animal was joined to it to define electrical experiments with an animal. This term, animal magnetism, eventually came to include the peculiar influence one person was able to exert over another by physical contact. In this sense animal magnetism is similar, if not identical, with the term mesmerism, referring directly to the experiments of Mesmer. The more modern term, hypnotism, has the peculiar significance of the power of mind over mind without the necessity of actual physical contact. . . . Through Mrs. Eddy's teaching, the term animal magnetism has become broad enough to include any and all action of the *human mind*, applying it to that peculiar power, influence, or force which is possessed by the creature in contradistinction to the Creator. Since Christian Science has introduced the proposition that God is the only real Mind, the carnal mind in all its varied manifestations is naturally, in the interest of self-preservation, arrayed against it. Therefore, every wilful phase of this human opposition which is created by the introduction of Science is malicious. Hence the use of the term malicious animal magnetism. It is magnetism because it refers to a supposed power independent of God; malicious, in keeping with the Scriptural declaration, "The carnal mind is enmity against God." Mrs. Eddy refers to it as "the human antipode of divine Science" [Science and Health, p. 484]. It is a term which is broad enough to include all that is opposed to God. It includes every phase of evil, every phase of human antagonism to truth. — From an interview with Alfred Farlow in *Human Life*, August, 1907.

Mrs. Eddy had nothing to do with the suit at law which was presently brought by Miss Brown. She has always shown herself not only just, but admirably sane, in all her worldly transactions. So, instead of advising this suit, she advised against it, but was not insistent to the point of rupture. She was engaged with her own affairs and would not permit the frightened students to encroach too heavily upon her time. The suit brought by themselves and in their own folly bore all the marks of haste and fear. The bill of complaint drawn up by Miss Brown reads:

Humbly complaining, the plaintiff, Lucretia L. S. Brown of Ipswich, in said County of Essex, showeth unto your Honors, that Daniel H. Spofford, of Newburyport, in said County of Essex, the defendant in the above entitled action, is a mesmerist and practises the art of mesmerism and by his said art and the power of his mind influences and controls the minds and bodies of other persons and uses his said power and art for the purpose of injuring the persons and property and social relations of others and does by said means so injure them.

And the plaintiff further showeth that the said Daniel H. Spofford has at divers times and places since the year 1875 wrongfully and maliciously and with intent to injure the plaintiff, caused the plaintiff by means of his said power and art great suffering of body and mind and severe spinal pains and neuralgia and a temporary suspension of mind and still continues to cause the plaintiff the same. And the plaintiff has reason to fear and does fear that he will continue in the future to cause the same. And the plaintiff says that said injuries are great and of an irreparable nature and that she is wholly unable to escape from the control and influence he so exercises upon her and from the aforesaid effects of said control and influence.

The students thronged to Mrs. Eddy's house before the suit was tried, beseeching her to join with
them, to at least attend the hearing at the Supreme
Judicial Court in Salem. She at last yielded to the extent of accompanying them on that morning in May,
1878. A new student, Edward J. Arens, argued the
case. Mrs. Eddy was amazed at his arguments, so contrary were they in their purport to her teachings, especially the argument that Miss Brown had no power to
withstand the injuries she complained of. Nor was
Mrs. Eddy at all surprised at the decision of the judge
that it was not in the power of the court to control Mr.
Spofford's mind. "Most certainly it was not in the
power of the court," Mrs. Eddy declared to her students. She rebuked them severely, pointing out that
the suit was but an exhibition of their own wilfulness
in attempting to protect mind and health otherwise
than as she had taught them. She returned to her
home to insist for the future more strenuously, more
decidedly, on her doctrine of meeting evil by resting
in the confidence of divine Love.

The student Arens, who argued what was called at
the time the "Ipswich Witchcraft case," had been received for instruction by Mr. Eddy in the fall of 1878.
He was a cabinetmaker of Lynn, an energetic, ambitious young man, and when he came into Christian
Science he found Mrs. Eddy's affairs in that languish-
ing and entangled state to which Daniel Spofford had
brought them. He wished to show his personal force,
to push the sale of the book, and to realize for the
cause of the book and the young society funds that
would put life into its circulation and thus permit of a

broader scope of activity. His efforts were more vigorous than well-advised, and two years later Mrs.
Eddy wrote thus of his activity in her affairs:

In the interests of truth we ought to say that never a
lawsuit has entered into our history voluntarily. We have
suffered great losses and the direst injustice rather than go
to law, for we always considered a lawsuit, of two evils, the
greatest. About two years ago the persuasions of a student
awakened our convictions that we might be doing wrong in
permitting students to break their obligations with us.
. . . The student who argued this point to us so convincingly offered to take the notes and collect them, without any participation of ours; we trusted him with the
whole affair, doing only what he told us, for we were
utterly ignorant of legal proceedings. It was alleged indirectly in the "Newburyport Herald" that we caused a bill
to be filed in the Supreme Court to restrain a student of
ours from practising mesmerism. That statement was
utterly false. It was a student who did that, contrary to our
advice and judgment, and we have the affidavit of the reluctant plaintiff certifying to this fact.[1]

The case directly referred to is "the Ipswich
affair," and the plaintiff, Miss Lucretia Brown.
Other cases which Arens brought in Mrs. Eddy's name
were the suits against Stanley and Tuttle, referred to
in a previous chapter, and a suit against Richard Kennedy brought in the municipal court of Suffolk
county, Massachusetts, in February, 1878, to collect
a promissory note made in 1870. The suit against
Stanley and Tuttle resulted unfavorably because the
defendants claimed that Mrs. Eddy had first instructed them to manipulate the head, and later

[1] Science and Health, third edition.

instructed them to treat differently, without touching the patient, and they claimed to have been confused and to have received no benefits. In the case of Kennedy, judgment was awarded in Mrs. Eddy's favor. The note for which suit was brought read:

In consideration of two years' instruction in healing the sick, I hereby agree to pay Mary Baker Glover one thousand dollars in quarterly instalments of fifty dollars, commencing from this date, February, 1870.

(Signed)   RICHARD KENNEDY

In April Arens arranged a suit against Daniel Spofford to collect from him a royalty on his practise for unpaid tuition fees. This suit was dismissed for insufficient service. Barry's suit against Mrs. Eddy was still dragging on and was not settled until October of the following year. Keeping in mind these suits at law, with their varying results for which the activity of Arens was responsible, the reader has a fairly clear idea of the maze of Mrs. Eddy's affairs in the spring and summer of 1878. Arens had arrayed against her in a definite way the minds of Kennedy and Spofford, and Barry who knew them both well was in opposition on his own account.

It was at this time that an apostate student wrote the following letter to Mrs. Eddy which, considering events about to befall, may illuminate what was always regarded as an inscrutable conspiracy. The letter shows the peculiar nature of this student and also, indirectly, the nature of others. It reads:

It is evident to me that you desire Dr. Kennedy to leave the city, and I think also it would be for your interest to accomplish this end. The relations between he and I

are probably of a different nature from what you suppose,
as I owe him a debt on the past, which, if driving him from
Lynn will accomplish, it can and shall be done. He thinks
I am your greatest enemy, and favor, if either, his side.
Let him continue to think so; it will do me no harm. For
my part I rather a person would come out boldly and fearlessly as you and I did facing each other, than to sneak like
a snake in the grass, spitting his poison venom into them he
would slay. I have said I owe Dr. Kennedy on an old score,
and the interview I had with him last night has increased
that debt, so that I am now determined, if it be your object
also, as two heads are better than one, to drive him from
Lynn. Why should we be enemies, especially if we have
one great object in common? Perhaps we can be united on
this, and the result may be that this city will finally be rid
of one of the greatest humbugs that ever disgraced her fair
face. All this can be accomplished, but as I said before, it
is necessary to be very cautious, and not let the fact of our
communicating together be known, as a friend in the
enemy's camp is an advantage not to be overlooked.

This thoroughly detestable letter is so artless in
its wickedness as to need no comment. It was without
the shadow of a doubt an effort to inveigle Mrs. Eddy
into a dishonorable correspondence with its wretched
author. Whether or not it was a part of the forthcoming inscrutable conspiracy can only be conjectured. Mrs. Eddy's reply to her erstwhile student
was very brief: "We will help you always to do right;
but with regard to your proposition to send Dr. Kennedy out of Lynn we recommend that you leave this to
God; his sins will find him out."

It was during this period, a period which may be
said to extend from 1872 up to and embracing this hour
of lawsuits and strife, when many students became

apostate owing to the influence of the very earliest students who had become recalcitrant over the teacher's denunciation of the laying on of hands, that Mrs. Eddy reexamined the nature of mental malpractise, mesmerism, and animal magnetism. In the third edition of Science and Health, Volume II, Chapter VI, is an analysis of the workings of mortal mind wherein she says:

We have never departed from one cardinal point of metaphysics, namely: never to encroach on the rights of mind; never to think to trespass in metaphysics more than in physics; never to enter another's thoughts more unceremoniously than his dwelling. In proportion to your advancement in metaphysics it becomes impossible for you to produce disease or to injure another with your mind, and you become a law to yourself never to infringe on the privacy of thought, and to read mind only when it appeals to you for help. We should speak audibly all that we would say to one inaudibly, with the single exception of treating disease. These fundamental rules admit of no exception, unless it be in rare cases, and from a motive to benefit the individual.[1]

In this same chapter Mrs. Eddy says:

Because this error [mental malpractice] was so remote from the border lands of metaphysical science we never fully fathomed its workings until the summer of 1880, and to our Father we owe it that we have found the facts of immortal Mind more than equal to meet the fables of mortal mind, that, like the silly moth, singeing its wings in the light, falls to dust. We rejoice that our experience from the malicious arrows aimed at us through the unseen and subtle agency aforesaid has helped others, enabling them to know how to meet this hidden element without having to learn their way.[2]

[1] Science and Health, third edition, Vol. II, p. 18.   [2] *Ibid.*, p. 34.

CHAPTER XVI

A STRANGE CONSPIRACY

DURING the summer which followed the lawsuits arranged and prosecuted by the student Arens, affairs at Number 8 Broad Street progressed more quietly. Both Mr. and Mrs. Eddy were teaching metaphysics. Mrs. Eddy's classes were held at her Lynn home, but Mr. Eddy taught in East Cambridge and in Boston, as well as in Lynn. The disaffected student Spofford was seldom seen in Lynn. He had opened an office in Boston and still retained one in Newburyport.

In October, 1878, the Boston *Herald* printed an article stating that Daniel Spofford had disappeared and his friends were greatly alarmed concerning him. A description of him was given and other papers were asked to copy it. A few days later the same paper stated that his body had been found and was lying at the morgue. On the twenty-ninth of October the *Herald* was able for the first time to print a fact in this case, relating that Asa Gilbert Eddy and Edward J. Arens were under arrest for conspiring to murder Daniel Spofford.

After the lapse of many years it is as difficult to form an opinion concerning this amazing charge as it was at the time of its occurrence. It is difficult because it requires one to follow the tangled threads of a conspiracy, a conspiracy so well wrought as at first to deceive the grand jury of the Commonwealth of Massachusetts, and, as was afterward found, too intricate to yield its prime mover even under legal scrutiny, and the indictment against Mr. Eddy and Mr. Arens was quashed by the district attorney, Oliver Stevens. It may be well to state at once that Mr. Spofford had not had a hair of his head harmed, and lived years, still rehearsing the strange features of this strange story which, without explanation, would throw discredit on the blameless life of Mr. Eddy, and by implication on Mrs. Eddy.

When the two innocent men were arrested they were held in three thousand dollars' bail for examination in the municipal court on November 7 for the crime of conspiring to kill Daniel Spofford. The preliminary hearing was held before Judge May. Counsel for the government submitted no argument after the hearing of evidence, but called the attention of the Court to a chain of circumstances established which he believed was strong enough to hold the prisoners. Judge May, after deliberation, declared it his opinion that the case was a very anomalous one, but that he would hold the defendants to appear before the Superior Court at the December hearing, and he again fixed the amount of bail, which would release them from the necessity of going to prison, at three thousand dollars each.

The case was called before the Superior Court in December, 1878, and an indictment was found on two counts. The first read: "That Edward J. Arens and Asa G. Eddy of Boston aforesaid, on the 28th day of July, in the year of our Lord one thousand eight hundred and seventy-eight, in Boston aforesaid, with force

and arms, being persons of evil minds and disposi-
tions, did then and there unlawfully conspire, combine, and agree together feloniously, wilfully, and of
their malice aforethought, to procure, hire, incite and
solicit one James L. Sargent, for a certain sum of
money, to wit, the sum of five hundred dollars, to
be paid to said Sargent by them, said Arens and
Eddy, feloniously, wilfully, and of his said Sargent's
malice aforethought, in some way and manner by
some means, instruments and weapons, to said
jurors unknown, one Daniel H. Spofford to kill and
murder against the law, peace and dignity of said
Commonwealth."

The second count charged the prisoners with
hiring Sargent "with force and arms in and upon
one Daniel H. Spofford to beat, bruise, wound,
and evil treat against the law, peace, dignity of said
Commonwealth."

The Superior Court record reads: "This indictment was found and returned into Court by the grand
jurors at the last December term when the said Arens
and Eddy were severally set at the bar, and having
the said indictment read to them, they severally said
thereof that they were not guilty. This indictment was
thence continued to the present January term, and
now the District Attorney, Oliver Stevens, Esquire,
says he will prosecute this indictment no further, on
payments of costs, which are thereupon paid. And
the said Arens and Eddy are thereupon discharged,
January 31, 1879."

This monstrous charge was thus dismissed without a trial. The men accused were made to appear too

insignificant in the world's affairs to warrant a full and clear exoneration. They were let go like guilty culprits who just escaped the sting of the law's lash. Their case is not singular. It is to be deplored that the law does not always make the vindication of a man, entangled in its meshes through the unwarranted suspicions of his enemies or neighbors, so clear and emphatic that he may stand innocent in reputation, unblemished, and without reproach, even as he did before the law laid hands upon him.

What would have happened had the process of law taken its full course? Doubtless the guilty conspirator would have been made to appear. To fasten a crime upon an innocent man is in itself a hideous crime, and by the very *nol. pros.* of this indictment a conspiracy was shown to exist which, had the district attorney of that day felt his whole duty, he would have disentangled by thoroughly sifting the evidence. He had a crime to fit to an individual. He should have gathered all the known details, examined every circumstance, however slight. He should not have lost a shred or tatter. For his work was to piece together a fabric of evidence to match a fabric of guilt. The garment would have fit but one man and that man the criminal.

In speaking of a district attorney's obligations to the people, James W. Osborne, a distinguished attorney of New York City, and a former assistant in the district attorney's office, says:

It is as much his duty to take care of the rights of one of the people as the rights of all. . . . Resting always on the evidence, his feet are fixed in the way they should go.

. . . A human being moves in certain well-defined circles, which, joined together, make up a complete history of the man's life. When you have a section of the arc of any man's history, you are pretty well able to follow it to its completion. It is like the key to a puzzle around which the broken pieces naturally group themselves. There is the social life, the religious life, the business life, — will these sections of the arc fit together? Can you complete the ring? When you have them all they fall into place naturally; all phases join by an imperceptible cleavage; the circle is completed by those who, with hands joined, encompass the life. You see the complex whole. Here is the individual. You know the mainspring of his thoughts, his desires, his habits, his acts. Taken together you have his character; you have the man.

I am not obliged to give you the motive for a crime to prove it to have been perpetrated. . . . The motives of the human heart are often beyond comprehension. But it is the most natural thing in the world to ask, "Who could have desired to do this deed?" Therefore a motive is a part of the evidence, and when you can prove a motive, it becomes of the greatest importance. It excludes other possible agents, all things being equal, and becomes like a finger pointing unswervingly and declaring to the shrinking and guilty person, "Thou art the man!"

As the district attorney of that day did not see fit to so handle his evidence, no unswerving finger ever pointed out the guilty person. It is therefore not possible to make any direct accusation at this late day either by surmise or inference, but that the reader may form his own opinion of the nature of the entanglement it is only necessary to tell the main facts of the story.

Mr. Spofford did disappear from Boston in October, 1878, and was absent from his office two weeks.

But he disappeared of his own free will and passed the
fortnight in the home of the man who claimed to have
been hired to kill him. Mr. Spofford told his story in
court. He said that a man, introducing himself as
James Sargent and describing himself as a saloon-
keeper, had come to him in the early part of the
month at his office, 297 Tremont Street, Boston. This
man first asked him if he knew two men named Miller
and Libbey. Being answered in the negative, he said,
"Well, they know you and they want to get you put
out of the way."

Then he related that these two men had employed
him to make away with Spofford. The plan was to get
Spofford to take a drive on a lonely road, and in some
remote spot to beat him over the head and kill him,
then to entangle his body in the reins and cause the
horse to run away. Having unfolded this marvelous
plot, Sargent acknowledged that he was to get $500
for his services. He told him that he had already received seventy-five dollars, and meant to try to get the
rest. But Sargent declared he had no desire to risk
his own life in such a business, although apparently
suffering no qualms from any moral scruple. He further stated that he had already been to a state detective,
Hollis C. Pinkham, and asked him to watch the case.

Mr. Spofford said that he himself immediately
went to this state detective, and found that Pinkham
did know of the matter, but apparently was so little
concerned that he had not even thought it necessary
to warn Spofford. In fact, the state detective expressed himself of the opinion that it was a trumped-
up story told by Sargent to ingratiate himself with

the police department, for this man, the detective told Spofford, was an ex-convict with a bad criminal record.

According to his own story, Mr. Spofford did nothing further until Sargent came again to call upon him, and when he again beheld the square-set, brutal-featured man in his office he was greatly alarmed. Sargent had come to tell him that the men, Miller and Libbey, were pressing him to complete his work; that he had put them off, saying their man was already dead; but they had sent an agent to his office and now accused Sargent of playing false with them.

Spofford conferred again with the state detective and on that official's advice disappeared. He chose a strange place to conceal himself. Mr. Spofford actually took the drive on the lonely road with the ex-convict and went with him to his house in Cambridgeport. Sargent did not even ask him to pay for the hired horse and buggy. Spofford remained in the home of the saloon-keeper of Sudbury Street for two weeks, reading the papers in which he was advertised as lost and later as lying in the morgue, never venturing to come forth and disclose his whereabouts to his anxious friends. This strange proceeding would seem to indicate that the depraved man, Sargent, had been employed by some one as an actor in a farce rather than a tragedy.

At the preliminary hearing in the municipal court of Boston there was a strange assemblage of witnesses brought to swear against the liberty of the teacher of moral science, Mr. Eddy, and his student, Edward Arens. The two men who had been summarily arrested and haled to court were astounded to behold

Daniel Spofford in such a company. Besides Sargent, the saloon-keeper of Sudbury Street, there were his sister, who kept a house of ill-fame at 7 Bowker Street, and several women inmates of this house; also George Collier, Sargent's accomplice, who was under bonds awaiting trial on some charge of evil doings of his own; Jessie MacDonald, a discharged servant from Mrs. Eddy's household; and the detectives employed on the case, Hollis C. Pinkham and Chase Philbrick, were of the company.

Sargent, with bold effrontery, professed to identify Mr. Eddy and Edward Arens as "Miller and Libbey." He then told a long and vivid story of his meetings with them, — how they had come into his saloon one morning and told his fortune and then, getting into confidential conversation, had asked him if he knew any one who could be hired to put a man out of the way; how he had said that he was ready himself for any such job, provided there was money in it; and how by arrangement he afterward met Mr. Eddy and Mr. Arens on the railroad track in East Cambridge on the seventeenth of August at five-thirty o'clock in the afternoon. There, he declared, being somewhat alarmed for himself, he had had his friend Collier conceal himself in a freight car to hear the details of the wicked conspiracy, and he stated how he had also provided himself with a revolver in case these desperate characters should attack him.

The presiding judge must have wondered at this on studying the calm, sweet eyes of Mr. Eddy, the astounded and fearless gaze of Mr. Arens, and then the shifty, cruel eyes of Sargent. But his perplexity must have increased on observing the guileless expression of Spofford. Collier testified to the truth of all Sargent had said; the women witnesses from the Bowker Street house declared that Sargent had come there and left with his sister the seventy-five dollars he had received for the murder; the detective, Pinkham, stated that he had listened to Sargent's and Spofford's stories, that he had seen Sargent talking to Arens on Boston Common, and that he had also seen Sargent approach Mr. Eddy's house and be refused admission. The testimony of the servant girl, Jessie MacDonald, was that she had heard Mr. Eddy say that Spofford kept Mrs. Eddy in agony and he would be glad if Spofford were out of the way; also she had heard Mrs. Eddy read a chapter from the Bible which says that all wicked people should be destroyed.

Russell H. Conwell was the attorney employed by Mrs. Eddy to conduct the defense of her husband and her student. The able lawyer had prepared a thorough analysis of the apparent facts, but as the case never came to trial, the defendants had no hearing. Mrs. Eddy, however, did not rest after the peremptory dismissal of the case, but remained active in the defense of her husband's honor until every charge was privately examined and affidavits secured covering every point. In these affidavits she was singularly fortunate in receiving the confession of the accomplice Collier which promised to clear up the entire matter had the *nolle prosequi* not been entered. Shortly after the police court hearing, this man wrote the following badly spelled letter now among Mrs. Eddy's bequeathed papers.

To Dr. Asa G. Eddy and E. J. Arens,—Feeling that you have been greatly ingured by faulse charges and knowing thair is no truth in my statements that you attempted to hire Sargent to kill Daniel Spofford, and wishing to retract as far as possible all things I have sed to your ingury, I now say that thair is no truth whatever in the statement that I saw you meet Sargent at East Cambridge or any other place and pay or offer to pay him any money; that I never herd a conversation between you and Sargent as testified to by me. Whether Daniel Spofford has anything to do with Sargent I do not know. All I know is that the story I told on the stand is holy faulse and was got up by Sargent.

GEORGE A. COLLIER

This letter led Mrs. Eddy to search out the man Collier and persuade him to make an affidavit before a justice in Taunton, December 17, 1878. His sworn statement is as follows:

I, George A. Collier, do on oath depose and say of my own free will, and in order to expose the man who has tried to injure Dr. Asa G. Eddy and Edward J. Arens, that Sargent did induce me by great persuasion to go with him to East Cambridge from Boston, on or about the 7th day of November last, the day of the hearing in the municipal court of Boston in the case of Dr. Asa G. Eddy and E. J. Arens for attempting to hire said Sargent to kill one Daniel Spofford, and that he showed me the place and the cars that he was going to swear to, and told me what to say in court, and made me repeat the story until I knew it well, so that I could tell the same story that he would, and there was not one word of truth in it all. I never heard a conversation in East Cambridge between said Eddy and Arens and Sargent, or saw them pay or offer to pay Sargent any money.

(Signed)   GEO. A. COLLIER

The other affidavits Mrs. Eddy secured were statements as to Mr. Eddy's whereabouts on the day and at the hour when the ex-convict Sargent declared he was conferring with him and giving him money on the railroad tracks. The statements made before justices and sworn to in all cases were that Mr. Eddy was teaching a class in metaphysics at the home of David Grey, 43 Clifford Street, Boston Highlands, from two-thirty o'clock until five-forty-five o'clock. The ride in the horse-cars of those days to East Cambridge from this address would have consumed an hour. Mr. Eddy, however, reached his home in Lynn about seven-fifteen in the evening, having gone from Boston Highlands to the Eastern depot and returned to his home on the six-thirty o'clock train. It took him three quarters of an hour to reach the Eastern depot from his class in Boston Highlands. That he arrived home at the hour stated does not rest on Mrs. Eddy's statement alone but is attested by Miranda R. Rice under oath, who was at 8 Broad Street with Mrs. Eddy, waiting to hear particulars from Mr. Eddy of his new class.

As to the detective's testimony that he had seen Sargent at Mr. Eddy's door, Mrs. Eddy wrote at the time:

The only time this man Sargent came to our threshold, to our knowledge, was the day the detective came to arrest Mr. Eddy; he preceded the detective a few minutes and had just been ordered from the door by Mr. Eddy because of his impertinent remarks, when the detective who had him in attendance rang at the front door and himself admitted Sargent into the house.

Though the state removed the detective, and Sargent and Collier subsequently went to jail on other charges, this case, which was built up on perjuries and which collapsed without a hearing, evidently had great villainy in it and it should have been made to appear. Mrs. Eddy never held Daniel Spofford directly responsible for involving her husband in the wicked conspiracy and causing him to appear at the bar of justice in the company of thieves and women of ill repute. At most she believed him blindly acquiescent in a design which it was never in his heart to originate. But she did point out, without naming, one who had motive and character for the instigation of the dastardly intrigue.

CHAPTER XVII

ORGANIZATION OF CHURCH AND COLLEGE

THE development of machinations usually has the result of clearing the atmosphere. The hostile plot related in the previous chapter operated in this manner. Its workings were like a chemical precipitation. Mrs. Eddy's spiritual genius was resisting the encroachments of the little group around her and preparing to deal with the larger needs of a great spiritual movement.

She foresaw the future prophetically, and that the hour had struck for a new movement in the history of human rationalism. In less than twenty-five years the century would close, and in the opening of the twentieth century a new era of mental life awaited humanity. Mrs. Eddy realized this; she desired to prepare for it, to have in readiness processes of amelioration for the miseries of an age more or less in the bondage of fear, an operative organization by which humanity might lay hold of the new hope which should thrill it. Christian Science must go forward, it must be presented to the world beyond this little city of Lynn, it must be organized.

To trace in any great movement, as Lecky the historian of rationalism has pointed out, the part which belongs to the individual and the part which belongs to general causes is an extremely delicate task. Mrs. Eddy had already made an amazing gift to her time

MRS. EDDY IN 1882, IN BOSTON, MASSACHUSETTS
When she lived in her first home, the little house in Broad Street,
where the First Edition of Science and Health was finished

which might well be deemed a sufficient work for any one individual to have perfected. In her treatise, Science and Health, she had given to the world a new conception of the nature of the Supreme Being and His eternal government of the universe. But having received a spiritual revelation, and having formulated this revelation into a treatise, Mrs. Eddy now apprehended that there existed a socially diffused sense throughout the world that a new age of reasoning was to appear with the dawn of the twentieth century. In apprehending this she realized a fresh work which was laid upon her, the work of bringing into the full glare of the world's thought a spiritualized realization of the Christian faith.

What then were the tasks of the hour? An effective church organization was the crying need. After that Mrs. Eddy foresaw the necessity of establishing a college of instruction which would serve as a strong center of dissemination. Her book must have a third edition and this edition must be effectively circulated. Teachers and practitioners must be sent forth. It was a great work which unfolded itself in her mind in the very face of the conspiracy to dishonor her in Lynn, directed at her through the persons of her husband and student.

During the summer of 1878 Mrs. Eddy had ventured to carry her work into Boston. She first gave lectures on Sunday afternoons in the Shawmut Avenue Baptist Church, and later lectured in Fraternity Hall of the Parker Memorial Building, Appleton Street side. This public meeting hall seated from three hundred to four hundred persons. At first her lectures drew but a few people, but very shortly the audiences grew and she was soon able to fill the larger meeting place.

The Boston audiences were a revelation to Mrs. Eddy. The listeners attracted to the new doctrine were distinctly of a cultivated world. While her long labors in Lynn had unfolded her own powers, they had attracted to her only disciples whose intellectual limitations caused them to be more or less disappointing. They had been able to follow her only a certain distance in philosophic speculation, whereupon a reaction of some sort of stubbornness would ensue, a stubbornness impossible to cope with. In Boston a new quality of mind responded to her. Those first Boston audiences revealed to her that the foundation of her church was to be laid in the city of liberal culture.

But the Founder of Christian Science was not yet done with her efforts in Lynn. Although the Eddys moved into rooms in Boston in 1879, the next year saw them back at their former home. There Mrs. Eddy continued her teaching, still lecturing in Boston. There were students whom she taught in Broad Street who remained loyal to the work; and when she went forth they followed her to Boston and became her aids. She could not personally do everything that lay before her; she must direct them to tasks by the faithful performance of which the struggles of the early church might have been greatly minimized.

Mr. and Mrs. Eddy lived a tranquil domestic existence. Their union was based on affection and mutual esteem. Their housekeeping was ideally simple and harmonious. Perfect orderliness, exquisite cleanliness, and gentle social courtesy were Mrs. Eddy's marked characteristics, while calm, upright, steadfast, a continual support and protection to his wife, Mr. Eddy has been likened to the late President McKinley in his individual traits.

A vivid idea of the interior of that home may be gained, which is pleasing to remember when one is tempted to think of it only as a storm-buffeted center, its inmates scandalized, ridiculed, and outraged by hirelings and plotters determined to molest its peace. The exterior of the little house with its balconied portico, its flowers and shade trees, has already been described. The first-floor rooms, so long occupied for classes and lectures, were now converted into a charming little parlor and study. Mrs. Eddy received her callers in the first room and did her literary work in the second.

The walls of the reception-room were finished in plain gray paper with gold cornices. The windows were hung with white lace draperies, looped back over high gilt arms. A crimson carpet covered the floor and the furniture was of black walnut. The tables always held vases of flowers, for Mrs. Eddy was devoted to the cultivation of plants in summer and winter, and her success with them was an evidence of her continual love of the beautiful. It is impossible to impart in such meager details the veritable charm of Mrs. Eddy's home, a charm which has existed in every home she has made; but those who have described the room speak of it as a place where one breathed the atmosphere of graciousness expressed in rare simplicity.

In this room Mrs. Clara Choate was received by Mrs. Eddy in January, 1878. She was one of Mrs. Eddy's devoted students during that troublous time, and her description of the home life shows that Mrs. Eddy was not overwhelmed by her difficulties, but calm and resolute. She also tells of a certain buoyancy and gaiety which at times characterized Mrs. Eddy, a gaiety which caused her to rally her students to cheerfulness and mirth, as years later she rallied the lawyers and journalists who assembled with awestruck countenances to catechize her on the rationality of her mind.

Mrs. Choate, whose husband belonged to the family which has given so many distinguished publicists to the American nation, and who was herself related to the Blaines, was an early reader of Science and Health. She secured a copy of the first edition and read it with wonder and delight, but she did not immediately become a Christian Scientist. Having sent from her home in Salem for a practitioner and having been greatly benefited in health, she determined to meet the author of the book and study its doctrine at first hand. She accordingly came to Lynn. When she was shown into the little gray-walled parlor, she looked about in some wonderment. Expecting to find austerity, she was surprised to behold harmony, beauty, and sunshine. Yet this presently appeared the natural environment for the religion of love. Her meeting with Mrs. Eddy was typical of many such meetings. She describes it thus:

When the double doors leading into the back parlor were at last opened and I saw her standing there, I was seized with a sense of great gladness which seemed to be imparted by her radiant expression. Mrs. Eddy instantly healed me of every ill that had claimed me. I cannot describe the exhilaration that rushed through my whole being. I was uplifted and felt a sense of buoyancy unspeakable. It was as though a consciousness of purity pervaded Mrs. Eddy and from her imparted itself to me, whereupon I felt as if treading on air to the rhythmic flow of music.

Mrs. Eddy was over fifty years old, but Mrs. Choate describes her as a graceful figure in a violet-colored house-gown finished with lace at the throat and wrists. Her hands were small and expressive, her hair rippled about her face and was dressed high at the back of her well-shaped head. Her cheeks glowed with color and her eyes were clear, unwavering, like wells of light.

Mrs. Choate was not much over twenty, a young wife and mother who had never been away from home before. Mrs. Eddy called her "child," and took her into that circle of friends which closely surrounded her. Later Mrs. Choate and her husband came to live across the street. She was much with Mrs. Eddy in and out of the house, and her happy spirits often relieved the strain of Mrs. Eddy's arduous days. It was in May that they came to reside in Lynn. Her husband, George D. Choate, entered a class during that month, his opposition to Christian Science having been swept away by his wife's marvelous healing and her enthusiasm for the cause of the new religious movement. They were later to aid in the establishment of college and church.

Other students who now came into the work were Miss Julia Bartlett, Mrs. Ellen J. Clark, Arthur True

Buswell, and James Ackland. Some of them lodged in the Broad Street house, occupying the several chambers of the second floor, but not living at the family table. Many incidents of the daily life of Mrs. Eddy were related by the students which show her never to have forgotten those sterling habits gained from the guidance of a mother remarkable throughout her life for housewifely virtue.

Though occasionally entertaining her students at table and serving them with the food she prepared with her own hands, she was ever the teacher, writer, lecturer, organizer. If she sometimes walked on a pleasant evening with them to her favorite retreat on the beach, she never relaxed into the idleness of mere diversion. Spiritual realization was the constant theme of her conversation. Those around her had found health, harmony, joy, in the Science of Being which she had taught them; they must help her to spread this gospel. The world was hungering for this truth; it must be fed. The world was sick in sin and error; it must be healed and taught truth. None of the students found in her a companion in idle thought and self-seeking. Sometimes they complained of it and would have had her merrier, more diverted, less contained and full of far-seeing plans. Because of her persistently maintained superiority to these human instincts some of the students were eventually estranged.

Organization was her word for the hour. It had become in her mind an imperative duty to organize the Christian Science Church. A tentative organization had been made. In 1875, it will be remembered, the little band of eight students had pledged themselves to raise money for church services, but their ranks had been broken by rebellion and that organization was disbanded. On July 4, 1876, the Christian Scientist Association was formed to hold the students together for work and occasional meetings. This proved effectual for its purpose for a number of years. Mrs. Eddy now urged the incorporation of a church society. This was accomplished in August, 1879, and a charter, issued August 23, was received from the state. The articles of incorporation stated that the Church of Christ, Scientist, was to be established in Boston, thus fulfilling Mrs. Eddy's prophetic vision.

The members of the new church numbered twenty-six and the organization and first service took place at the home of Mrs. Margaret Dunshee in Charlestown. The officers and directors were: Mrs. Eddy, president; Edward A. Orne, clerk; Mrs. Margaret J. Dunshee, treasurer; Mrs. Eddy, Mr. Orne, James Ackland, and Arthur T. Buswell, directors. They elected and ordained Mrs. Eddy pastor after the Congregational method of New England.[1] This is not the basis of the present Christian Science church, but the organization continued in existence for ten years, at the end of which time it was dissolved.

For some six weeks the Church of Christ (Scientist) carried on public meetings in the parlors of various members. Then on November 30, 1879, the first regular service of the church was held in a public hall. It was convened at Hawthorn Hall on Park Street, Boston. That hall, which had recently become a pub-

[1] Mrs. Eddy was ordained November 9, 1881.

lishing-house, was the real cradle of the church. Mrs. Eddy was the active pastor from the date of organization and regularly preached a Sunday afternoon sermon. Even before the church had been organized for services she had preached at Fraternity Hall, making the trip to Boston from her Lynn home for this purpose. On the morning of each Sabbath her students would seek her and find her sitting with closed eyes, deep in meditation. Urging her to eat, to dress, to make preparation for the delivering of her sermon, they expressed much love in solicitation. She would, however, send them away, demanding silence and time for thought. On the railway train from Lynn to Boston the students would join her. She was always faultlessly dressed and usually in a mood of spiritual gaiety.

In the pulpit there was never a trace of fatigue. It has been said that her sermons were exhilarating and moved her audiences to emotional exaltation; yet in the same breath critics add that she brought forward only the healing phase of her teaching, seldom touching on religious questions, such as repentance, humility, or prayer. They say that she was cold or indifferent to such topics. These two statements are not consistent, nor is the latter founded on fact. Some of her sermons are included in "Miscellaneous Writings" and are essentially spiritual. Prayer, Mrs. Eddy teaches, is the realization of the omnipresence of God and the aspiration for purity. Silent realization has always been an impressive ceremony of her church. As for repentance, she taught the very essence of it, which she declared was the forsaking of sin.

The seeds of rebellion were in the first church organization. The reactionary effect observable in many of the early students was to repeat itself. Kennedy had persisted in the use of mesmerism, Spofford endeavored to wrest the leadership from the church's founder, now Arens conceived the idea of writing a book on the topics he had studied, and for that purpose stole bodily from Mrs. Eddy's writings. He preceded her to Boston and opened an office not far from where Kennedy had established himself. Rebellion now broke forth with violence in a group of students who walked out in a body. They prepared the following statement as their reason for so doing:

We, the undersigned, while we acknowledge and appreciate the understanding of Truth imparted to us by our teacher, Mrs. Mary B. G. Eddy, led by Divine Intelligence to perceive with sorrow that departure from the straight and narrow road (which alone leads to growth in Christlike virtues) made manifest by frequent ebullitions of temper, love of money, and the appearance of hypocrisy, cannot longer submit to such leadership. Therefore, without aught of hatred, revenge, or petty spite in our hearts, from a sense of duty alone, to her, the cause, and ourselves, do most respectfully withdraw our names from the Christian Science Association and Church of Christ, Scientist.

This document, dated October 21, 1881, was signed by eight protesting students whose names need not be commemorated here. Their statement is interesting because of a state of consciousness presented to view.

Examining the charges summed up in this statement, it can readily be seen how the fresh impetus at work in Mrs. Eddy's mind had wrought upon these narrow-visioned artisans. The Boston lectures had seemed to take the work beyond their sphere; the influx of new students from beyond Lynn had detached the teacher's attention from their immediate concerns; the necessity to provide funds for promotion had put an end to the easy-going communistic methods of the primitive movement; and, above all, Mrs. Eddy had commanded an implicit obedience from her later students and they had yielded it. Mr. Choate went to Portland where she sent him to teach, heal, and lecture, Mr. Buswell went on a similar errand to Cincinnati, Joseph Morton was sent to New York. These were the signs of a burgeoning of the work which alarmed the first students, and some of them retaliated, as has been shown, by malediction.

Had Mrs. Eddy been the virago and the avaricious hypocrite that they in their suspicion and jealousy brought themselves to believe, her work would have died in Lynn, and the greatest religious movement of modern times would never have been known. But instead of receiving its death-blow from the carefully worded epistle of apology, it was rebaptized and confirmed, and the young church was in reality purged of the strong elements of opposition and encumbrances of ineffectuality which had hampered its growth.

In a sense it proved a transfiguration of her lifework. The signed apostasy was read at a regular meeting of the Christian Scientist Association. The Founder and Leader was both grieved and astounded, all unaware as she was that disaffection of so serious a nature had arisen among them. Not one of the dissenters was present at the meeting when the letter was read. The remaining students drafted a reply to be sent to each signer of the letter, and then withdrew — except for two new students who remained with her and Mr. Eddy all night.

In the morning the group was joined by another student shocked to learn of what seemed the burial of their Cause. But Mrs. Eddy rose above this stunning blow with calm assurance as one baptized with a new vision. She spoke to them of the future work of the church in such inspired sentences that they all shared with her the sense of a transfiguration and wrote her words upon their hearts to be ever remembered. Their reply to the apostates was to propose the ordaining of Mrs. Eddy as pastor of the Church of Christ (Scientist). This was formally done on November 9, 1881, after the method of the early Congregational Church of the American Colonies, the solemn approbation of the elders.

During one week she waited in almost continual prayer for the return of the lost sheep, sending messages by the faithful, even going herself like a shepherd to seek a possible repentant one. Finding that her appeal did not meet with the response which would have shown the rebellious students merely the victims of a temporary delusion, sorrowfully she took from them the right to resign by expelling them from the ranks of her church. It was a masterly decision, for she thereby preserved the church's charter. The apostates had made themselves liable to expulsion by failing to comprehend the meaning of her appeals to them to remain faithful to their commitment.

Her act had a most salutary effect on the loyal students. Dismay had at first threatened them. They now rallied around her and in a few weeks published in the Lynn papers a reply to the seceders in the form of resolutions. In these they expressed their heartfelt love and gratitude for their teacher and acknowledged her as their Leader in Christian Science, saying that she alone was able to protect the work she had founded; they denounced the charges brought against her as utterly false and deplored the wickedness of those who could abuse one who had befriended them in their need and rebuked them with honesty. They expressed their admiration and reverence for her Christlike example of meekness and charity, and declared that in future they would more faithfully obey her instructions in appreciation of her Christian leadership.

Thus Mrs. Eddy preserved the organization of her church and she had already laid the foundation for the college of instruction she purposed to establish in Boston. The Massachusetts Metaphysical College was the name she selected for that institution, which she organized in January, 1881, ten months before the struggle in her church. She drew up an agreement with six students to teach pathology, ontology, therapeutics, moral science, metaphysics, and their application to the treatment of diseases, and for these purposes the college organization received a charter from the Commonwealth of Massachusetts. Mrs. Eddy was named president and the six students directors.

To thoroughly understand the force of Mrs. Eddy's character it is only necessary to view the difficulties of the situation in which she was placed when she perfected these two basic organizations. She had been so pressed for money that she had been obliged to go upon her knees and cleanse her own floors, she had had to make over the garments she wore to present a faultless appearance of good taste to the public; she had protected her husband by her own energetic conference with counsel and witnesses in a conspiracy to charge him with murder; she had seen her oldest and most trusted women students plot against her and desert her; she had lectured and taught, and sent out missionaries to the North, South, and West; she had sent Mrs. Choate as a precursor to Boston.

In the midst of such activities the third edition of Science and Health had been prepared and was in press. It was issued in 1881, and contained those chapters whose mere captions arouse to-day in her thousands of followers the enthusiasm of faith. Footsteps of Truth, Science of Being, Recapitulation, Creation, Prayer and Atonement were in its contents. This edition retrieved the blundering workmanship of the second edition and is in some respects a clearer statement of her doctrine than she had yet made. With such comprehensive and effective efforts for the future, she prepared to leave Lynn and to step into the full current of the life of her times in the city conceded to have the greatest culture in America.

Thus very shortly after the purging of the early church of disloyal members in Lynn by her faithful students, in January, 1882, the furnishings of the Broad Street house were packed and stored until determinate arrangements should be made for a future residence. On the last evening before leaving Lynn a meeting of the church was held in the denuded rooms, the members seated on packing-cases for their final deliberations. At this meeting Miss Julia Bartlett was received into the church. She later performed an important work of teaching and healing in New Hampshire. Miss Bartlett was probably the first member of the Christian Science Church who remained unfaltering in loyalty to the cause. She was a remarkably successful healer and it was through her work in New Hampshire that many students, among them the family of Ira O. Knapp, were interested in Christian Science.[1] Mr. Knapp became a director of The Mother Church.

Before settling in Boston Mr. and Mrs. Eddy made a visit to Washington and on this occasion Mr. Eddy performed a service of inestimable value for his wife and the cause to which she was dedicated. This was the thorough investigation of the subject of copyrights. Through the labors of her husband, Mrs. Eddy was thoroughly enlightened on this most important matter, important to the security of all her subsequent work. It has been remarked again and again, sometimes critically by those who saw only the worldly advantage of protection to property, again admiringly by those who perceive that every act of Mrs. Eddy's business career was established in sanity and adherence to the law, that her copyrights have been iron-clad and infrangible and never neglected. Perhaps to her follow-

---

1 Mr. and Mrs. Knapp gained their healing from another student of Mrs. Eddy's, Mrs. Mary E. Harris, subsequently Mrs. Curtis.

ers alone the real value of her copyrights is apparent. Their value to Christian Scientists is that they preserve Christian Science unadulterated for the years to come.

The necessity for investigation into this highly abstruse and perplexing subject was made apparent by the perfidy of the student, Edward J. Arens. He, some time in 1880, became imbued with the idea of metaphysical authorship, doubtless planning to turn his energies to the same purpose that had been threatened by a former student, namely, to wrest the leadership of Christian Science from its discoverer. He issued a pamphlet "Christianity; or, The Understanding of God, As Applied to The Healing of the Sick."

The preface to the third edition of Science and Health was written by Asa G. Eddy, and in writing it Mr. Eddy dealt vigorously with Arens. He states that while Arens says he has made use in his pamphlet of "some thoughts contained in a work by Eddy," he for over thirty pages repeats Mrs. Eddy's words verbatim, having copied them without quotation and filching, among other passages of the book, the very heart of Christian Science. This is the scientific statement of being which Mr. Eddy calls "that immortal sentence," and which reads: "There is no life, truth, intelligence, nor substance in matter. All is infinite Mind and its infinite manifestation, for God is All-in-all. Spirit is immortal Truth; matter is mortal error. Spirit is the real and eternal; matter is the unreal and temporal. Spirit is God, and man is His image and likeness. Therefore man is not material; he is spiritual." [1]

[1] Science and Health, p. 468.

Mr. Eddy very tersely says in his arraignment of Arens: "If simply writing at the commencement of a work . . . 'I have taken some thoughts from Ralph Waldo Emerson,'" gave one the right to walk over the author's copyrights and use pages of his writings verbatim, and publish them as his own, any fool might aspire to authorship and any villain become the expounder of truth. He then makes this statement concerning his wife: "Mrs. Eddy's works are the outgrowths of her life. I never knew so unselfish an individual, or one so tireless in what she considers her duty." He dismisses Arens with this emphatic characterization: "It would require ages and God's mercy to make the ignorant hypocrite who published that pamphlet originate its contents. His pratings are colored by his character, they cannot impart the hue of ethics, but leave his own impress on what he takes."

The federal courts subsequently enjoined Arens not to publish or circulate his pamphlets, and all printed copies were destroyed by order of the court. This did not happen until after Mr. Eddy's death, or until process of law dealt with Arens, as shall be presently recounted. But Arens' perfidy wrought upon Mr. Eddy seriously. He suffered real anguish of mind from it, being far more disturbed than was his wife, for he regarded it as a culmination of bitter attacks upon her work and an exhibition of malicious animal magnetism.

Speaking in a purely human sense, Mr. Eddy resented the unfaithfulness of one whom Mrs. Eddy had taught and trusted very largely with her business affairs. He felt it keenly that one who had gone through such an experience of unjust prosecution as Arens had suffered jointly with him in the Lynn conspiracy and who had been defended by his wife's faithful energies should now array himself against the cause. Arens was living in Boston not far from the house on Columbus Avenue which Mr. and Mrs. Eddy leased in the spring of 1882. He was teaching and preaching adversely to Christian Science, and as yet had not been restrained from circulating his pirated writings.

Whether or not it was as a result of sorrow engendered in his heart or distress arising in his mind over the continual harassment brought by attacks on the work to which he had given his energies, Mr. Eddy visibly failed in health. His heart became weak; he lost his appetite and could not sleep. He complained of a sense of suffocation, an oppression of the suggestion of evil. Mrs. Eddy summoned Dr. Rufus K. Noyes, a graduate of the Dartmouth Medical School, who was then a resident of Lynn, and many years a distinguished Boston physician. He was known to Mrs. Eddy as a young man of brilliant achievements for his years, and had recently served as a resident physician in the city hospital.

She summoned Dr. Noyes to diagnose her husband's case, for much perplexity had arisen among her students concerning his condition. She told the physician she believed her husband was suffering from the suggestion of arsenical poisoning, because, to her, the symptoms appeared to be those of actual or material arsenic. Some of her household had believed Mr. Eddy was suffering from cancer of the stomach. Dr. Noyes diagnosed the case as disease of the heart. He advised rest and tonic, digitalis and strychnia. But

Dr. Noyes believes that his prescription was not adhered to and no medicines were administered.

It may be asked why Mrs. Eddy called a regular physician, especially if she did not intend to administer the medicines prescribed. A great deal of excitement was aroused by her husband's illness, both among her friends and her critics. She desired a diagnosis at which no man or woman could cavil. She did not believe that her husband had cancer, or that his heart was defective, but that he was suffering from suggestion. She believed that a practising physician, trained in natural science, would bear her out in this and thus clinch her own diagnosis. But she was ahead of her age. Experimental psychology had not then made the important discovery that the deadliest poison is a secretion engendered by the working of hatred.[1]

[1] The Washington *Herald* in August, 1907, printed an article descriptive of the experiments of Professor Elmer Gates in his laboratory of psychology and psychurgy. The article was also printed in the Chicago *Tribune*. It states: "Professor Gates has shown the causative character of thinking in a long series of most comprehensive and convincing experiments. He found that change of mental state changed the chemical character of the perspiration. When treated with the same chemical re-agent the perspiration of an angry man showed one color, that of a man in grief another, and so on through the list of emotions, each mental state persistently exhibiting its own peculiar result every time the experiment was repeated.

"When the breath of Professor Gates' subject was passed through a tube cooled with ice, so as to condense its volatile constituents, a colorless liquid resulted. . . . He made his subject angry and five minutes afterwards a sediment appeared in the tube which indicated the presence there of a new substance produced by the changed physical action caused by a change of the mental emotion. Anger gave a brownish substance, sorrow gray, etc. . . . Each kind of thinking produced its own peculiar substance which the system was trying to expel. . . . Professor Gates undertook to discover the character of the substances which he obtained by condensation of the breath of his subjects. The brownish precipitate from the breath of any persons administered either to men or to animals caused stimulation and excitement of the nerves. Another substance, produced by another kind of discordant thinking, when injected into the veins of a guinea pig or a hen, killed it outright. . . . The deadliest poison known to science is hate. Professor Elmer Gates is the man who has found it out, . . . who has demonstrated it."

That Mr. Eddy suffered greatly, and that Mrs. Eddy suffered with him in her deep affection and sympathy is vouched for. A student who came and went in Mrs. Eddy's house with the freedom of a sister has drawn a picture of the hour of sorrow which is tenderly beautiful. Mrs. Eddy had the work of her church to carry on; her room was littered with books and papers; there was no order there at this time, for she could give but snatches of attention to affairs while her husband was lying stricken in an adjoining room. He breathed with agony and with physical sobs. Sitting by him, Mrs. Eddy would lay her face close to his and murmur, "Gilbert, Gilbert, do not suffer so," and under her silent treatment he would be relieved for a time and sleep.

But Mr. Eddy observed that he distracted his wife from her pressing business and heroically declared, "My sickness is nothing; I can handle this belief myself." He steadfastly declared he was coping with the attack and urged his wife to leave him. When she had reluctantly done so, he experienced a depression, but refused to have her called to relieve him. Just before his death he cried out, "Only rid me of this suggestion of poison and I will recover." Mrs. Eddy had retired but was called; her husband expired, however, before she could reach him. This was before daybreak on Saturday morning, June 3, 1882.

If there is any truth in the old saying, died of a broken heart, it might well be applied to the death of this good man. Because of the persistent rumors concerning his illness and death, rumors that he had had a cancer, that he had been taking arsenic, and even that some one had actually given him a dose of poison, Mrs. Eddy again called Dr. Noyes, this time to perform an autopsy. Dr. Noyes exposed the heart and exhibited the physical organ to Mrs. Eddy, pointing out the valvular difficulty. He found no traces of arsenic whatsoever, no cancer or other disease of the stomach.

In so far then as the surgeon's knife can prove anything, Mr. Eddy died of heart exhaustion. But the surgeon's knife cannot find everything; it cannot find love, for example, in the noblest heart that ever beat; nor can it find hate in the cruelest. Who can with authority deny Mrs. Eddy's statement that poison mentally administered killed her husband? "Not material poison," she declared, "but mesmeric poison."

It may not be the term that natural science would admit, but natural science acknowledged readily that grief, disappointment, and profound depression will cause heart failure. Remembering the wicked charge of wilful attempt to murder falsely brought against Mr. Eddy, and the cruel assaults upon his wife, whom he loved and cherished, by the seceding students, and the attempt at a veritable overthrow of the work to which he was devoted, it may be very easily understood why Mrs. Eddy declared that her husband was mentally poisoned, and in that statement doubtless she was scientifically exact. It should be remembered that this happened in the early days of Christian Science practise and at a time when Mrs. Eddy was just awakening to the pernicious mental influence of hate. Christian Science presents a doctrine of love which antidotes hate. "Divine Love always has met and always will meet every human need," says Mrs. Eddy in Science and Health.[1]

Mr. Eddy's remains were taken to Tilton, New Hampshire, and interred in the cemetery on a branch of the Merrimac River in the shadow of the beautiful foot-hills of the White Mountains. A granite shaft marks the spot. Mr. George D. Choate accompanied the body and Mrs. Clara Choate remained with Mrs. Eddy, who arranged for her the topics of the eulogy which Mrs. Choate delivered on Mr. Eddy in Hawthorne Hall. Her subject was: "Blessed are the dead which die in the Lord from henceforth: . . . their works do follow them."

[1] Science and Health, p. 494.

CHAPTER XVIII

FOUNDATION WORK IN BOSTON

WITH the death of her husband Mrs. Eddy suffered a severe blow, having lost a devoted co-worker and friend in whom she had found great satisfaction through a most exalted human relationship. A new chapter now opens in her life, a period of world activity in the cause of religion. She becomes the founder and the organizer, the teacher and promulgator of Christian Science and in this character transcends her former self as the kind hostess and sympathetic friend. Girlhood, widowhood, wifehood vanish, are swallowed up, in a complex but unified individuality which reveals her preeminently as the Founder, Mary Baker Eddy.

The most cynical critics of this illustrious woman have made the comment that she was never so commanding a figure as when she bestirred herself in the face of calamity. Although these critics have essayed to portray her in the sad moment of her bereavement as a woman prostrated, hysterical, and exhausted, afraid to go out of her house and afraid to stay in it when in the quiet upper chamber the mortal remains of her husband lay draped for the grave, the events of those days will not harmonize with such a characterization.

Mrs. Eddy was self-controlled in the face of her bereavement, so calm that she in every way conformed to the usages and standards of the world, and yet bore herself with the composure of one acting in sublime faith. As there had been unwarranted rumors concerning Mr. Eddy's illness and death, she had permitted an autopsy. That grim function completed and the verdict of heart failure rendered, Mrs. Eddy summoned such friends and students as she could rely upon. Mr. Eddy's interment was lovingly arranged for and carried out and her tribute to his life and work was pronounced for her in a public service. She then took steps to withdraw from active work through the summer and rearranged her plans for a campaign of several years, looking to the establishment of the church on a firm foundation.

Before leaving Boston for a summer's rest, a period which the world would call a time of mourning, but which to Mrs. Eddy was a spiritual retreat for the restatement in her consciousness of the deep things of love and truth and immortality, she gathered together her students and gave to each his work. She received representatives from the press and granted an interview in which she refuted the popular notion that consternation had seized her with the swing of death's pinion. She declared with superb affirmation, "I believe in God's supremacy over error, and this gives me peace."

Mr. Arthur True Buswell, the student whom Mrs. Eddy had sent to Cincinnati to teach and practise, came to her house on Columbus Avenue, summoned by telegram to join in an advisory council. He suggested that she make use of his home in Barton, in the northern part of Vermont, for her vacation, and she accepted. Her house in Boston she left in the care of her students, Miss Julia Bartlett and Mrs. Abbie Whiting. She took with her as companion for the summer Miss Alice Sibley, a young woman of great beauty of character who was much endeared to her.

Although she had exhibited heroic qualities of energy and fortitude, neglecting nothing of direction and command before leaving Boston, she showed on the journey traces of nervous exhaustion and at times the hysteria of grief threatened to overwhelm her. With her wonderful faith she battled against the thoughts which assailed her, holding herself to her great purpose with the energy of a saint. Mr. Buswell relates that her great struggle was known to his household, but that she carried it through alone, though they often watched outside her door. After a night of agony she would emerge from her struggle with a radiant face and luminous eyes, and they would hesitate to speak to her for fear of disturbing the peace which enveloped her.

However great the struggle of the night, day found her ready to discuss the work of the movement. During the brief summer she constantly considered the situation in Boston. She planned the reorganization of her household, the reopening of the college, discussed what new students should be admitted to the fall classes, arranged for lectures to be given by the old students, and above all discussed the founding of a periodical which she resolved to call the *Journal of Christian Science.*

In such practical matters Mr. Buswell could help her, and together they discussed the proposed new

organ for dissemination. Mr. Buswell was appointed
to form the company to publish this new periodical.
The undertaking required a great deal of thoughtful
consideration and the vital needs of its conception fo-
cused and controlled her thought, leaving her grief to
yield more gently to the ministration of divine agency.

An almost equally important matter for consideration was the future conduct of her household
which she purposed establishing on an institutional
basis. She turned over in her mind the qualifications
of students in order to settle upon one in whom she
could repose the trust of steward of her household.
One day she requested Mr. Buswell to telegraph to
Calvin A. Frye of Lawrence, Massachusetts. Directly
afterward she resolved to return to Boston, and what
had been in many respects a pleasant summer interval
of inspirational drives and walks shared with Alice
Sibley and of practical conferences with Mr. Buswell
now came to an end.[1]

Hastening to answer Mrs. Eddy's summons, Mr.
Frye met the returning party at Plymouth, New
Hampshire. Mrs. Eddy requested him to make the
journey to Boston with them and on the train she unfolded in part her plans and her needs of efficient
stewardship. She put to him searching questions concerning his own life and his willingness to serve the
cause of Christian Science. To all her questions he
replied sincerely and declared himself ready to perform whatever lay in his power. Mrs. Eddy did not
tell him at the time what she later revealed to him,

---

[1] From notes of an interview with A. T. Buswell by the author in October, 1907. Printed in *Human Life*.

that Mr. Eddy had gone to Lawrence some months before his death and inquired into Mr. Frye's record with the possible idea of summoning him to this very position. He had anticipated his wife's need. The Rev. Joshua Coit, Mr. Frye's pastor in the Congregational Church, had so spoken of Mr. Frye that Mr. Eddy recommended him to his wife as a man to be trusted with her intimate affairs.

Mr. Frye entered Mrs. Eddy's household on her arrival in Boston and from that hour remained faithful in her service. There is no term that will cover the manifold duties which devolved upon him. He was usually spoken of as her private secretary because of the enormous amount of correspondence of which he relieved her. He was her bookkeeper, her purchasing agent, and her personal representative on many important occasions. Those who would make a reproach of his faithfulness have referred to him as her butler and her coachman. Indeed, he did not hesitate to occupy the box of her carriage to guard her on her daily drives.

But a few words concerning Mr. Frye's history will correct the impression that the titles of servitude were warranted by his natural social status. The Frye family is an old one, as American ancestry goes. His grandfather and great-grandfather fought in the wars of 1812 and the Revolution. Frye Village, now a part of Andover, Massachusetts, was named for his grandfather, who had a prosperous milling business there in grist and lumber. His father, Enoch Frye, prepared for college in Phillips Andover Academy and graduated from Harvard in the class made famous by Ralph Waldo Emerson. Calvin Frye received his edu-

cation in the district school of Frye Village. His father
was in moderate circumstances, having contracted a
lameness which unfitted him for active life work, and
it was not possible for him.to educate his sons as he
had himself been educated. There were five children
of Calvin's generation, a brother who died in infancy,
one who lost his life in the Civil War, another who
was a business man of Boston, and a sister who with
Calvin became a Christian Scientist.

Calvin married at the age of twenty-eight, but his
wife lived only a year after the marriage and they had
no children. He thereafter lived at home with his
parents and sister in Lawrence, working in the Natick
mill as an overseer of machinery. His family all belonged to the Congregational Church, his father and
grandfather before him having been members of the
choir. For fifteen years Calvin was an active church-
worker, librarian, class leader, and usher. He and his
sister Lydia became interested in Christian Science at
the same time through Mrs. Clara Choate who carried
the new teaching into Lawrence. She healed a relative
of the Frye family and was then invited to their home.

Mr. Frye's mother had suffered from mental de-
rangement for many years and Mrs. Clara Choate
restored her to sanity which continued for four years,
when under a sudden return of her malady she expired. But her marvelous restoration made firm con-
verts of brother and sister, and Calvin Frye went to
Lynn and studied Christian Science in the autumn
of 1881 and practised healing in Lawrence until Mrs.
Eddy summoned him to Boston. Lydia Frye Roaf
joined her brother and was for a time in charge of

Mrs. Eddy's domestic affairs. She returned to Lawrence and practised Christian Science until her death. The Fryes were a singularly united family, neglecting none of the filial duties and paying each other the attention of yearly visits. Calvin Frye was a quiet, earnest man with a clear and placid countenance, and he was not without a mild mirthfulness which made him an agreeable companion. His education was broadened by the habit of reading. In practical matters he was an active, careful agent and the quality of faithfulness was preeminently his.

The house which Mr. and Mrs. Eddy had taken in Boston before Mr. Eddy's death was at 569 Columbus Avenue. After two years, in March, 1884, she removed to the house next door at 571. It, too, was a four-story dwelling with gray stone front. It was very simply furnished, for Mrs. Eddy curtailed and modified the views of the enthusiastic students who would have had her (as one of them regretfully expressed it to the author) "lay carpets the feet would sink into or hang draperies of rich lace and velvet and decorate with bronzes and paintings which would reflect her taste in art." The students who desired and urged such appointments were of two temperaments, those who loved her devotedly in a very human way and wished to exalt her before the world of Boston; others who had decidedly florid views of what metaphysics should manifest in worldly appearance and would have turned the modest gray institute into a miniature Vatican palace, with oratories, perpetual altar lights, and chapel incense as its features, had they had their way.

Mrs. Eddy had previously expressed her views on these matters. Mrs. Choate had given her a reception at her house in Tremont Street at the corner of Upton Street on her return with Mr. Eddy from Washington early in the spring of 1882. Through the efforts of a student who had a large social acquaintance the parlors were filled with fashionable Bostonians. Mrs. Eddy was simply garbed in a quiet gray silk with a black lace shawl draped over her shoulders. When she appeared the babble was quieted and she made a brief address. She then shook hands with a few of the guests, and retired from the scene of festivity. She afterward told her disappointed students that Christian Science could not be forwarded after that method.

Governed by ideas of simplicity, she now gave orders for the fitting out of the college. The class-room on the second floor was laid with oilcloth. The wealthy and fashionable students, of whom there were now a good many, lifted their hands in amazement and despair. Mrs. Eddy further ordered a small platform built in one corner on which her table and chair should be placed. The entire house was furnished with like austerity and had the plainness of an office even in the front parlors, though it was always garnished throughout with the shine of perfect order.

Miss Julia Bartlett and Mrs. Abbie Whiting were living in the house. Alice Sibley came and went with the freedom of a daughter. Mr. Edward H. Hammond of Waltham, who later introduced Christian Science into Baltimore, Mr. Hanover P. Smith, who wrote a book of appreciation of Mrs. Eddy, and Mr. Arthur Buswell also resided there. The house was run on the cooperative plan and the residents all used the parlors for receiving patients, each having his specified office hours.

On the front door of the house was affixed a silver plate bearing the inscription, "The Massachusetts Metaphysical College," and students soon began to overflow the parlors. They were attracted through the public services at which Mrs. Eddy usually presided, or through the accounts of her own or her students' healings which were frequently printed in the papers of Boston. Mrs. Eddy's classroom became the center and soul of the house. She was teaching two or three hours a day. Of the work of the college she bore the entire burden.

So much did she pour her genius into it that when its doors were finally closed in 1889 she wrote that the college drew its breath from her and, as the reason for closing it, asked who else could sustain the institute in its vital purpose on her retirement. No one had helped her carry on the work of teaching up to this time. Asa G. Eddy, it is true, taught two terms in Lynn; Dr. E. J. Foster-Eddy taught one term in Boston, and General Erastus N. Bates taught a class just before the institute was closed. But aside from this assistance, Mrs. Eddy taught all the classes that passed through the college during the eight years of its existence. Throughout this period there were more than fifty classes, not only for primary students, but also for those more advanced who wished to become teachers of Christian Science. The task was herculean, the work accomplished amazing, for in addition to the periodic classes she was teaching she was also lecturing every Thursday evening in the parlors of the college and preaching almost every Sunday. During the first few months of the year (1883) Mrs. Eddy was arranging for the establishment of the *Journal,* which made great demands upon her time.

The *Journal of Christian Science,* afterwards called *The Christian Science Journal,* made its first appearance April 14, 1883. The little magazine, destined to become the organ of the church, was at first an eight-page paper, issued every other month. It was an attractive publication from the first moment of its birth, and to-day those first numbers are so rare and so eagerly desired that the bound volumes are worth their weight in gold. In the prospectus Mrs. Eddy stated the purpose of the *Journal,* or rather her purpose in founding it. She said it was the desire of her heart "to bring to many a household hearth health, happiness and increased power to be good, and to do good"; and "to kindle all minds with a common sentiment of regard the new idea that comes welling up from infinite Truth needs to be understood."

It was not a great literary output in its first issues nor did it leap at once to financial self-sufficiency. Rather was it a shy, modest little pamphlet which required the sinking of a good deal of capital to get it on its legs, and it was a great drain on the attention of the founder. But it was seen at once that it had a sufficient *raison d'être.* It conveyed rare touches of sympathy for lives shut in, lives that were desolate, lives that had seemed to spell failure. It was not sent to the mighty or the learned, nor was it designed for such, but for the needy. It contained articles on how to keep well, on prayer as a spiritual aspiration, on sunshine in the home, on the folly of having nerves, the fallacy of that tired feeling, the abuse of will power. Its pages sparkled with witty sayings culled from great authors, and nuggets of gold from philosophic minings. It showed in every column the earnest, diligent work of its editor.

Some of the articles from Mrs. Eddy's pen in these early numbers have been reprinted in her book "Miscellaneous Writings," which have served as the stepping-stone to many of her followers in a comprehension of the text-book, "Science and Health with Key to the Scriptures." There is no doubt that her personality is revealed in them in more vivid colors than elsewhere. From time to time in the *Journal* appeared a poem from her hand, and from these devout versifications were chosen some which have become the best beloved hymns of the church.

Mrs. Eddy did not write the entire contents of the *Journal*, far from it; there were numerous excellent articles by her students and coworkers. But her impress is strongly visible, and in glancing through its pages one can almost see her at work at her desk, so direct and vital is the editorial contact. It is journalism which has the keen and bracing atmosphere that was felt in the old days from such great dailies as Horace Greeley's New York *Tribune*. To be sure it is journalism in a limited sphere and with its own direct appeal, but it is of that sort which brings into a home the highest sense of a socialized life.

The founding of the *Journal* proved to be one of the most effective moves Mrs. Eddy made in the establishment of Christian Science. The magazine could go cheaply where it would cost a great deal of money to send lecturers and practitioners. Moreover, it carried in a peculiar way the personal touch of the founder of Christian Science. And yet the *Journal* was in no sense a personal organ. To so style it is to confuse its aims with those of a political or biased publication. Its appeal was to the spiritual sense of the reader.

The *Journal's* history is singular in that it had a series of editors and publishers who fell away from Christian Science into strange apostasy. The first assistant manager, Arthur True Buswell, was expelled from the Christian Scientist Association. His case was a peculiar one and difficult to explain, for he has declared to the author that Christian Science in his opinion is the vital truth of the world. On March 1, 1883, Mr. Buswell was appointed to care for the advertising of the proposed paper.

Mrs. Emma Hopkins, wife of an Andover professor, was editor for a period from September, 1884, until March, 1885, and afterward assistant editor until the late autumn of 1885, her name first appearing in the *Journal* in February, 1884. Mrs. Hopkins was a student of Mrs. Eddy. She came to her in trouble and sickness. She was healed, taught, and provided with employment congenial to her mind. But after the most extravagant happiness in her new-found field of usefulness, she became the victim of a flattering woman from Detroit who came to study at the college. This woman was Mary H. Plunkett, known later in New York as an advocate of marriage by selection of soul affinity without regard to marriage and divorce laws. Mrs. Plunkett departed for New Zealand with her affinity, leaving her husband behind, and was later reported to have wearied of her companion or to have been deserted by him and to have experienced a tragic end.

This woman succeeded by flattery and cajolement in turning the head of Emma Hopkins. She told her she would make her the greatest woman on the planet and succeeded in making the Andover professor's wife believe herself a feminine genius whose name would go down the ages as another Hypatia. It was strange that a student could sit for two or three hours in a classroom under the spiritual teaching which led all into a rapt sense of the higher life, and then make her way to the office of a recognized malcontent, and there plot desertion and heresy.

However, it was so. Mrs. Hopkins left with Mrs. Plunkett for the West and began teaching a system of so-called metaphysics under her management in Detroit, Chicago, and other western cities. Her teaching was a perversion of the doctrine she had learned from the founder of Christian Science, though the perversion was at first so subtle that it was scarcely possible to detect it. It was, however, the old heresy of hypnotism clothing itself in religious terms. Under the tutelage of the clever *déclassée,* for such Mrs. Plunkett was known to have been in Detroit, it is not surprising that Mrs. Hopkins found the singularly pure ideals of Mrs. Eddy to appear reversed or that she was presently joining the chorus of Christian Science deserters in declaring her selfish and tyrannical. The two women published for a time a magazine which they called *The International Magazine of Christian Science,* a deceptive name which caused considerable annoyance to the management of the *Journal.*

In July, 1885, Mrs. Sarah H. Crosse became publisher and manager[1] and remained in that position until the appointment of Dr. Silas J. Sawyer in September, 1886. She too left Christian Science with a group of other students, some of whom departed from the Association in 1888 for the very strange reason that they desired to study medicine. This disaffection will be spoken of in another chapter. The Rev. Frank Mason was at that time serving as manager. He later went to New York and founded a church in Brooklyn which was non-Christian Science. Mr. William G. Nixon[2] took the business management of the *Journal* in 1889 and his apostasy will be described in connection with the building of The Mother Church. During that year Mr. Joshua Bailey was editor, and the year following Miss Sarah J. Clark of Toledo acted in this capacity,—both loyal students. Finally, in 1892, the charge of the *Journal* was assumed by Judge Septimus

[1] In January, 1883, Mrs. Crosse was appointed one of the Board of Directors of the Christian Scientists' Publishing Company. In March, 1883, she was made assistant to Mrs. Eddy, who was to be the editor of the proposed paper. Mrs. Crosse was a contributor to the pages of the *Journal* over the signature "X" for several years. In July, 1885, Mrs. Crosse became publisher and manager, continuing under Mr. James H. Wiggin, who became editor in January, 1886. At Mr. Wiggin's retirement the Rev. William I. Gill became editor. Mr. Gill's editorship was only from September through November, 1886. Mr. Wiggin then resumed this office and served until January, 1889. From December, 1886, to July, 1888, The Christian Science Publishing Company was the publisher of the *Journal.* Mr. Mason served as manager from August, 1888, to August, 1889.

[2] See footnote, p. 328.

J. Hanna, who stood like a rock and for ten years edited it with ability and discretion. He was relieved of his duties in 1902 that he might become active in the lecture field, and Mr. Archibald McLellan of Chicago was then appointed editor.

During all these years the little magazine, in spite of precarious storms, under the masterly superguidance of Mrs. Eddy, grew into a powerful organ for the church. In its early days its life was more than once threatened by such sinister means as the publication of a counterfeit which just escaped the infringement of copyright. But of the use of copyrights Mrs. Eddy had been wisely educated by both investigation and experience. It was in 1883, shortly after founding the *Journal*, that she exercised her knowledge of the law in this respect and brought to an end the encroachments of Edward J. Arens which have been previously referred to.

Mrs. Eddy sued Arens for infringement of copyrights by filing a bill in equity in the United States Circuit Court at Boston in April, 1883. Arens filed an answer in which he alleged that the copyrighted works of Mrs. Eddy were not original with her, but had been copied by her, or by her direction, from manuscripts originally composed by Phineas Quimby. This extraordinary statement he was called upon to substantiate with proofs. He was unable to present the slightest evidence, since his appeals to George Quimby of Belfast, Maine, met with no response. Arens therefore gave notice to the court, through his counsel, that he would not submit testimony, that he had none to submit. Thus Arens' defense fell to the ground and his failure to prove the old and worn statement that Mrs. Eddy's book was Quimbyism became a veritable vindication of her authorship. The United States Court issued a perpetual injunction against Arens, restraining him from printing, publishing, selling, giving away, or distributing in any manner his pirated works under pain of a fine of $10,000. Furthermore, his printed books to the number of 3800 were "put under the edge of the knife and their unlawful existence destroyed." The costs of the suit which were $113 were taxed against Arens.

Thus the seal of the United States Court was put upon Mrs. Eddy's rights as an author, and those copyrights which Mr. Eddy secured in her name were never again disputed. This signal triumph came at a time when Mrs. Eddy needed such a perpetual guarantee from justice for her right of way. Having secured it, no one could again with propriety publicly or privately dispute her authoritative claim as discoverer of the science she was establishing.

CHAPTER XIX

THE WIDE HORIZON

THE modest appeal of *The Christian Science Journal* very early began to create results which were first apparent in the arrival of students from the West at the Metaphysical College in Boston. And no sooner had the first Western students returned to their homes than they began to insert their cards as practitioners in the *Journal,* and thereafter letters of inquiry poured in from Milwaukee and Chicago, and Mrs. Eddy's morning mail began to assume bulky proportions. She published a notice in the magazine referring the inquirers to her western students, but they were not to be satisfied with anything but information from headquarters.

Late in the year 1883 a pressing demand came from Chicago that a teacher of Christian Science be sent there — if Mrs. Eddy herself would not come. So manifold were the demands on Mrs. Eddy's time that the idea of a western trip seemed out of the question. Her correspondence, her classes, her Thursday evening lectures and Sunday morning sermons, to say nothing of the editing of the *Journal,* left her no time for the slightest recreation and seemed too imperative to be laid down for a fraction of an hour. Conducting a class in Chicago would mean a month's absence. In the emergency she looked about her for a suitable and capable person to send out to the Macedonia of the West.

THE MASSACHUSETTS METAPHYSICAL
COLLEGE

One of a series of gray stone residences
on Columbus Avenue, Boston, occupied by Mrs. Eddy in 1882

Among the names that suggested themselves to her was that of Mrs. Clara Choate, a student who had occasionally taken her place in the pulpit and who had performed excellent work as a practitioner and teacher. But when she broached the subject to Mrs. Choate she found her unwilling to go. Mrs. Choate had a large practise in Boston, her home ties seemed strong. She had living with her an aged parent and her child was in school. Mrs. Eddy recognized the weight of the objection and did not urge the request upon her, but it became something for discussion among the students that Clara Choate was at variance with her teacher. A situation not exactly harmonious appeared to be arising. To dispel this Mrs. Eddy called together the students resident in her house for a prayerful consideration of the duties of all and their obligations to her as faithful disciples. She foresaw that the work was growing with such giant strides that faithfulness to duty must be exacted and yielded if the call for missionaries was to be answered.

It was not possible for Mrs. Eddy to call a conference in this somewhat overeager community of students without enormous significance attaching itself to the occasion. Realizing this, she requested the students of the house to regard the meeting for counsel as a private meeting, and directly the name Private Meeting was coined. The Private Meeting society, or the "P. M.," as it was immediately dubbed, became talked about among the students outside the house who felt that something was being planned from which they were to be excluded. The P. M. society met but twice, but so widely was its existence discussed that Mrs. Eddy was obliged four years later to write an account of its deliberations. She related that the meetings had considered two topics, first, "There is no Animal Magnetism"; second, "God is All; there is none beside Him." These topics were given out without instructions and the students who joined in the meeting were expected quietly to treat the disharmony in their midst.

"If harm could come from the consideration of these two topics," Mrs. Eddy wrote, "it was because of the misconception of those subjects in the mind that handled them. . . . I dissolved the society, and we have not met since." [1]

In April Mrs. Eddy decided that she herself would go in response to the increasingly urgent call from the West. She temporarily handed over the *Journal* to Mrs. Hopkins, arranged for a suspension of her Thursday night lectures, and provided for certain of her students to take the services in her absence. Class work in the college was likewise suspended. The arrangements for the journey were left to Mr. Frye, who was to travel with her as secretary while Mrs. Sarah Crosse attended her as a companion. She spent a month in Chicago teaching a class in a private house on the West Side. Double parlors were taken for the class work, besides the suite of rooms engaged for her party.

Students came from towns outside of Chicago as well as from various parts of the city. The parlors soon proved inconveniently small, but the work was successful for her teaching met with enthusiasm. The

1 "Miscellaneous Writings," p. 350.

great Christian Science movement of the West resulted from that early visit of Mrs. Eddy, a visit un-
dertaken in such perplexity as this call, colliding with
her stress of work, had brought about. But by business punctiliousness and executive command she had
been able to lay down the duties which had at first
seemed imperative of personal direction. Few of her
followers could then understand the amazing fortitude
this required. But the western field in the years following justified its demand upon her time. Its response was an abundant harvest of idealism in the
midst of vaunting materialism.

When she returned to Boston it was with vision
rested by that far horizon which was presently to
stretch to the Pacific. Some two years later there
appeared in the *Journal* this notice: "The California
Metaphysical Institute affords an opportunity on the
Pacific Coast for receiving a course of instruction in
the rudiments of Christian Science. Those desiring
to enter a class, or to obtain further information, will
address Sue Ella Bradshaw, C. S. B., San José, California." [1] And one month later a similar card advertised the establishment of the Illinois Christian
Science Institute, incorporated, at Chicago. This was
but the beginning of what rapidly grew into a network
of academies and institutes for the dissemination of
her doctrine.

When the church showed signs of outgrowing its
Boston and New England environment it became nec-

---

[1] Miss Sue Ella Bradshaw, C. S. B., of San Francisco, studied with Mrs.
Eddy at the College in Boston in the fall of 1885. In the spring of 1886 she took
the Normal course at the College and later began her teaching in California.

essary to look to the needs of the field at large. Mrs.
Eddy realized this need almost before it was apparent,
certainly before it was obvious to other eyes than hers.
She had done everything hitherto to promulgate her
doctrine; now it was forced upon her that she must
safeguard it from adulteration and heresy. In her
very first class in Chicago there arose a mind to lead a
rebellion. Mrs. Ursula Gestefeld was the student who
subsequently led a movement of mental scientists in
the Western city, and her innovation, counterfeiting
the teaching she had received, was but a type of what
might and did occur in other localities.

"For many successive years," Mrs. Eddy writes,
"I have endeavored to find new ways and means for
the promotion and expansion of scientific Mind-healing, seeking to broaden its channels and, if possible,
to build a hedge round about it that should shelter its
perfections from the contaminating influences of those
who have a small portion of its letter and less of its
spirit. At the same time I have worked to provide a
home for every true seeker and honest worker in this
vineyard of Truth.

"To meet the broader wants of humanity, and
provide folds for the sheep that were without shep-
herds, I suggested to my students, in 1886, the propriety of forming a National Christian Scientist Association. This was immediately done, and delegations
from the Christian Scientist Association of the Massachusetts Metaphysical College, and from branch associations in other States, met in general convention at
New York City, February 11, 1886." [1]

1 "Retrospection and Introspection," p. 52.

Thus Mrs. Eddy describes how, from her address to the association in Boston which held its tenth annual meeting on January sixth of that year at the college building, the action was immediately taken to carry out her views and wishes for the associations in other cities to be drawn into a unity of purpose. On February eleventh the first regular meeting of the national association was held in New York City with delegates present from Boston and Chicago. This national association held four subsequent meetings and was of tremendous aid in the formative period of the church. It held its second meeting in Boston, its third meeting in Chicago, its fourth meeting in Cleveland, and its final meeting in New York, when Mrs. Eddy requested its members to adjourn for an indefinite period. She had then other plans for the church which unfolded successfully and harmoniously.

It was somewhat in consequence of the forming of the national association, somewhat from the gradual missionary work of the *Journal*, and largely because of the healing work of the students, who went out from the college month after month, that the Christian Science doctrine spread to every part of the country. This book is not a history of the Christian Science movement, hence it is not within its province to show how it came about that thirty academies were in existence in 1888. But so it was, and these schools were in Colorado, Kansas, California, Iowa, Nebraska, New York, the District of Columbia, Pennsylvania, Illinois, Wisconsin, Ohio, Missouri, and Kentucky.

This inspiring growth of adherents in all parts of the country did not result instantaneously or miracu-

lously from Mrs. Eddy's visit to Chicago, but grew
with a healthy, sturdy activity during the four years
intervening between the spring of 1884 and 1888.
Mrs. Eddy was meantime faithfully pursuing her work
at the college on Columbus Avenue. Her house became the center of much interest and was for several
years a very notable residence in Boston. It was substantial without being pretentious, its arrangement
was typical of modern city residences and Mrs. Eddy
relaxed somewhat the rigid order of its furnishings
as the months passed and her financial resources were
more abundant and secure. On the first floor was a
suite of parlors continuous with a small reception-
room. These rooms could all be thrown together by
opening sliding doors, and this was done on Thursday
nights when the curious Boston literary folk came to
hear the new doctrine. For, had they not read what
Bronson Alcott said of this new teacher of metaphysics, and was not Bronson Alcott a prophet to
be heeded? [1]

So it became a common question in the drawing-
rooms of the eighties, "Have you met Mrs. Eddy, have
you heard her lecture, have you been to her college?"
And to Mrs. Eddy's home came many distinguished
persons during the years from 1884 to 1887. It was
not then so difficult a matter to meet the founder of
Christian Science as it became later. One had only to

---

[1] "The sacred truths which you announce sustained by facts of the
Immortal Life, give to your work the seal of inspiration—reaffirm in modern
phrase, the Christian revelations. In times like ours so sunk in sensualism,
I hail with joy any voice speaking an assured word for God and Immortality.
And my joy is heightened the more when I find the blessed words are of
woman's divinings."—*Bronson Alcott in a letter to Mary Baker Eddy, dated
Concord, Mass., January 17, 1876.*

ring her bell and state his purpose of inquiry to a student on duty, and as soon as Mrs. Eddy could lay aside the work of the moment she would come to the reception-room, a kindly and sympathetic hostess with the rare charm of perfect composure through which shone a radiant readiness to believe the highest and best and noblest of whoever presented himself. Among such callers and inquirers into her teaching was Louisa M. Alcott, author of "Little Women." This woman, since crowned with literary laurels and embalmed for the future with a fame all her own, went one day, as was related by a literary woman of Boston, to meet Mrs. Eddy and learn of her doctrine from her own lips. Although the famous children's classic appears in harmony with Christian Science, the lady who described this visit, herself then an associate editor of a journal and of wide literary acquaintance, commented on the incident of the visit thus: "But Miss Alcott, though her father was a transcendentalist and some years before had more than half avowed a faith in the new system of metaphysics, did not take to it. She was of a very practical, matter-of-fact mind. She had had enough of idealism and was determined to keep her feet upon terra firma. But she was impressed with Mrs. Eddy's personality." [1]

If Miss Alcott was impressed with her personality, she certainly did not correctly apprehend the doctrine, as she revealed her understanding of it in an article written for the *Woman's Journal*, a magazine devoted to woman's suffrage and conducted by Miss Alice Stone Blackwell. Mrs. Eddy replied to her arti-

---

[1] Katherine Conway, of *The Pilot*, in an interview.

cle in *The Christian Science Journal,* kindly pointing
out the difference between hypnosis and her own
teaching. It is interesting to note that Miss Blackwell
was herself a contributor to *The Christian Science
Journal* on the subject of suffrage in April, 1887.

In printing the article on woman suffrage in her
journal, in frequent references to the educational advancement of women, and in reviewing books on diverse subjects, Mrs. Eddy revealed a broad interest in
woman's work all over the world. She likewise maintained an active, alert interest in the sermons and public speeches of eminent men, and, either by herself or
through her editors, she reviewed philosophic treatises
that came from the press.

Of Madame Blavatsky and theosophy the *Journal*
had a year earlier printed an article which, while it
radically disagreed with theosophic occultism, gave
the Russian woman credit for broad scholarship. On
the other hand, in a review of a publication on George
Eliot's essays and verse by Rose Elizabeth Cleveland,
Mrs. Eddy praises Miss Cleveland for her felicity as
an editor and in a genuine outburst of sincere appreciation of the great English novelist declares her womanly and heroic with "firm, unfaltering adherence to
honest conviction and conscientious reasonableness.
. . . Her metaphysics purge materialism with a single
sentence," declares Mrs. Eddy, quoting the sentence
as follows: "One may know all that is to be known
about matter and nothing that needs to be known
about man."

Lilian Whiting, author of "The World Beautiful," then a Boston journalist and correspondent for

western papers, described a visit to Mrs. Eddy in an
article for the Ohio *Leader,* dated July 2, 1885. As
Miss Whiting was not a Christian Scientist her description is edifying as to how Mrs. Eddy appeared to
the casual visitor of those days. Miss Whiting wrote
that her note requesting permission to call was replied
to with a courteous invitation to do so at an hour
named. She continues:

"Accordingly at eight o'clock on that evening I
rang the bell of the large and handsome residence on
Columbus Avenue near West Chester Park, known as
the Metaphysical College. A maid ushered me into a
daintily furnished reception-room where pictures and
bric-a-brac indicated refinement and taste. Presently
Mrs. Eddy came in and greeted me with a manner
that, while cordial and graceful, was also something
more, and had in it an indefinable element of harmony; and a peace that was not mere repose, but
more like exaltation. It was subtle and indefinable,
however, and I did not think of it especially at the
time, although I felt it. The conversation touched
lightly on current topics and finally recurred to the
subject of metaphysical cure."

Describing her singular experience as a result of
the call, she says: "I remembered afterwards how
extremely tired I was as I walked rather wearily and
languidly up the steps to Mrs. Eddy's door. I came
away, as a little child friend of mine expressively says,
'skipping.' I was at least a mile from the Vendome and
I walked home feeling as if I were treading on air. My
sleep that night was the rest of Elysium. If I had been
caught up into paradise, it could hardly have been a

more wonderful renewal." Miss Whiting continues as though loath to cease the description and, with many adjectives, dwells on her "exalted state," the "marvelous elasticity of mind and body," and "an utterly unprecedented buoyancy and energy I was feeling." She then remembers to state that all this was the result of a half hour's conversation on metaphysics with "the most famous mind-curer of the day."

Such were some of Mrs. Eddy's experiences with the sisterhood of writers who now rendered grave or excited appreciation and anon intellectual disparagement. But whether they were critical or effusive of praise, Mrs. Eddy never turned one of them away, or refused an audience to any inquirer. To doctors, clergymen, and philosophers she gave intellectual attention and while she lived in the world of affairs, she lived in it broadly, deeply, generously, acting her own part as a leader wisely, but yielding courteous consideration to all other leaders in whatever movement and without regard to sex.

The increasing number of her students, their teaching and healing in the wider field, now opening up for the establishment of the new church, created an ever-increasing demand for her text-book, "Science and Health with Key to the Scriptures." The book had been through fifteen editions, and there were therefore fifteen thousand copies in circulation, but letters came to her from the West complaining that the book was not obtainable. It was necessary to put forth a fresh edition, and Mrs. Eddy determined to revise the book and give to it the benefit of her experience in elucidating many of its statements.

On her return from the visit to Chicago she did not take up the active editorship of the *Journal,* but contented herself with supervising its columns, applying herself in all spare moments to the rewriting of Science and Health. For many months she worked on the manuscript and by summer, 1885, she had prepared a completed first draft. This manuscript contained all the essential matter of the earlier editions, — as a comparison will show, — but it had been amplified and clarified and given illuminating touches throughout by Mrs. Eddy's higher unfoldment in metaphysical understanding.

Having completed the first draft of her work, Mrs. Eddy engaged the Rev. James Henry Wiggin to read the manuscript with a view to indexing it and also to preparing it for the printer with the privilege of making proper technical emendations such as are usually given all manuscripts by the editors of a publishing house. Mr. Wiggin was a man whom many Boston authors had employed for such work, and, because of his reputation for honor and ability, she believed that her book might be entrusted to his hands without fear that he would overstep his privilege and tamper with its subject-matter or context. Such proved to be the character of his workmanship.

Mr. Wiggin was a prominent figure in Boston literary circles during the eighties and nineties. He was a retired Unitarian clergyman and for a time an editor for the University Press. While he was, in a sense, a man of the world, that is to say, a social fraternizer with the literary, musical, and artistic Bohemia of two continents, — for he traveled somewhat in Europe,—he was a man of character and enjoyed the friendship of men highly esteemed. John Wilson and Edward Everett Hale were his friends.

It is difficult to understand why the claim was made that Mr. Wiggin practically rewrote Science and Health. Those at the printers, University Press, knew otherwise; and Mr. Wiggin, himself, was amused at the claim. It may be sincerely doubted if he would have considered it honorable to strike so vitally at the integrity of any writer for whom he had worked as to cast a doubt upon the product of his mind. Even to make the claim of polishing and giving style to a writer's expression is, as it were, to assert that he has something to say and does not know how to say it. The fact that Mrs. Eddy's book had gone through fifteen editions before Mr. Wiggin came on the scene proved that she both had something to say and knew how to say it.

Mr. Wiggin used the pseudonym Phare Pleigh in writing for *The Christian Science Journal*, and it is doubtful if Mr. Wiggin would think it fair play to print his personal letters after his death. He was a friend of Mrs. Eddy, though never a convert to Christian Science, and being a man of the world, he expressed himself on the subject of the new religion at various times in various ways according to his mood and the character of the friend he was with. But what Mr. Wiggin thought as to Mrs. Eddy's authorship he expressed in an extensive review published in 1886 entitled "Christian Science and the Bible." In this review the following passage occurs:

"Now in this century there has arisen a sect called

Christian Scientists. Their founder and corner-stone is Mrs. Mary Baker Glover Eddy. Born in Concord,[1] New Hampshire, and afterwards a resident of Sanbornton[2] and Lynn, she has been for several years a resident of Boston, where she is pastor of the Church of Christ, Scientist. She is also president of the Massachusetts Metaphysical College, a school of the prophets whose students are taught Mrs. Eddy's views as they are set forth in Science and Health, a book which she first published ten years ago, and which has since passed through many editions, though she practised and taught the Science years before the book was printed or the college established."

Through a period of four years Mr. Wiggin wrote many articles for *The Christian Science Journal* and he used his brain and talents in its defense, taking up the cudgels against clergymen in all parts of the country who essayed in sermon or magazine article to ridicule the new faith. Is it necessary to assume that he was acting the part of a hypocrite or merely enjoying a tilt with professional theologians under his pseudonym like a masked knight at a medieval tournament?

It is possible that he was more strongly attracted to Christian Science than some of his worldly associates knew. In one of his articles in the *Journal*, "Heard at the Clubs," he tells how a political discussion in which he was interested was interrupted by a reference to Christian Science and how an editor, an actor, and others testified to its benefits to the astonishment of a noted literary divine from Great Britain. He declared, "The talk everywhere turns on Chris-

1Actually, Bow; 2Sanbornton Bridge, now Tilton.

tian Science and whoever has met the founder has been impressed with her integrity of purpose." His various articles and editorials may be found in volumes three through six of the *Journal*.

Men of great parts have elsewhere and often been attracted to a cause, served it for a time earnestly and faithfully, and then fallen away from it. But in such instances it is seldom asserted that they gave it its life blood and then grew ashamed of it and ridiculed it. Such men do not give life blood to anything. They may be clever and gifted, but they are never the inspiration of a movement.

After Mr. Wiggin had proofread Mrs. Eddy's revision it appeared as the sixteenth edition of her book and was announced in the *Journal* for January, 1886: "Attention is called to this volume. It is worth the notice, not only of Christian Scientists, but of all who are interested in the progress of truth. It is from the University Press, Cambridge, and this is a guaranty for its typographical appearance. All the material of the other editions is herein retained; but all of it has been carefully revised and rewritten by Mrs. Eddy, and greatly improved. The arrangement of the chapters has been changed. One new chapter has been added, on the Apocalypse, giving an exposition of the bearings on Christian Science of the twelfth chapter of Revelation, to which it is believed by Mrs. Eddy to particularly relate. A special feature is a full Index, prepared especially for this edition by a competent gentleman. In these days no important book has any right to come before the public without a proper Index."

When four years later Mrs. Eddy was preparing another major revision she again had the benefit of Mr. Wiggin's literary training in proofreading the fiftieth edition. She paid him fittingly for his work and cherished a kindly regard for him. It is regrettable that a revelation of his personal vanity as shown in private correspondence should have been given to the world in recent pamphlets — since vanity and egotism are common weaknesses shared in some degree by all mankind. In a playful protest against his learned profundities exhibited on one occasion in a philosophic review printed in the *Journal*, Mrs. Eddy wrote:[1] "Now, Phare Pleigh evidently means more than 'hands off.' A live lexicographer, given to the Anglo-Saxon tongue, might add to the above definition the 'laying on of hands,' as well. Whatever his *nom de plume* means, an acquaintance with the author justifies one in the conclusion that he is a power in criticism, a big protest against injustice; but, the best may be mistaken."[2]

[1] See also "Miscellaneous Writings," p. 216.

[2] "It is a great mistake to say that I employed the Rev. James Henry Wiggin to correct my diction. It was for no such purpose. I engaged Mr. Wiggin so as to avail myself of his criticisms of my statement of Christian Science, which criticisms would enable me to explain more clearly the points that might seem ambiguous to the reader.

"Mr. Calvin A. Frye copied my writings, and he will tell you that Mr. Wiggin left my diction quite out of the question, sometimes saying, 'I wouldn't express it that way.' He often dissented from what I had written, but I quieted him by quoting corroborative texts of Scripture.

"My diction, as used in explaining Christian Science, has been called original. The liberty that I have taken with capitalization, in order to express the 'new tongue,' has well-nigh constituted a new style of language. In almost every case where Mr. Wiggin added words, I have erased them in my revisions.

"Mr. Wiggin was not my proofreader for my book 'Miscellaneous Writings,' and for only two of my books. I especially employed him on 'Science and Health with Key to the Scriptures,' because at that date some critics de-

With Mrs. Eddy's own gentleness of characterization and generosity of appreciation, Mr. Wiggin may fall into his rightful place in the story of her life as an aid and not a marplot, and his memory need not be stigmatized with the reproach of literary caddishness.

During August, 1888, Mrs. Eddy visited Fabyans, New Hampshire, staying several days at the White Mountain House. Her student, Mrs. Janette E. Weller, traveled with her. She gave an informal address at the Fabyan House to the summer guests, who gathered from various resorts in the mountains when they learned that she was sojourning a few days at this hotel. She afterward withdrew with her secretary and traveling companion to the farm of Ira O. Knapp for a few days of quiet. She had just closed an eventful year in which she had formulated the subject-matter of a new book, written during the winter and put forth in May, 1888, changed her residence, and paid an eventful visit to Chicago.

"Unity of Good and Unreality of Evil" was advertised in these words in the *Journal*: "This little book is at last ready for the public. Next to 'Science and Health' it is the most important work she has written." And it remains to-day the most important because of its absolute metaphysics. Her entire list

---

clared that my book was as ungrammatical as it was misleading. I availed myself of the name of the former proofreader for the University Press, Cambridge, to defend my grammatical construction, and confidently awaited the years to declare the moral and spiritual effect upon the age of 'Science and Health with Key to the Scriptures.' . . .

"I hold the late Mr. Wiggin in loving, grateful memory for his high-principled character and well-equipped scholarship." [See Miscellany, p. 317.]

MARY BAKER EDDY

Pleasant View, Concord, New Hampshire, Nov. 20, 1906.

— Statement printed in the *New York American*, November 22, 1906.

of publications in that year included "Science and
Health with Key to the Scriptures," "Unity of Good,"
"Christian Healing," "People's Idea of God," "Chris-
tian Science, No and Yes," "Mind Healing, an His-
torical Sketch," and "Rudiments and Rules of Divine
Science."

It was becoming well-nigh impossible for Mrs.
Eddy to have even an hour of her waking time to herself for the purpose of meditation, deliberation, or
consideration of the larger plans that were now imperative. How "Unity of Good" was written is a
mystery, for while she lived at the college whoever
sought her had but to knock on her door. The large
chamber over the parlors at the college was more of a
library, a study, an office, than a quiet chamber for
rest. Her door was thronged from early morning until
late at night, and the uselessness of such distraction
was that the most insistent besiegers were those with
the least important business.

For such reasons, and because the field actually
demanded her wisest deliberations, Mrs. Eddy took
steps to remove from the college building. During
the Christmas season of 1887 she left Columbus Avenue to reside in a house she had purchased at 385 Commonwealth Avenue. This was the first house she had
owned since the Broad Street house in Lynn, for she
leased the college building at a rental of one thousand
dollars annually. Her new home was on the outskirts
of Boston, overlooking from the rear in those days the
Charles River and fronting on a boulevard parkway
where stands to-day the superb Anne Whitney statue
of Leif Ericsson. The house included twenty beauti-

ful rooms. It was fitted up suitably, though not extravagantly, and Mrs. Eddy established herself here with her secretary and her companion. Her life was fixed by a very punctilious order; she wrote at certain hours, received at certain hours, attended the college to teach her classes, and began to take the daily drive which was to be the only recreation she insisted upon from that time until her earthly departure.

The West was calling for her again. Letters which poured in told her that she must go out to the field once more. The National Christian Scientist Association was to meet in Chicago in 1888, and Mrs. Eddy determined to deal with all her students' needs and wants at that focal point and meet them for the purpose of satisfying their insistent claims upon her attention. In order that the occasion might be a gratifying one to the entire field, and that the church might be renewed and refreshed for its pioneer work, Mrs. Eddy issued a call for this convention which was printed in the *Journal* for June. She said:

Christian Scientists: For Christ's and for humanity's sake, gather together, meet *en masse*, at the annual session of the National Christian Scientist Association. Be "of one mind, in one place," and God will pour you out a blessing such as you never before received. He who dwelleth in eternal light is bigger than the shadow, and will guard and guide His own. Let no consideration bend or outweigh your purpose to be in Chicago on June 13.

This call was not without its effect. Hundreds journeyed to Chicago to attend what was anticipated as a "week's jubilee of spirit." It was the first great gathering of Christian Scientists from many parts of the United States. The knowledge had gone abroad that Mrs. Eddy would herself attend the convention, and this served to draw together not only the students who had graduated from her classes, but also hundreds who had been healed by her students and who wished to know more of her philosophy. Mrs. Eddy made the journey accompanied by Captain and Mrs. Eastaman, and her secretary Calvin Frye. Dr. E. J. Foster, a young physician who had studied with her, and whom she afterwards legally adopted as her son, joined the party in Chicago.

The national association held its business meetings in the First Methodist Church of Chicago, then situated on Washington and Clark Streets. On the second day the convention assembled at Central Music Hall for a program of addresses to be delivered by practising students. The doors being opened to the public, much to the astonishment of the eight hundred delegates, there assembled an audience of about four thousand, among whom were many prominent Chicagoans, for the newspapers had not failed to advertise the fact that the Boston prophetess, as they chose to call her, was in the city. All unaware of the curiosity her coming had aroused, Mrs. Eddy attended the meeting, expecting to occupy a seat upon the platform among her students, but to take no part in the program. Her purpose was to greet and cheer her students.

Destiny was not to have it so. The Rev. George B. Day, pastor of the Church of Christ (Scientist) in Chicago, had decided to introduce her as the speaker of the day, and on his own authority had inserted a notice in the papers that she would make an address. As he led Mrs. Eddy through the anteroom to escort her to the stage, he acquainted her with his purpose. His fear that she would refuse to accede had led him to delay telling her until the last moment before she stepped upon the platform. A student much beloved of Mrs. Eddy, who was standing near the door, saw her protest with an outward sweep of her hand and a slow negative shake of the head, and declare with emphasis that she was in no way prepared to speak. The clergyman, all excitement and nervousness, persisted and Mrs. Eddy halted for a moment on the threshold of the stage and lifted her eyes as though for inspiration and guidance. A newspaper report of what followed says:

Without a subject selected and without notes she entered the platform when, as by some preconcerted plan, the whole vast audience rose to its feet and welcomed her. She walked to the center of the stage and after being introduced recited the first verse of the ninety-first psalm and in the address which followed her voice filled that immense auditorium so that those most remote from her could hear distinctly.

The address thus delivered without preparation, outline, or text has been pronounced by many of her students to be one of the greatest statements of Christian Science ever made from a rostrum. Like Lincoln's great unreported speech, delivered in Bloomington, it came upon the delegates as a surprise, and so spellbound were the hearers that the very reporters forgot to take notes. It was inadequately reported, and though the substance of it was sent out to the

papers, and was printed in the *Journal*, and the report
was subsequently reprinted in "Miscellaneous Writings" under the subject, Science and the Senses, it is
certain that something of the spirit of her utterances
was lost in the transcription, for the amazing effect of
her address cannot entirely be understood from reading it to-day.

When she ceased speaking, the scenes which immediately followed were intensely dramatic, extraordinary, unprecedented. In the audience were many
who had been healed from grievous illnesses by reading her book, and scarcely any of her hearers but
had known of marvelous cures; hence the audience
was anticipating a miraculous wave of health and it
received it at flood-tide. Whatever had been on the
program was forgotten for the time, swept aside by an
impetuous forward rush of that audience to the platform, indifferent to the chairman's attempts to get
a hearing.

It was well Mrs. Eddy was elevated above the
throng or she would have been borne down by it. As
it was, men leaped to the stage and assisted women
to follow. They wanted to take her hand, to tell
her of wonderful healings, to touch her dress if
nothing more. A babble of rejoicing broke forth
above which came the cries of many who were
crowded to the rear, beseeching attention to themselves. A mother who failed to get near held high
her babe, an old woman held up palsied hands, crying, "Help me!" Some persons declared the address
had healed them spontaneously. Men and women
wept together.

So carried away by the tide of emotion as to neglect details, the newspaper correspondent who reported these events for a Boston paper declared simply that many were healed there and then. As a matter of fact the cases verified were actually eleven. The Boston *Traveler* reporter said that "the people thronged about Mrs. Eddy. . . . Meekly, and almost silently, she received all this homage from the multitude, until she was led away from the place, the throng blocking her passage from the door to the carriage."

While in Chicago Mrs. Eddy lived at the Palmer House, and access to her being easily gained, importunate callers besieged her doors. It was no part of her plan to hold a public reception in Chicago, or in fact to do anything of a public nature. Her amazement at the publicity thrust upon her left her without choice, and how to satisfy the sudden demand for personal greeting was a difficult question to decide. In the evening of the day on which she experienced such an ovation, she decided to go to the parlors for a short time to satisfy the persistent callers.

Learning of her decision, the hotel hurriedly decorated the rooms with a profusion of flowers, giving a festive and brilliant appearance for an impromptu reception. This was to prove a singular function. Men and women of wealth and fashion crowded and elbowed persons from the humblest walks of life. The parlors, the corridors, the stairways were thronged. When Mrs. Eddy came from her private suite and entered the drawing-room, the assemblage almost immediately lost its head in one concerted, intense desire to touch the hand of the woman who had so eloquently

preached God's love as to make the sick well at the
sound of her voice. They pressed forward upon her
regardless of each other. Silks and laces were torn,
flowers crushed, and jewels lost. Mrs. Eddy drew
back from the pressure of humanity and as she looked
upon the flushed faces she seemed to shrink within
herself, as if asking, "What came you here to see?"
She turned to her secretary and companion for assistance and almost immediately withdrew by a side
door. When the company learned that she had withdrawn they gradually and disappointedly dispersed.

From such scenes Mrs. Eddy had always shrunk
with peculiar sensitiveness. As she had told her students when first coming to Boston, she now reiterated
to her immediate helpers, "Christian Science is not
forwarded by these methods." Months later in Stein-
way Hall, New York City, Mrs. Eddy had a similar experience. There the audience was requested to file by
her across the stage, and obedience to the request was
enforced by the ushers. In the confusion of the reception, however, strange scenes occurred. Faithful students were startled to see Mrs. Mary H. Plunkett press
forward, take Mrs. Eddy's hand, and leaning forward,
dramatically kiss her cheek. Thus she publicly associated herself with the teacher whose work she had
misrepresented and whose trust she had betrayed.

Public functions and such scenes of worldly ambition had much to do with a resolve which was growing in Mrs. Eddy's mind to withdraw entirely from
public life that the adulation of her personality might
cease and the truth she taught have opportunity to
make its way through the work of her students.

CHAPTER XX

WITHDRAWAL FROM THE WORLD

WHILE the "jubilee of spirit" was being celebrated in Chicago during June, 1888, a quite different order of mental activity was causing fomentation in the Christian Scientist Association at Boston. Some of Mrs. Eddy's students had become inoculated with the theories of Mr. Julius Dresser and Dr. Warren F. Evans. Both of these men had been patients of Quimby during the early sixties and both undertook to establish systems of healing. Both men printed and issued books on mental science. They attracted a small following which in later days came to be known as the New Thought movement.

It was not so much the teaching of these writers on mental suggestion which attracted Mrs. Eddy's students,—for those who had passed through her classes well knew that mental suggestion and Christian Science were as divergent as a chimeric dream and a scientific discovery,—but rather was it the thought that they might carry Christian Science itself outside the walls of its citadel and become writers and teachers and leaders among the philistines. Christian Science within the fold was too stringent in its demands. Not satisfied with manna, they would return to the flesh-pots of Egypt. The meat desired was intellectual divertissement; not only that, they would handle the things of God with more careless ease and

roll the jewels of the temple upon the street for the
delectation of the curious.

Thus it was that a group of rebels had coalesced
within the Christian Scientist Association. They were
not without examples for their dereliction. The group
of students who departed from the church in Lynn had
preceded them by seven years and gone their ways.
Others, too, had left the movement. Mrs. Plunkett,
Mrs. Hopkins, Mrs. Gestefeld, had emulated Kennedy, Spofford, and Arens. But these examples were
not edifying as solutions of the problem of finding
happiness by returning to intellectual speculation
after avowing allegiance to a spiritual ideal. Therefore this new group of Christian Science deserters
would find a more plausible reason for their conduct.

In order that they might manage their departure
without the shame of expulsion they took advantage
of the absence of Mrs. Eddy and the secretary of the
Association, William B. Johnson, to possess themselves of the Association's books. These they placed
in a lawyer's hands and notified Mrs. Eddy on her return from Chicago that the books would not be surrendered until they had received an honorable dismissal from the Association. Expulsion, they felt,
would be dishonorable, carrying with it the implication of unworthiness.

While the unmannerly abstraction of the Association's books was the *modus operandi* of their rebellion, the *casus belli* announced was the Corner case.
In the spring of 1888 Mrs. Abby H. Corner, a student
and member of the Association, had attended her
daughter in childbirth and the accouchement termi-

nated fatally to both mother and child. Mrs. Corner was prosecuted for malpractise by the state but was acquitted when the facts were brought out that the cause of death was one which a medical practitioner could not have averted, namely hemorrhage. Certain members of the Association disagreed with Mrs. Eddy in respect to the propriety of certain proceedings relative to Mrs. Corner's defense.

Although Mrs. Eddy did not approve of her students' taking charge of the surgical part of obstetrical work unless they were surgeons or midwives duly qualified by the state requirements, she did not desert her student in time of trouble, and although the Association paid Mrs. Corner's expenditures for defense, — a matter of two hundred dollars, — the disagreement over the Corner case was what the restless element in the Boston church needed for a plausible excuse to seek the world and its freedom, and to desert the pure ideality of the fundamental statement of Christian Science found in the scientific statement of being. Mrs. Eddy did not engage in any spiritual wrestling with these rebellious students, though she did ask them to come to her in Christian love and state their grievances to her personally. As none of them did so, they were eventually dismissed, thirty-six members going out of a congregation of about two hundred.

Although their tactics had been successful in securing the so-called letters of dismissal, after their expulsion the seceding students declared they had considered a plan for expelling Mrs. Eddy from her own church and the Christian Scientist Association. However, the points held by Mrs. Eddy on this occa-

sion and with which the belligerent students disagreed
are to-day reckoned among the common-sense practises
of Christian Science, and this incident is an example of
the numerous instances where the short-sightedness of
the pupil has attempted to brush aside the more ma-
ture and accurate judgment of the teacher, and where
Mrs. Eddy proved her worth as the Leader of the
Christian Science movement. With such deep-boring
desire to explode the citadel of Christian Science faith
and blow into the heavens its foundation stones, the
insurrectionists would have accomplished destruction
had it been in human power to do so, and the dust of
centuries might again have settled over the spiritual
revelation, as Spofford had once foretold would be the
result if Christian Science were demolished.

"Under divine Providence there can be no acci-
dents,"[1] Mrs. Eddy says in Science and Health, and
the rebellion in the Boston church in 1888 was no
more a fortuitous or calamitous occurrence than the
rebellion in Lynn which resulted in the transplanting
of the work to Boston, the establishment of the college and *Journal,* and the creation of the National
Christian Scientist Association. Mrs. Eddy had safe-
guarded the text-book of Christian Science by copyrights, and in the months in which she waited for the
culmination of the conspiracy in the Boston church
she turned over in her mind the many-sided problem
of safeguarding the organization. She was once more
submitting herself for divine guidance, and in the sacred secrecy of such communion was evolving a plan
by which security should be attained against explosive schism.   [1] Science and Health, p. 424.

Now the first step toward the masterly solution of this great problem of organization which confronted her was a loosening of all the bonds which apparently held her students together. With absolute reliance upon the underlying, irrevocable compact of Spirit, which constitutes the "church invisible," Mrs. Eddy dissolved the Association of her students in September. Then she closed the Metaphysical College and dissolved the organization of the Boston church.

She had discontinued teaching classes at the college in May, 1889, and on October 29 of that year she closed its doors. Its dissolution was accomplished after due deliberation and earnest discussion by a vote of the board of directors of the college corporation. In announcing its purpose the board presented to the public resolutions in which it thanked the state for its charter, the public for its patronage, and declared its everlasting gratitude to its president for her great and noble work. The teaching was henceforth to be done by the qualified students.

In "Retrospection and Introspection" Mrs. Eddy has given her clearly defined argument for this procedure and it is an unmistakable disclaimer of delight in personal success. She says: "The apprehension of what has been, and must be, the final outcome of material organization, which wars with Love's spiritual compact, caused me to dread the unprecedented popularity of my College. Students from all over our continent, and from Europe, were flooding the school. At this time there were over three hundred applications from persons desiring to enter the College, and applicants were rapidly increasing. Example had shown the dangers arising from being placed on earthly pinnacles, and Christian Science shuns whatever involves material means for the promotion of spiritual ends." [1]

It was the first way-mark of withdrawal. The dangers arising from personal adulation were in a thousand ways made apparent to Mrs. Eddy and the more she requested her students to look away from her and fix their eyes on Truth, the more she was made to feel that danger of apotheosis which desired to set her on "earthly pinnacles." Appealing to Cæsar seemed to be a fixed concept of a human sort among the students which required the most thorough-going denial. As the Romans would have made Nero a god, so the students seemed bent on making their spiritual leader a Cæsar of egotism, a peculiar reversal in human deduction. Mrs. Eddy finally was obliged to publish in the *Journal* the following notice: [2]

I shall not be consulted verbally or through letters as to the following: Whose advertisement shall or shall not appear in the *Journal*.

The matter that should be published in the *Journal*.

On marriage, divorce, or family affairs of any kind.

On the choice of pastors for churches.

On disaffections if there should be any between students of Christian Science.

On who shall be admitted as members or dropped from the membership of Christian Science churches.

On disease, or the treatment of the sick.

But I shall love all mankind and work for their welfare.

Each and every one of these disclaimers of absolutism was sincere; they were avowals of a stead-

1 "Retrospection and Introspection," p. 47.
2 *The Christian Science Journal*, September, 1890.

fast purpose to refuse to ascend a dictator's throne. If it had for a time seemed wise for her to direct and guide the affairs of the church and association, experience had shown her in no unmistakable way the misconstruction which wilful human perversion may place upon such direction. The rebellious students of 1888 had announced as one of their grievances the opinion that Mrs. Eddy was too arbitrary in the conduct of the Christian Scientist Association. Such a statement she received as a premonitory signal. It was a mailed hand threatening Love's dominion. Between those who would set her up and those who would drag her down, the founder of Christian Science stood serene in the consciousness of spiritual insight. She would not desert her post or be driven from it until she had led her students into the ways of self-direction.

But withdrawal was not desertion, and withdrawal more and more occupied her thoughts as a means to the end of establishing the impersonal guidance of the church. Certain personal and family matters crowded upon her for attention. She who had given so much to the world must consider somewhat her own affairs before taking up the problem, the great problem of the "church visible."

During the difficulties of 1888 which may be realized as the clamoring of hundreds of disappointed students who would have Mrs. Eddy to teach them and no other and the thirty-six rebellious students who would rend the Cause of Christian Science, George Glover, Mrs. Eddy's long-wandering son, was present in Boston with his wife and children. Mrs. Eddy had

seen her son but once before since he had been separated from her in his infancy. Having located him in
1879 in South Dakota, she had sent him a telegram requesting him to come to her. He was then a man
thirty-five years of age. He came to Boston and
visited her and Mr. Eddy at the home of the Choates
where she was then residing temporarily.

While on his brief visit to Boston, Mrs. Eddy had
studied the character of her long-alienated son with the
eyes of maternal solicitude, and also the detached sense
of independent individuality. Was this boy a Baker or
a Glover? Moreover, was he a teachable man? In rehearsing his experiences on this visit to his mother in
1879, Glover is said to have since related to a newspaper correspondent that for some strange reason his
mother would not hear of his returning to his western
home and that he stayed on for several weeks with her
while she endeavored to teach him Christian Science, — which he modestly acknowledged he "made
a mess of." But having heard considerable about
Richard Kennedy and his misuse of the science of
Mind, and feeling that Kennedy was harassing his
mother with false reports of her teaching, Glover one
day, without revealing his plans to his mother, visited
Kennedy's offices and, according to Glover's alleged
statement, threatened him with a revolver. According
to the newspaper which quotes Mr. Glover he declared
that he told Kennedy he knew of his "black art tricks"
to ruin his mother and he meant to stop him.

"Mother seemed very much surprised when I told
her what I had done," George Glover is said to have
stated in March, 1907, referring to the visit of 1879.

"But she did not scold me and in a few days she consented to let me return home to the West and to my wife and little son."

How clearly George Glover had shown to his mother after weeks of effort to educate him, to teach him Christian Science, the ungovernable, untameable spirit of the man of the plains, no one but himself had ever told, if indeed he did relate his experiences on his visit East as quoted. Richard Kennedy absolutely denied the occurrence. But whether George Glover did bully him or did not, and whether or not he recounted a fiction to his mother and later to the press, his nature is shown to have been alien to her nature, to have been impervious to her doctrine. Destiny still parted them with an insurmountable barrier. Hungering for the plains, restless for the saddle, his leathern holster bulging beneath his coat, his hand nervously seeking his hip at the slightest altercation, what could a woman of sixty do with a man of middle age, settled in his habits? Here was no longer the problem of mother and son. Authority and obedience were as a dead letter. Time had set its seal upon him as a man and an individual.

Departing for the West, he went over the great divide in human concepts for another nine years, but in 1887 sent his mother a characteristically casual note stating that he intended coming East to pay her a visit. In a letter which Glover says he received from his mother dated October 31, 1887, she replied to her son in words pregnant of her apprehensions with regard to his character. "I must have quiet in my home," she wrote, "and it will not be pleasant for

you in Boston." She told him that the Choates were
no longer with her. "You are not what I had hoped
to find you," she continued, "and I cannot have 'you
come. . . . The world, the flesh, and evil I am at
war with. . . . Boston is the last place in the world
for you or your family. When I retire into private
life, then I can receive you if you are reformed, but
not otherwise. I say this to you, not to any one else.
I would not injure you any more than myself."

But this letter which speaks volumes of maternal
regret appears to have had no effect in deterring
George Glover from seeking the mother whom he had
disregarded for years. She was now sixty-six years of
age, spiritualized by years of self-abnegation and religious devotion. He was in his forty-fourth year
and hardened in the ways of the flesh. He presented
himself with the confidence of filial relationship. Yes,
he was her son, and she received him as such. She
provided for him a residence in Chelsea. With his
children he visited her at her home and he attended
the church and was cordially received by its members.
Mrs. Eddy lovingly presented her son and his children
at the fair held in December, 1887, to raise funds for
building a church.

After several months of enjoying himself in the
reflected glory of his mother, George Glover with his
family again returned to the West. He had taken no
step to come to his mother's standard of life and she
had not urged him or repelled him. But she had
studied him and reflected on the joy it would have
been to her to have been able to find in him a son
fitted to carry out certain demands of her work. Such

reflection carried with it regret and finally resulted in an effort to find among her students one who could bear to her the relation of a dutiful, obedient, and worthy son, one who would perform the acts of filial respect and service that would insure her the nucleus of a spiritual household. In the enjoyment of such a home, quiet domesticity would take its natural course and as the years revolved she might withdraw to the heights of contemplation, putting off one by one the claims of the world.

Pursuing this idea in November, 1888, Mrs. Eddy legally adopted Dr. Ebenezer Johnson Foster in the Suffolk County (Massachusetts) Probate Court, stating as her reasons in the proceedings before Judge Mc-Kim that he was associated with her in business, home life, and life-work, and that she needed his interested care and relationship. The plea was granted and Dr. Foster added Eddy to his name and became her son. This effort toward parental relationship was not a success, and may be briefly set forth.

Dr. Foster came from a small town in Vermont. He was a graduate of the Hahnemann Medical College in Philadelphia and for two years a member of the clinics of the Blockley Hospital and of the Pennsylvania Hospital. He was later a member of the Vermont State Homeopathic Medical Society. Holding diplomas from both the regular and the homeopathic schools of medicine, he was attracted to Christian Science by the healing of a close friend who had been an old army comrade. He came to Boston an enthusiastic inquirer in the fall of 1887 and took a course of lessons under Mrs. Eddy's instruction at the college.

Before its close he taught one term in the college. Previous to his adoption he resided in her Commonwealth Avenue home together with other students. He was one of that group of intimate students among whom were Julia Bartlett, Calvin Frye, Captain and Mrs. Eastaman, and William B. Johnson.

Dr. Foster-Eddy was an agreeable and accomplished man of forty with a clear, well-trained mind and the enthusiasm for work which was so necessary in the multitudes of duties pressing upon all. He remained with Mrs. Eddy until 1896. In 1893 she made him her publisher when she removed William G. Nixon from that office. Dr. Foster-Eddy then lived at the Commonwealth Avenue house, though Mrs. Eddy was residing in Concord. Away from her personal influence, he was not as attentive to business as the requirements of his office demanded, and he indulged in certain fopperies which brought down upon him from other students scathing criticism not entirely unwarranted. It became necessary for Mrs. Eddy to remove him from the publishing business in the summer of 1896, when she made Joseph Armstrong, a former banker of Kansas, her publisher. Mr. Armstrong had been manager of The Christian Science Publishing Society since January 1, 1893.

Mrs. Eddy then directed Dr. Foster-Eddy to go to Philadelphia to carry out certain plans in the work of the church. She gave him a letter to present to the Philadelphia church and minute instructions, but he did not carry out her directions. As her personal agent he misrepresented her and became *persona non grata* in that city. The Philadelphia church wrote a

letter concerning him to Mrs. Eddy and she recalled
him, but he did not return to her at once. He first
went to Washington on a pleasure trip and finally
presented himself at Pleasant View, bursting with a
story of his fancied wrongs. Mrs. Eddy received him
in the library and heard him out; then she left him in
silence. He quitted the house and returned to Boston
where she sent him a letter of admonition, kindly
worded, but unmistakable in its rebuke. Instead of
returning to Pleasant View, Dr. Foster-Eddy went
West, traveled for a long time, and eventually returned to his old home in Vermont. Mrs. Eddy made
no charge against him, nor did she ask for an explanation. She did not, however, erase him from her memory
and in due time made monetary provision for him.

It was after the adoption of Dr. Foster that Mrs.
Eddy began looking about for a permanent home removed from Boston. In the early spring of 1889 Dr.
Foster persuaded her to go to Barre, Vermont, with a
view to spending the summer in the mountains. He
preceded her there and engaged a furnished house,
and Mrs. Eddy with Miss Martha Morgan, who was
then her housekeeper, and Mr. Frye followed when
arrangements were completed. She did not, however,
remain long, for the surroundings were not desirable.
Dr. Foster returned to Boston and selected a house in
Roslindale, a suburb of Boston. This house was purchased in April, 1891. Mrs. Eddy lived there three
weeks of June following, but finding it too accessible
to visitors she returned to Concord, N. H., where she
had been living quietly since June, 1889. Her removal
from Boston had come about simply and naturally.

While on her way to and from Barre, Mrs. Eddy had passed through Concord, New Hampshire, known in childhood. Its beauty and its dignity appealed to her so powerfully that she sojourned for a time there while the Roslindale property was being negotiated for. When Roslindale failed as a satisfactory habitation, her agreeable experience in Concord returned to her mind as an argument for its selection as an abiding-place. But she would not again make a hasty decision or permit others to do so for her in so important a matter as a permanent home. So she decided to live for a time in a furnished house in Concord and look about her for the desirable home.

It was in the summer of 1889 that she retired to Concord, carrying out her purpose of withdrawal from the personal direction of the students in Boston. In Concord she resided at 62 North State Street for three years. While living there she took her daily drives in and around the little New Hampshire capital, so dear to her because of her earliest recollections of childhood. From one of those drives she returned by the road (now, through her gift to the city, a macadamized avenue) which stretches along the crest of a valley to the southwest from the city. Halting her carriage about three quarters of a mile outside the capital, she looked out over the valley in contemplation. Mrs. Eddy saw here the vision of a home remote and yet accessible. She saw Bow, her birthplace, nestling in the ridge of blue hills away to the east and she discerned the hazy outline of Monadnock, far to the southwest, rearing its august and lonely head. Below the pleasant upland upon which she stood lay all the broad valley, like the Valley of Decision, which her years had spanned, and doubtless she saw with the eloquent prophet of old "multitudes, multitudes in the valley of decision."

What Mrs. Eddy beheld in vision she brought to pass. Land was bought uniting two estates, and the old house encumbering the spot where she stood when she made her determination was moved back and under the direction of her student, Mr. Ira O. Knapp, rebuilt into a modest, modern country home. This place Mrs. Eddy named Pleasant View, and there she resided from 1892 until 1908, a period of about fifteen years. Those who have never seen this charming, idyllic spot can picture it by imagining a broad sweep of green acres, sloping gently to a little lake, a ribbon of river, and a line of hills away to the east. The house standing back from the road, surrounded by a well-kept lawn, was given the picturesque addition of a small tower and broad eastern veranda, with an unpretentious portico over the front entrance.

Within the soft gray-green walls of the simple frame dwelling a shining order, peace, and dignity came to prevail. Mrs. Laura Sargent, a student of Mrs. Eddy's first class in Chicago, came from her home in Wisconsin to reside with Mrs. Eddy, and remained with her almost continuously. And to her loving attendance much of the quiet order of that home may be attributed. A gentle veil of seclusion descended over Pleasant View, securing to it a quiet and dignity necessary to the detached life of contemplation, a life wherein things temporal may stand forth in their relation to things eternal as types

PLEASANT VIEW, CONCORD, NEW HAMPSHIRE
Where Mrs. Eddy resided from June, 1892 to January, 1908

of spiritual significance. It was the life of brooding love, a life of the highest rarity in human experience, wherein heaven leans and kisses earth. Here Mrs. Eddy spent the years of perfecting the type of organization under which she conceived the spiritual compact of her church to rest.

It was not without action, however, that she brought about the firm foundation of a Christian Science church which should be unassailable as the rock of her doctrine. Mrs. Eddy had been clearing the way before her for an activity which was to eventuate in the building of The Mother Church in Boston, not simply as a structure of stone, but as a structure wherein its organization would be so constituted as to assure the permanent and orderly conduct of its affairs. Her first step in this direction was to request that the Boston church be dissolved. This dissolution was accomplished on December 2, 1889, and from that time until September 23, 1892, the church functioned as a voluntary association, its affairs being managed by Mrs. Eddy and its Board of Directors.

With the adjournment in New York in 1890 of the National Christian Scientist Association, the bonds of organization were entirely loosed and what the future held in store for them Christian Scientists were unable to discern. They had now to live the life and perform the works which a living faith demanded of them, and to trust that their teacher, withdrawn from the clash of petty affairs, was working out a plan by which they might manifest to the world a perfect unity of purpose. And she was working out such a plan, — meantime by letters and communications in the *Journal* encouraging her students all over the country to organize local churches. Thus detached organization was progressing with wonderful strides throughout the country.

In Boston the church was homeless, but still holding meetings, which now convened in Chickering Hall. This church had endeavored to purchase a lot of ground in Falmouth Street as early as 1886 with the idea of erecting an edifice thereon, but through various dissensions and rebellions it had been unable to complete its purchase, so that in 1889 a heavy mortgage still hung over its head. In December, 1889, Mrs. Eddy personally satisfied this mortgage and gave the lot in trust to her student, Ira O. Knapp. Mr. Knapp reconveyed the property to three trustees, namely, Alfred Lang,[1] Marcellus Munroe, and William G. Nixon. The purpose of forming this trusteeship was that donations might be received for a building fund from loving students throughout the field.

The building fund had been growing slowly but surely; now a hitch in the mind of one of the trustees brought it to a sudden stop. It was William G. Nixon[2] Mrs. Eddy's publisher, who could not be satisfied with the ultimate purpose of the trusteeship, and demanded that the title of the land be scrutinized by legal eyes. A paroxysm of doubt among his fellow trustees followed with the result that all surrendered their trusteeship and returned to the donors the funds which had accrued for the church building.

[1] Alfred Lang later founded the branch church in Lawrence, Mass.

[2] Mr. Nixon, who left the Christian Science movement at this time, later renewed his allegiance by attendance both at The Mother Church and a branch church.

MRS. EDDY AT THANKSGIVING IN 1891
About a year before the organization of The Mother Church in Boston

Undismayed by this action Mrs. Eddy employed an attorney to search the statutes of Massachusetts for a law by which her contemplated gift to the church might be made good and valid. Her lawyer very shortly put his finger on a statute seldom resorted to, which seemed a providential decree for this emergency. This statute provided that trustees might be deemed a body corporate for the purpose of holding grants and donations without the formal organization of a church. So on September 1, 1892, Mrs. Eddy again conveyed through a Deed of Trust her gift of ground, which was now valued at twenty thousand dollars, to Ira O. Knapp, William B. Johnson, Joseph S. Eastaman, and Stephen A. Chase. They were to be known as The Christian Science Board of Directors. These Directors pledged themselves to erect upon this lot a church building.

That no doubt might exist in the minds of her students throughout the United States and elsewhere that her purpose was entirely unselfish and that it was for the ends to which they all looked, Mrs. Eddy now counseled the organization of a universal church to be known as The Mother Church, The First Church of Christ, Scientist, in Boston, Massachusetts, which should draw its membership from Christian Scientists throughout the entire world. Thus on September 23, 1892, by her advice twelve students came together and organized under her jurisdiction the present church. This church so satisfied the wishes of her students that over fifteen hundred members united before the first annual meeting, held in October, 1893.

Now the building fund began to grow as it had

not done before. The donations returned by the
doubting Thomas were sent back doubled and trebled.
To secure the more rapid completion of The Mother
Church edifice forty-two students each contributed
one thousand dollars in 1894.[1] Mrs. Eddy summoned
her student, Joseph Armstrong, to Pleasant View,
placing in his hands the power of decision in vexa-
tious questions that might arise. Through his patient
direction and the co-operation of his able and
loyal co-members of the directorate, the original
Mother Church was completed the night of December 29, 1894.

Thus was the great labor of her mind during the
first five years of her retirement brought to a satisfactory conclusion. The little Boston church, which in
1888 had threatened to eject its Founder, was no
more; it had been dissolved; however, its continuity
of purpose remains unbroken in the present church.
Through the provisions of the Deed of Trust, The
Mother Church was to have nothing within the walls
of its edifice which was not in strict harmony with
the doctrine and practise of Christian Science as set
forth by Mary Baker Eddy in "Science and Health
with Key to the Scriptures." The church was dedicated January 6, 1895. Three months later Mrs. Eddy
accepted the Directors' invitation to become its Pastor
Emeritus.

So had Mrs. Eddy ably directed her students by
love that was wise and counsel that was firm in the
midst of dereliction, stubborn opposition, revolt, and
schism to that state of mind and that perfection of

---

1 "Miscellaneous Writings," p. 143.

organization that they found themselves self-operative under provisos which would prevent their straying from her teaching. And in doing this she succeeded in withdrawing her own personality from the clashing world of events, leaving only Truth enthroned for ruler. What wonder that her devoted followers lovingly call her Leader!

CHAPTER XXI

THE LEADER IN RETIREMENT

ALTHOUGH Mrs. Eddy had withdrawn from active participation in the work of her church, her withdrawal was in the nature of retirement and not seclusion. She did not go into a selfish privacy at Pleasant View, but remained actively engaged in many duties which her position required of her. She no longer edited the *Journal*, preached from a pulpit, or taught regular classes, but she continued to contribute articles to the *Journal*, to send annual messages to her church, and to receive those who had the right to her counsel. She made several visits to Boston in the interest of The Mother Church and received annually for several years large numbers of its members from many parts of the country. She prepared articles for the press on request, and, besides continuing to clarify the text of Science and Health, she gathered together and edited some of her scattered articles which she published under the title "Miscellaneous Writings." She also wrote "Christ and Christmas," 1893; Church Manual, 1895; "Christian Science *versus* Pantheism," 1898; Messages, 1898–1902; and published "Pulpit and Press" in 1895.

Mrs. Laura Sargent, her companion, took active charge of the household régime, and her sweet-tempered direction of the servants, her ceaseless inspection of the domestic machinery, made affairs move with pleasant exactness. Miss Clara Shannon of Montreal was another inmate of the household who devoted special attention to Mrs. Eddy's personal wants. Mrs. Pamelia J. Leonard of Brooklyn spent many months of several years at Pleasant View assisting in the work of church advancement, work which Mrs. Eddy never neglected. Mr. Frye continued in his faithful service of steward and secretary combined, and his duties were of the most diverse nature, varying from ordering supplies, keeping accounts, and transmitting Mrs. Eddy's directions to her gardeners and coachman, to assisting in handling her heavy mail.

If Mr. Frye and Mrs. Sargent were the most constant of Mrs. Eddy's attendants in her daily life, there were many other students called upon to serve their Leader, and such service was always regarded in the nature of an honor. Many served as assistant secretaries or companions from time to time, but as to the personnel of that roll of honor it is not necessary to make any further statement than the plain and straightforward one once made by Mrs. Eddy, that no one was ever called to Pleasant View for discipline. They were called there because they had shown by their work elsewhere a high order of usefulness.

Mrs. Eddy maintained her habit of rising early through all the years of retirement. She rose about six o'clock in summer and before seven o'clock in winter. She had an hour for prayerful meditation three times daily, morning, noon, and night. In the morning it was her custom to walk through the various rooms of her house on a tour of friendly inspection, whereon she not infrequently directed some change in the adjustment of furnishings and draperies; but mainly the tour was one of cheerful sociability when she talked with every member of her household, the laundress and the gardener's assistant not being neglected in words of commendation and sallies of wit or spiritual admonition. The love and reverence in which all held her made her coming an anticipation of each day.

After her regular morning exercise (which at Pleasant View was in fine weather frequently a walk about the artificial pond which some of her students had caused to be built in the lower garden, and on less agreeable days an hour's pacing of the covered veranda) Mrs. Eddy returned to her study where her secretary brought her letters. After dinner, which it was her custom to take in the middle of the day, she usually went for a drive. As the daily drive was the only occasion on which she was seen in public for many years, it became a matter of public interest, and her Concord neighbors took pleasure in meeting her brougham, drawn by a sober pair of black horses. They would bow their friendly salutations or occasionally, when she ordered her coachman to stop and summoned them with a kindly and courteous gesture, would approach her carriage and shake hands with the venerable religionist.

During the eighteen-nineties Mrs. Eddy made several visits to Boston. After the completion of the original Mother Church she made a journey especially to inspect it, her heart yearning over this gift which she had so generously shared with her students in presenting to the organization. On April 1, 1895, she went to Boston unannounced, with her companion and her secretary, and spent that night in the rooms designed for her especial use. These rooms are in the tower of the church and consist of a study, an alcove, and a dressing-room. Under the direction of Maurine Campbell they were exquisitely fitted with every appointment, a gift of many Christian Science children.

On May 25 she again occupied her rooms in The Mother Church and the next day preached from its pulpit. In January, 1896, she also preached in The Mother Church, returning the same afternoon to Concord. On Monday, June 5, 1899, Mrs. Eddy came to Boston from Concord and spent the night at her Commonwealth Avenue house, then occupied by Septimus J. Hanna, the first reader in The Mother Church at that time. The church held its annual meeting in Tremont Temple the following day and in the afternoon she appeared on the platform and addressed the meeting. Judge Hanna escorted Mrs. Eddy to the platform and introduced her, the students arising and quietly saluting her with waving handkerchiefs. She spoke briefly on the text from Malachi, "Prove me now herewith, saith the Lord of hosts, if I will not open you the windows of heaven."[1]

Mrs. Eddy avoided a public reception by withdrawing from the platform before the meeting adjourned and returning the same afternoon to Concord. This does not mean that she was unwilling to receive her students when she could fittingly arrange to do so. When the Christian Scientist Association — her students — met on Communion Sunday, June 5, 1895,

[1] "The First Church of Christ, Scientist, and Miscellany," p. 131.

she invited all members who desired to call upon her to go to Pleasant View the next day. The one hundred and eighty responded to this invitation, and Mrs. Eddy threw her house open, receiving them with great kindness, shaking hands with all, and conversing with many at length. This invitation was extended to all in 1897, when she was obliged to receive nearly three thousand guests. She could not personally greet such a large company, so she received them *en masse*, making a lengthy address and having refreshments served upon her lawn.

Mrs. Eddy sent no message of invitation in 1898, but a great many students made the pilgrimage to Concord nevertheless, and were obliged to content themselves with seeing her start on her drive. It became generally known to her church that their Leader was not pleased to have these annual visits take the appearance to the world of a pilgrimage of adoration, for it had begun to be spoken of as though she had withdrawn from daily intercourse with them only to secure a personal adulation greater than that accorded to any living woman. This of all things Mrs. Eddy desired to avoid, for the charge of apotheosis lurked behind any demonstration of her students' affection. So for several years such visits were discouraged.

But in 1901, the year in which Mrs. Eddy was eighty years of age, she again permitted the students to gather at Pleasant View after the June communion. On this occasion three special trains, leaving Boston for Concord, carried her guests. In June, 1903, about ten thousand Christian Scientists arrived in Concord, many from distant points. As the great multitude ap-

PLEASANT VIEW, CONCORD, NEW HAMPSHIRE
Mrs. Eddy speaking from the balcony to 10,000 Christian Scientists

proached Pleasant View members of her household
went to the gates and requested the students to enter
the grounds and Mrs. Eddy sent word that she would
address them from the balcony outside her study.
When she entered the balcony she stood looking down
on the great throng of people for a moment in silence,
then stretched out her hands to them in a gesture
characteristic of her great heart's love, seeming to say
in that mute appeal, "All that I have I give unto you."
She spoke briefly, addressing them as though they
were indeed the lambs of the Lord whom she would
feed with heavenly manna. Here and there a student
wept; all hung upon her words and her voice carried
to the remotest listener. As she stepped back into her
room, many began to write down the words they remembered, and as they compared their notes, each
one seemed to have caught a special and personal
message. This was the last time Mrs. Eddy received
her students *en masse* at Pleasant View.

There was, however, in 1904 a large concourse of
students in Concord to celebrate the dedication of the
Concord church, a structure of virgin granite near the
central square of the capital. This church edifice was
the gift of Mrs. Eddy to her students in that city, and
is one of the most beautiful of the many beautiful
Christian Science churches in America. About two
thousand students gathered for this occasion, but they
respected Mrs. Eddy's wish not to haunt her drive or
to visit Pleasant View. They assembled expectantly
on the lawn close by awaiting her arrival. From her
carriage she made an address which the perfect silence
of the assemblage made clearly audible. She directly

addressed herself to the president of The Mother Church, who was present, and donated a wooden gavel, symbol of her spiritual call to her church.

When Mrs. Eddy published "Miscellaneous Writings" in 1897, she requested in the March *Journal* that her students cease teaching Christian Science for one year. She had labored assiduously on this new publication, gathering almost entirely from the *Journals* since 1883, numerous of her addresses, messages, Bible lessons, even special letters and poems; and she believed the book would better prepare the minds of persons coming into the faith to understand the Christian Science text-book than the efforts of students. The book met with great success, for it was like a personal meeting with the Leader, full of the animated flashes of her wit and the quiet touches of her sympathetic understanding.

Although this work was sent out as a sort of primary class-book, it was eagerly read by the students who had gone through classes with her as teacher, and it soon became the most cherished of her writings after Science and Health. In the fall of 1898 Mrs. Eddy decided once more to personally teach special students selected and called by her. A class of sixty-seven members assembled in Concord — not knowing why they had been summoned. Among those who were called were members from England, Scotland, and Canada. Mrs. Eddy refused remuneration for her instruction, which she gave in the Concord Christian Science Hall, and she taught but two sessions. The lessons occurred on November 20 and 21, the first lasting for two hours, the second for four. The students were abundantly

MRS. EDDY

As she looked when she taught her last class in 1898

satisfied with what was pronounced her "wondrous teaching."

Among the members of this last class was the editor of a newspaper in Concord, a personal friend formerly from Tilton. Another editor became her student by reading her text-book, and they were ever after during her residence there welcome guests at her house. This close relationship with two eminent journalists of the city made Concord feel that the whole city was on terms of intimacy with the venerable Leader of the Christian Science Church. Her views on many public questions were obtained by them and printed in their papers and, whereas she had been too modest to acclaim her benevolences, they were not slow to do so, and Concord became aware that Mrs. Eddy was supplying gifts of shoes to needy children of Concord through a local shoe store and donations to religious associations outside her church. In addition, several of Concord's streets were paved and state projects initiated as the result of Mrs. Eddy's interest and support. She was no longer a private personage, but one of the capital's best known and most public-spirited citizens.

The world which had been so long in recognizing her seemed at last ready to acknowledge her work as an important factor in the progress of latter-day civilization. It was women who conferred the first general honor upon her, an honor quite apart from that accruing to her by reason of her religious leadership. The Daughters of the American Revolution made her a member of their body in the year 1894, when the wife of the President of the United States, Mrs. Harrison, was chief officer of the organization. And it was at Mrs. Harrison's request that the honor was bestowed.

Newspapers and magazines now frequently besought her for interviews and communications on important matters. She occasionally acceded to the latter requests, giving her views on the Spanish-American War, and, after the death of President McKinley, paying her tribute to his noble life. On the occasions of public festivals and celebrations she also gave on request her views as to the meaning of the Puritan Thanksgiving Day and its significance to this generation and the true meaning and best celebration of the spirit of Christmas. On such questions of public morals as marriage and divorce she responded to requests for her opinions.

But to the interviewer in person, Mrs. Eddy was not accessible. Her reasons for refusing to receive press correspondents in general were not based on selfishness or indifference to public interest, but rather that she might not be represented as self-seeking. She had established a publication committee[1] and its work was expanding into every state in the United States and even to countries overseas. It was not Mrs. Eddy's wish to perform an act of supererogation in giving out news of the church. Concerning her own life, she did not think it necessary to admit the world too intimately into her personal affairs, for to admit the world would be to make a parade of the simplest private virtues and devotions. Acting as she believed with the highest propriety, she consistently refused an audience to the special correspondent.

[1]Later known as the Committee on Publication.

Because of this insistent privacy at Pleasant View a rumor grew up in the newspaper offices that the founder of the new religious faith, which was established on the tenet that God is able to heal all our infirmities, was herself a victim of infirmity. What that infirmity might be could only be surmised and speculated upon by the fertile brains of ingenious reporters. In May of 1905 Mrs. Eddy broke her long continued rule and granted an interview to a representative of the Boston *Herald*. On that occasion she said: "All that I ask of the world is time, time to assimilate myself to God. I would take all the world to my heart if that were possible; but I can only ask my friends to look away from my personality and fix their eyes on Truth." So gracious, so gentle, so detached, so luminous was her personality, that the interviewer could not press upon her the many questions framed for the occasion, but submitted them to Mrs. Eddy's secretaries for her to take up in a more leisurely way with them, when she could dictate her replies. So humbly cognizant of this yielding on the part of the reporter was Mrs. Eddy, that she sent to the Boston *Herald* a kind tribute of appreciation.

But this interview did not satisfy a certain element of the press of America. The picture of a saintly character, living a contemplative and spiritual life of retirement did not accord with its preconceived notion, false as its own mental vision was. It yearned to press home upon the minds of the world its own image in a dramatic first-page "story," and for that end a newspaper of New York decided to make such a powerful demand for an audience that it should not be gainsaid.

The occasion for making this demand seemed to the newspaper mind to arise after dedication of the new Mother Church structure in Boston.

In 1902 Mrs. Eddy had suggested in her message to the church the need for a larger church edifice in Boston, and at the annual meeting the church voted to raise any part of $2,000,000 required for the erection of such an edifice. The work of clearing land adjacent to the original Mother Church began in October, 1903. The corner-stone of the new church building was laid in 1904, and like a miracle the great structure of white granite and Bedford stone began to arise from the heart of the city. In 1906 it lifted its white dome, a serene symbol of faith, above all the surrounding buildings, visible from far and near, a crown of peace. This church was dedicated in June, 1906, when about thirty thousand Christian Scientists filled the city of Boston and took part in the six successive services of communion.

The Christian Scientists who had come to Boston to see The Mother Church dedicated remained to attend the Wednesday evening meeting at which testimonies of Christian Science healing were given. The great temple was crowded from floor to dome, and overflow meetings were held in the original Mother Church and in five public halls. Many who were not Christian Scientists were amazed listeners to the outpouring of testimonies from every part of the great auditorium. Men and women arose in their places on the floor of the church and in the first and second balconies. As each arose he called the name of his city and waited his turn to tell of the miracle of health

THE MOTHER CHURCH

The Original Edifice with the Extension and the Christian Science Publishing House

and virtue wrought in his life as a result of the study of Christian Science. The names of the cities called up the near and the far of the civilized world — Liverpool, Galveston, St. Petersburg, San Francisco, Paris, New York, Atlanta, and Portland. There were negroes as well as white men in that audience; there were French, German, and Scandinavian; there were army officers from Great Britain, and members of the British nobility, Americans of great wealth, jurists, former doctors and clergymen, teachers, clerks, day laborers. It was like a jubilation of an army with banners. And not only of the vanquishment of cancers, consumption, broken limbs, malignant diseases, and paralysis did these votaries of Christian Science testify, but of poverty overcome, victory gained over drunkenness, morphine, and immoral lives. It was a triumphant assertion of the health and power of spiritual living.

Who now would lay finger upon the character of the founder of such a living faith? Who now would say that she had not taught a creed by which men can live and ennoble their lives? Who would begrudge her her hard-won right to retirement, peace, and serenity? It would be difficult to believe, did not all the world know, that in October of this same year two representatives of a New York newspaper did present themselves at Pleasant View and demand an audience with the venerable founder then in her eighty-sixth year. So churlish and so threatening was their demand, so steeped were they in a strange suspicion, that the faithful protectors of Mrs. Eddy's home life knew not what to say. The preposterous assertions that Mrs. Eddy was no longer living seemed to require the reproof of her presence, and yet to introduce such violent accusers to the saintly Leader seemed out of the question. Mrs. Eddy herself solved the difficulty, when the matter was laid before her, by saying that she would see not only them, but with them her neighbor across the way, that by his testimony the unbelieving reporters might be convinced that they were talking with the veritable Mary Baker Eddy.

The interview was brief, but the reporters were given ample time to ask the questions they desired. The turbulence of their quest, the malignity of their purpose, caused the venerable woman a slight tremulousness as she arose to greet them; a flush mounted her cheeks and she leaned momentarily upon the table at which she had been writing when they entered. Upon such evidences of natural emotion they based a story of absolute decrepitude and they did not spare her silvered head from indignity. The lurid story these writers gave to the world was that Mrs. Eddy could not possibly drive abroad in her carriage and therefore must be impersonated by some other grayhaired woman many years her junior. They declared that she did not manage her business, and was controlled mentally and physically by a designing clique who lived in her house and humbugged her church.

The vilification of a blameless life smote the public consciousness of the entire country. Far from feeling that the New York paper had performed a clever journalistic feat, the press of the country repudiated it with loathing and scorn. But with characteristic American enterprise, it sent representatives to Concord, New Hampshire, on the very day of the publication of the story, Sunday, October 28, 1906. The Associated Press, the Publishers Press, all the large newspapers of Boston and New York had representatives at Mrs. Eddy's home within twenty-four hours. In this emergency Mrs. Eddy summoned Mr. Alfred Farlow, head of the Christian Science Publication Committee. To meet the gathering newspaper men he sent to Concord an able representative, Mr. H. Cornell Wilson, of New York. Mr. Wilson conferred with Mr. Frye and his assistant, Mr. Lewis C. Strang, a former dramatic critic of Boston. From men of affairs in Concord who were not Christian Scientists Mr. Strang and Mr. Wilson secured affidavits as to Mrs. Eddy's social and business character. The affidavits were from the treasurer of the Loan and Trust Savings Bank of Concord, Fred N. Ladd; the president of the National State Capital Bank, J. E. Fernald; a lawyer who stands at the head of the New Hampshire bar, General Frank S. Streeter; the mayor of Concord, Charles R. Corning; and the editors of the two most prominent New Hampshire papers, M. Meehan of the Concord *Patriot* and George H. Moses of the *Monitor and Statesman.*

The affidavits covered the points that Mrs. Eddy had personal and business relations with her bankers, that she was the person who rode out in her carriage daily, and that she was not an invalid, or in any way mentally impaired, as she had received within the week for a call of a half-hour's duration Mayor Corning and General Streeter. Mr. Moses declared that he possessed in Mrs. Eddy's handwriting a budget of more than a hundred letters written to him during the past few years (the last one bearing a recent date), letters concerning printing which he had done for her. Affidavits were also furnished from members of the Pleasant View household; the two secretaries, Calvin A. Frye and Lewis C. Strang; the two companions, Mrs. Laura Sargent and Mrs. Pamelia Leonard, refuting the charge that Mrs. Eddy had any organic disease.

The assembled press representatives accepted with thanks the data supplied them, but united in the request for a personal interview with Mrs. Eddy. Their request was not only united but individual, and the most persistent of the reporters besieged the front door of Pleasant View, while photographers and artists stood at the gateway and haunted the driveway. Recognizing the situation as imperative, Mrs. Eddy decided to receive them all on Tuesday, October 30. They were bidden to come at one o'clock, when she would give them an audience just before taking her drive.

Accordingly, about fifteen newspaper men and women drove to Pleasant View and assembled in her drawing-room. There were also present her banker, her lawyer, the mayor, and a few men prominent in The Mother Church. The dainty rose drawing-room was quite filled with an official-looking assemblage, and many of the faces were intense with expectation of what they were about to behold. When Mrs. Eddy came down her own stairway and stood for a moment in the entrance, confronting the cynical and skeptical world, a world which refused to believe in disinterested virtue, she caught for a moment at the portière and an expression of pained comprehension slowly swept her face, a crimson stain burned her cheeks, and her eyes flashed a look of reproach over the assemblage.

Professor H. S. Hering, first reader of the Concord church, courteously and briefly stated the purpose of the gathering. Mrs. Eddy bowed. To the first question, "Are you in perfect bodily health?" she replied clearly and firmly, "I am." When the second question was put, "Have you any physician beside God?" Mrs. Eddy loosed her grasp upon the portière, took a step forward, and stretching out both hands in a sweeping, open gesture, declared solemnly and with magnificent energy, her voice thrilling all who heard her, "Indeed, I have not! His everlasting arms are around me and support me, and that is enough."

After answering in the affirmative another question about her daily drive, Mrs. Eddy indicated that the interview was at an end. She withdrew and Mr. Frye and Mrs. Sargent escorted her to her carriage which was waiting under the porte-cochère. As she left the house the newspaper men crowded the windows to watch her drive away. When her carriage disappeared, they asked to be shown the house, and were escorted over it. They entered the quiet study on the second floor, looked at the pictures on the walls, the books in the cases, stood where she so often did to survey the broad valley. They went through the simple little bedroom adjoining and surveyed the plain austerity of its furnishing with frank curiosity. The women reporters asked to see her wardrobe, and were shown the orderly clothes-room where her garments hung. In the dining-room they saw where she sat at table, the chocolate service she used, and inquired who sat on her right and left. They saw the library, her special chair, the table where books of reference were consulted. They examined the rugs and hangings of the drawing-room, the souvenirs, certificates of honor, the paintings. They did not ask to see her account-books, or if there were any special spot where she spent time in prayer.

On the whole the investigation of the private life and character of the venerable Leader was satisfactory to the newspapers. The journal which had printed the disagreeable article was discredited. It had failed to substantiate the story that Mrs. Eddy was in feeble health, and could produce no one to bear it out in the statement that she was mentally incapable. Her home life was shown to be simple and her relations with the citizens of Concord open and honorable.

But one important circumstance of Mrs. Eddy's life remained uncanvassed, her relation with her son, George W. Glover. Herein the New York newspaper which had aroused the recent inquiry thought it saw an opportunity again to challenge public attention and prove that the life upon which public scrutiny had been bent was not blameless. On Thanksgiving Day of 1906 a representative of the paper called on Mr. Glover in his home in Lead City, South Dakota, carrying a letter from Senator William E. Chandler of New Hampshire which stated that he had consented to act as legal counsel concerning certain questions which had arisen in connection with Mrs. Eddy's life. In its subsequent story of the interview with George Glover, the newspaper stated frankly that it found the son a loyal champion of his mother, and that it was necessary to impress upon him his legal opportunity and to make him believe that his aid was necessary to extricate his mother from being "detained in the custody of strangers against her will."

The clever New York newspaper man sat down in George Glover's home, a home with which Mrs. Eddy had presented her son, and drew from the guileless Westerner the story of his life and his relations with his mother. It was a story which must have surprised the reporter, for in spite of skilful manipulation of the facts, the truth was made apparent and stood forth in unblemished purity a witness to the mother's faithful consideration for her only child. He related the circumstances of his several visits to his mother while she was living at Pleasant View, how his mother had given him $5000 at one time to further his mining interests, how she had built for him the finest house in Lead City at an expense of $20,000 and had sent him $1100 additional to make alterations which he desired after occupying it, how she had interested herself in the education of his children and had sent money to him for that purpose.

To be sure, George Glover's story was filled with personal grievances. He did not like it that he could not always have direct access to his mother when visiting her at Pleasant View. He would have liked to realize for days the pleasure he experienced for a few hours in seeing her embrace and caress his children and make merry with the youngest in a relaxed mood.

He recounted how she had once permitted him in a sportive spirit to ring her electric bells and summon her secretary. It was the presence of a secretary which seemed particularly to have aggrieved the son. A secretary was to him an unnecessary personage, a man of affairs who scanned his demands upon his mother's love with an unemotional business eye and offered advice where Glover thought he would have benefited had advice not been given. As a matter of fact Calvin Frye never acted as adviser but as executor of Mrs. Eddy's wishes.

Playing upon this prejudice toward the secretary, the newspaper representative appears to have found it easy to induce Glover to exaggerate in his own mind the sense of his grievances and to catch the fear that he would eventually be wrongfully deprived of his inheritance by those men of affairs with whom his mother had so long associated. Glover was induced to believe that he was in a pitiable condition of neglect and that powerful friends had been raised up by the newspaper to aid him. Thus he beheld his "legal opportunity" to interfere in the management of his mother's affairs.

As soon as George Glover consented to act in a suit at law nominally for his mother's interests, but in reality against her every wish and purpose, her only other heirs were sought out by this same agency and persuaded to join the issue. These heirs were her adopted son, Ebenezer Foster-Eddy, and George W. Baker, her nephew. The suit was brought by the sons and nephew, together with Glover's oldest child, Mary Baker Glover. It was called the petition of next

friends, or exactly, "The petition of Mary Baker
Glover Eddy who sues by her next friends George W.
Glover, Mary Baker Glover, and George W. Baker
against Calvin A. Frye, Alfred Farlow, Irving C. Tom-
linson, Ira O. Knapp, William B. Johnson, Stephen
A. Chase, Joseph Armstrong, Edward A. Kimball,
Hermann S. Hering, and Lewis C. Strang."

The particulars of the complaint are too largely a
matter of legal technics to be recounted save in sum-
mary. It is sufficient to say that it was set forth
in the bill that Mrs. Eddy was forcibly detained and
constrained to do the will of strangers, that her large
estate was manipulated improperly by her secretaries,
and that she was in a feeble mental state which prevented her comprehending what disposition was being
made of her affairs. The plaintiffs prayed that the defendants be required to give account of all their business transactions, and if they had wrongfully disposed
of any property that they be made to restore it; that
they be restrained from any further business dealings
in Mrs. Eddy's name, pending the suit, and that a re-
ceiver be appointed to take possession of all Mrs.
Eddy's property.

So this son, who was alienated from his mother in
childhood because his rugged health and boisterous
spirits were declared by relatives to be unendurable
in a home where she was an invalid, was now in her
advanced years stirred up against her by what motive
it is difficult indeed to determine, but by the method
of arousing a false fear for her welfare through his un-
familiarity with the enormous social interests involved. But Mrs. Eddy was not supine under the

peculiar and extraordinary attack. She came forward to meet the issue with the deliberation of a superbly clarified intellect and her procedure was so wise in every detail as to win the applause of the most judicial as well as the most worldly of her critics.

Her first act was to employ an expert accountant to go over her books and ascertain if any charge of mismanagement or malfeasance could be brought against her trusted secretary, Calvin A. Frye. When her books which had been audited yearly were found to be substantially correct, save for a slight error in bookkeeping which defrauded not her, but the secretary himself, she created a trusteeship, transferring all her property to three men for their management and disposition, subject to clearly defined conditions. These three men were her cousin, the Honorable Henry M. Baker, her banker, Josiah E. Fernald, and the editor of *The Christian Science Journal* and *Sentinel* (also member of the Board of Directors of The Mother Church), Archibald McLellan. But one of these men was a Christian Scientist; the others were prominent business men of Concord, her cousin having represented his district in Congress.

With a view to taking this step she had caused to be created a trust deed for the benefit of her son, George W. Glover, and his family, by which she conveyed securities valued at $125,000 to the guardianship of her lawyer, General Frank S. Streeter, Archibald McLellan, and Irving C. Tomlinson. The provisos of the trust guaranteed a liberal annual income to her son during his lifetime and to his wife during hers, a smaller annual income to each of her grandchildren, and the expenditure of money for the education of those who had not completed their schooling, and its maintenance in force until her youngest grandchild should reach his majority. On the death of her son and his wife, and the arrival of the grandchildren at years of majority, the trust was to be paid over in equal shares to her grandchildren. This trust bore the proviso, however, that the beneficiaries should not directly or indirectly contest her last will or other disposition of property.

This arrangement did not satisfy George Glover, whose suspicion was now thoroughly aroused by misrepresentations of his mother's property. He was led to believe that her fortune was enormous and that he was faring but ill in its benefits. The petition was filed March 1, 1907, and on April 2 the trustees of Mrs. Eddy's property begged leave to intervene and be made substitutes in place of the "next friends." Thereupon the complainants amended their petition and considerable legal delay ensued. On June 5, Judge Robert N. Chamberlin of New Hampshire denied the motion of the trustees to intervene, but on June 27 he constituted the Honorable Edgar Aldrich a master of the court to hear all pertinent and competent evidence and determine whether Mary Baker G. Eddy on the first day of March, 1907, was capable of intelligently managing, controlling, and conducting her financial affairs. Co-masters were subsequently appointed, these being Dr. George F. Jelly of Boston, an alienist, and the Honorable Hosea W. Parker of Claremont, New Hampshire, an eminent lawyer.

354   THE LIFE OF MARY BAKER EDDY

Accordingly, when all the details of qualifying for masters had been completed, Judge Aldrich began the hearing in Concord. The hearing opened on Tuesday, August 13, 1907. It was continued for six days, with a recess for Saturday and Sunday, and on the sixth day the complainants withdrew their suit by motion of their counsel, without asking from the masters any finding upon the questions submitted to them by Judge Chamberlin. The withdrawal of the suit came suddenly and was in the nature of a collapse. It followed shortly upon the heels of a visit paid to Mrs. Eddy at Pleasant View by the masters' court and counsel for both defendants and plaintiffs which was a courtesy extended to her, because of her years, by Judge Aldrich. Senator Chandler, the lawyer for George W. Glover, had endeavored to have the court command Mrs. Eddy's presence in the court-room, but Judge Aldrich decided that the court could convene as well in the library of Pleasant View to protect Mrs. Eddy from the unnecessary strain of appearing in a court-room among the throngs of the curious and at such a season as mid-August. During the visit to her home she exhibited such mental alertness and ability in discussing financial, civic, and social topics, that it was a foregone conclusion that the masters' findings would adjudge her eminently capable of administering her own affairs. Apprehending this clearly from long legal experience, the astute lawyer for the complainants decided upon withdrawal.

Therefore, after six months of unjust prosecution, Mrs. Eddy was permitted to regain the privacy which she desired and the conduct of matters relative to the welfare of the church in which her life-work had centered. Her first public utterance came through her trustees when she made public her intention of creating a fund for the education of indigent students along lines of Christian Science inquiry. The details of her project had not been worked out, but the public was satisfied that the fortune derived from the sale of her various books was designed for the betterment of humanity.

On Sunday, January 26, 1908, Mrs. Eddy changed her residence from Pleasant View, Concord, to Chestnut Hill, in the suburbs of Boston. Her new home was established in a cheerful gray stone mansion, situated in twelve acres of well-wooded ground, commanding a view of the Blue Hills. The commodious house, containing twenty-five rooms, was adapted for the use of a larger household than was Pleasant View. Mrs. Eddy's contemplated projects required the additional attention of extra clerks and secretaries, and she also desired to be in closer touch with the headquarters of the church in furthering her philanthropic purposes.

The move was kept secret and made by special train. She was accompanied by a small party of her Concord household. Her drive to the station from Pleasant View was somewhat of a farewell to her birth-state and was on the whole a rather sad one; but the journey aroused her spirits to the work before her, and she entered her new home blithely and cheerfully. Her energy was unusual and within a few hours she had established the routine of her life in her new home. The arrangement of its rooms is not unlike that of Pleasant View, except for a greater spaciousness and more agreeable accommodations for her assistants and visiting friends.

When it became known in Concord that Mrs. Eddy had decided to make her home in Massachusetts, the city council met and passed resolutions of regret at her departure and of appreciation for the kindly relations that had existed for nineteen years between her and Concord people and also of her beneficence to the city of Concord. The mayor and the clerk were authorized to attest the testimonial of esteem in behalf of the city. This was done and the resolutions forwarded to Mrs. Eddy. She replied to their cordial recognition in the following words:

To the Honorable Mayor and City Council, Concord, N. H.

GENTLEMEN: — I have not only the pleasure, but the honor of replying to the City Council of Concord, in joint convention assembled, and to Alderman Cressy, for the kindly resolutions passed by your honorable body, and for which I thank you deeply. Lest I should acknowledge more than I deserve of praise, I leave their courteous opinions to their good judgment.

My early days hold rich recollections of associations with your churches and institutions, and memory has a distinct model in granite of the good folk in Concord, which like the granite of their State, steadfast and enduring, has hinted this quality to other states and nations all over the world.

My home influence, early education, and church experience, have unquestionably ripened into the fruits of my present religious experience, and for this I prize them. May I honor this origin and deserve the continued friendship and esteem of the people in my native State.

Sincerely yours,

MARY BAKER G. EDDY

By this letter she affirmed her continued interest in all who had been associated with her in early life and throughout her later years of usefulness and noble living; and by the projects to which she now gave her attention, declared her purpose of rising above the criticism of an unjust world into the pure atmosphere of brotherly love, fulfilling the commandments of her only acknowledged Master, to love God with all her heart and her neighbor as herself.

CHAPTER XXII

LIFE AT CHESTNUT HILL

RETURNING to Boston in her eighty-seventh year to take up her residence at Chestnut Hill, Mrs. Eddy caused the world to wonder what she could have in mind to accomplish by this change of base for her household. The average commenter regarded the move as hazardous for one of her advanced years and believed that she could find no contentment in a new home after her long residence in Concord. But such commenters were basing their judgment on the facts of an ordinary life. An ordinary life has ceased to be concerned with the affairs of this world after entering the eighties and is willing to drift quietly with the tide. But Mrs. Eddy had purposes as yet unrevealed to the world, among which was one great purpose, a purpose cherished for twenty-five years, namely, the establishment of a daily newspaper.

The germ of this enterprise lay in the seed that was planted in 1883 in the first issue of the eight-page paper, at first sent out only once every two months, the paper called the *Journal of Christian Science*, whose early fortunes for twenty years have been traced in the chapter dealing with foundation work in Boston. During this time the *Christian Science Sentinel* had been established as a weekly publication of Christian Science news, dealing with affairs of the church, with the lecturers, and printing letters and testi-

MRS. EDDY'S HOME AT CHESTNUT HILL, MASSACHUSETTS

monies of healing, the *Journal*, which had become a
monthly, retaining the special province of publishing
articles and essays on metaphysical subjects from the
pens of the students. There was also established
Der Herold der Christian Science, a monthly in the
German language.

All these publications were then housed at 250
Huntington Avenue. Ground was broken for the erec-
tion of the Christian Science publishing house in the
autumn of 1907 and the work was actively pushed, for
Mrs. Eddy's attention was now largely concentrated
upon the publications of the church, and her cherished purpose was yet to be unfolded to her followers.
This came in the first few months of her residence in
Boston. The new publishing house had gone up
speedily at the corner of St. Paul and Falmouth
Streets, a handsome, three-storied structure of Bed-
ford stone. The Publishing Society occupied its new
quarters in August, 1908. During July Mrs. Eddy
communicated to the Board of Directors her wish that
in the near future a daily newspaper be started, and
on August 8 she sent the following letter to the Board
of Trustees:

August 8, 1908

Christian Science Board of Trustees,
        Boston, Mass.

BELOVED STUDENTS: — It is my request that you start
a daily newspaper at once, and call it The Christian Science
Monitor. Let there be no delay. The Cause demands that
it be issued now.

You may consult with the Board of Directors, I have
notified them of my intention.

Lovingly yours,
MARY B. G. EDDY

On September 19 a request was sent out through the *Sentinel* to the field for subscriptions to a fund to enlarge the publishing house. No explanation was offered at this time of the Leader's purpose, but a response indicative of the confidence and support of the church for Mrs. Eddy's projects was instant, — money began to come in immediately. There was need of it, for much work had to be done. The land adjoining the existing structure was occupied by a block of flats in which were numerous tenants. These tenements had to be cleared and razed before construction could be begun. All this was accomplished rapidly and without friction or lawsuit. No men of affairs ever had a more active, earnest director behind them than the woman of eighty-seven in her quiet retreat in the Newton hills, just outside the limits of Boston.

As the structure went up the city wondered, editors of newspapers were watching, and reporters continually strove to elicit information as to what the Christian Science Church was going to do with such a commodious building. While the building operations were still going on the great modern presses were placed in position, wrapped in tarpaulin for protection. Continual speculation went on in the other newspaper offices of the city, and many conjectures were printed. But the inquirers were obliged to possess themselves in patience until October 17, 1908, when there was published in the *Sentinel* an editorial leader entitled *"The Christian Science Monitor."* In this article Mr. McLellan said:

We are pleased to announce that, with the approval of our Leader, Mrs. Eddy, The Christian Science Publishing

Society will shortly issue a daily newspaper to be known as *The Christian Science Monitor.* In making this announcement we can say for the Trustees of the Society that they confidently hope and expect to make the *Monitor* a worthy addition to the list of publications issued by the Society. It is their intention to publish a strictly up-to-date newspaper, in which all the news of the day that should be printed will find a place, and whose service will not be restricted to any one locality or section, but will cover the daily activities of the entire world.

As to the motive which has led to the establishment of a daily paper of this character, there is nothing we could say that would be so forceful or so timely as the announcement made by Mrs. Eddy when she established *The Christian Science Journal.* We quote as follows from her article, "A Timely Issue," as it appears in "Miscellaneous Writings":

"Looking over the newspapers of the day, one naturally reflects that it is dangerous to live, so loaded with disease seems the very air. These descriptions carry fears to many minds, to be depicted in some future time upon the body. A periodical of our own will counteract to some extent this public nuisance; for through our paper, at the price at which we shall issue it, we shall be able to reach many homes with healing, purifying thought." . . .

It will be the mission of the *Monitor* to publish the real news of the world in a clean, wholesome manner, devoid of the sensational methods employed by so many newspapers. There will be no exploitation or illustration of vice and crime, but the aim of the editors will be to issue a paper which will be welcomed in every home where purity and refinement are cherished ideals.

A notice was published in the *Sentinel* asking for Christian Scientists who were professional journalists to volunteer their services for the new publication. A very large number of responses came, more than could be accepted. But a wise and sufficient selection of applicants was made. The first issue of the *Monitor* appeared November 25, 1908, the day before Thanksgiving. In that issue appeared an editorial leader written by Mrs. Eddy entitled, "Something in a Name." In it she said:

I have given the name to all the Christian Science periodicals. The first was *The Christian Science Journal*, designed to put on record the divine Science of Truth; the second I entitled *Sentinel*, intended to hold guard over Truth, Life, and Love; the third, *Der Herold der Christian Science*, to proclaim the universal activity and availability of Truth; the next I named *Monitor*, to spread undivided the Science that operates unspent. The object of the *Monitor* is to injure no man, but to bless all mankind.

Thus Mrs. Eddy assumed full responsibility for the new publication, reaffirming the motto of her life as the motto of the new paper. If any doubt lay in the mind of the world as to who was the actual founder of the new paper it should have been dispelled by the editorial in the issue of the *Sentinel*, October 24, 1908, in which the editor thanked the Boston *Herald* for the respects paid to the forthcoming *Monitor*. The *Herald* had printed this paragraph:

Good luck to the coming Christian Science newspaper. Starting a daily paper is an enterprise that usually tests the courage and resources of the bravest and most resourceful souls. The graveyards are full of their remains.

"We hope," said the editor of the *Sentinel*, "we shall not be considered boastful when we say that the progress of the Christian Science movement from its very beginning has been not one only, but a series of steps such as 'usually test the courage and resources of the bravest and most resourceful souls;' and that as an incentive to high endeavor we could have nothing better than the example of our Leader, Mrs. Eddy, under whose guidance these steps have been taken successfully."

And they were taken successfully. The new paper was cordially received by the press in all parts of the country, its appearance was veritably a demonstration of brotherhood, and this was the title of an editorial which appeared in the second number, closing with these words:

To count the various items of good-will that went to build up the *Monitor* would be impossible. The architect was devoted, and his representative, the superintendent of the work, was indefatigable; the contractors were industrious in trying to meet the time limit. The builders of the press gave night and day labors. Those who had to provide materials brought in supplies, disregarding their own convenience. There was much more than buying and selling involved. There was the urgency of kindness in much of the work done. There was fine fidelity to promises given. There was honesty that rose above the claim of policy. Some might have seen confusion, but to the seeing eye, taking form among the clouds, was the vision of man serving man in a brotherhood of service. And through this demonstration of brotherhood the Leader of the Christian Science movement finds her labors for the world now assisted by *The Christian Science Monitor*.

"No wonder," commented Frederick Dixon of London in the *Outlook*, a British publication, after the passing of Mrs. Eddy, "no wonder Mrs. Eddy was an ever-inspiring leader to work for, and no wonder there

grew up around her a body of devoted assistants. No
matter how hard they might work, she worked harder
still; and for months and years, while they were receiving her constant and incisive instructions, they
read with mingled amusement and amazement the
stories of her mental incapacity and the failure of the
movement, which then, very much as now, constituted
in the Press the news of Christian Science."

The body of devoted assistants had presented in
the march of events differing types of men with differing talents and qualifications for work. These men
were under the survey of her active mind, they were
constantly being tried and tested in various services,
and time was making it necessary for her to place her
hand on the shoulder of some of these men and summon them to the post of the most urgent fidelity the
church could require. Changes in the personnel of
the Board of Directors were made necessary by the
death of two members and the resignation of a third
whose long and faithful service had given him the
rightful privilege of retiring.

Joseph Armstrong, fifteen years in Boston as business manager of The Christian Science Publishing Society, publisher of Mrs. Eddy's works, and a director of The Mother Church, passed from life in this
world at his home 387 Commonwealth Avenue, Boston, on Monday evening, December 9, 1907. He had
been a very efficient man, both as director of the
church and as manager of the Publishing Society. His
departure from this earth did not take place until he
had performed his duty in accounting for his stewardship at the Concord hearing of the suit brought

against the estate by George W. Glover. Mrs. Eddy wrote the following tribute to his memory the day after his departure:

"Hear, O Israel": The late lamented Christian Scientist brother and the publisher of my books, Joseph Armstrong, C. S. D., is not dead, neither does he sleep nor rest from his labors in divine Science; and his works do follow him. Evil has no power to harm, to hinder, or to destroy the real spiritual man. He is wiser to-day, healthier and happier, than yesterday. The mortal dream of life, substance, or mind in matter, has been lessened, and the reward of good and punishment of evil and the waking out of his Adam-dream of evil will end in harmony, — evil powerless, and God, good, omnipotent and infinite.[1]

In December, 1907, Mrs. Eddy appointed Allison V. Stewart as her publisher. He had been a member of the Board of Trustees since September, 1906. In January, 1908, Mrs. Eddy also nominated Mr. Stewart for the vacancy on the Board of Directors of The Mother Church and he was elected a member. With Mrs. Eddy's consent David B. Ogden was elected business manager of The Christian Science Publishing Society.

On May 31, 1909, William B. Johnson, for nineteen years Clerk of The Mother Church and member of the Board of Directors, and a loyal student for twenty-five years, lovingly desired of Mrs. Eddy the privilege of resigning from the post which had become one of the most exacting offices of the church. He expressed the wish to devote his time to the practise of Christian Science healing. His request was granted and a tribute to his long years of service appeared in the editorial columns of the *Sentinel* as a leader, entitled,

[1] Miscellany, p. 296.

"Well Done." The vacancy caused by Mr. Johnson's retirement was filled by the election of John V. Dittemore, who took his seat as a member of the Board of Directors and as Clerk of The Mother Church at the annual meeting, June 7, 1909. In answer to an invitation extended to Mrs. Eddy by the Board of Directors to attend the annual meeting, Mrs. Eddy sent the following letter:[1]

The Christian Science Board of Directors, Beloved Students:

I thank you for your kind invitation to be present at the annual meeting of The Mother Church on June 7, 1909. I will attend the meeting, but not *in propria persona*. Watch and pray that God directs your meetings and your lives, and your Leader will then be sure that they are blessed in their results.   Lovingly yours,

MARY BAKER EDDY

The *Sentinel* of November 19, 1910, in an editorial leader commemorated the services of Ira O. Knapp, C. S. D., who passed from earth November 11, 1910, at his home in Batavia Street, Boston.

Adam H. Dickey, who for nearly three years had been Mrs. Eddy's secretary, was unanimously elected a member of The Christian Science Board of Directors to fill this vacancy in accord with the following letter, received November 21, 1910, which it is interesting to note was the last official communication of Mrs. Eddy to any of the officers of her Church. It read:

Board of Directors:

BELOVED STUDENTS: — Please appoint Mr. Adam H. Dickey member of the Board of Directors.

Lovingly yours,

MARY B. EDDY

[1] Miscellany, p. 142.

Thus during Mrs. Eddy's residence at Chestnut Hill was the personnel of the Board of Directors changed by three members. Her attention had been very much centered upon the directorate and its deliberations. She had heartened it by special messages sent to its meetings, she had given it very important work to do in the investigation of the practises of certain of the branch churches, and she had sustained it by messages to the field. In one particular instance, she had written the following letter:[1]

BROOKLINE, MASS., Nov. 13, 1909

To the Board of Trustees, First Church of Christ, Scientist,
New York City.

BELOVED BRETHREN: — In consideration of the present momentous question at issue in First Church of Christ, Scientist, New York City, I am constrained to say, if I can settle this church difficulty amicably by a few words, as many students think I can, I herewith cheerfully subscribe these words of love: —

My beloved brethren in First Church of Christ, Scientist, New York City, I advise you with all my soul to support the Directors of The Mother Church, and unite with those in your church who are supporting The Mother Church Directors. Abide in fellowship with and obedience to The Mother Church, and in this way God will bless and prosper you. This I know, for He has proved it to me for forty years in succession.   Lovingly yours,

MARY BAKER EDDY

To support the directors of The Mother Church meant that the members of The Mother Church and of branch churches should be loyal to the tenets and by-laws of The Mother Church as set forth in the Church Manual; for it is the work of the Board of

1 Miscellany, p. 360.

Directors to administer the discipline of this Manual. When Mrs. Eddy wrote this letter, she did not write an absurdity but the veritable truth concerning her long experience of forty years. In Science and Health, page 107, Mrs. Eddy says: "In the year 1866, I discovered the Christ Science or divine laws of Life, Truth, and Love, and named my discovery Christian Science." For Mrs. Eddy these divine laws were Immanuel. Moreover, she had supported the tenets and been governed by the tenets since 1879, the charter for the first church organization having been obtained in August of that year. It is true that Mrs. Eddy from time to time had to revise and amend the by-laws and tenets of The Mother Church, as the experience of the church "walking through deep waters" many times revealed a necessity for regulation. But her authorship of the Manual was as inspired as her authorship of "Science and Health with Key to the Scriptures"; she studied both writings and she also submitted her life to the guidance of the Manual as well as the textbook.[1]

An important part of the labors performed by Mrs. Eddy after removing to Chestnut Hill was a revision of the Manual. In the Sentinel for June 20, 1908, this letter appeared:[2]

[1] On the twenty-third day of September, 1892, at the request of Rev. Mary Baker Eddy, twelve of her students and Church members met and re-organized, under her jurisdiction, the Christian Science Church and named it, The First Church of Christ, Scientist. At this meeting twenty others of Mrs. Eddy's students and members of her former Church were elected members of this Church,—those with others that have since been elected were known as "First Members." The Church Tenets, Rules, and By-Laws, as prepared by Mrs. Eddy, were adopted. A By-Law adopted March 17, 1903, changed the title of "First Members" to "Executive Members." (On July 8, 1908, the By-Laws pertaining to "Executive Members" were repealed.)
Historical Sketch, Church Manual, p. 18.
[2] See also Miscellany, p. 139.

My Beloved Brethren: — When I asked you to dispense with the Executive Members' meeting, the purpose of my request was sacred. It was to turn your sense of worship from the material to the spiritual, the personal to the impersonal, the denominational to the doctrinal, yea, from the human to the divine.

Already you have advanced from the audible to the inaudible prayer; from the material to the spiritual communion; from drugs to Deity; and you have been greatly recompensed. Rejoice and be exceedingly glad, for so doth the divine Love redeem your body from disease; your being from sensuality; your soul from sense; your life from death.

Of this abounding and abiding spiritual understanding the prophet Isaiah said, "And I will bring the blind by a way that they knew not; I will lead them in paths that they have not known: I will make darkness light before them, and crooked things straight. These things will I do unto them, and not forsake them."

(Signed) Mary Baker Eddy

On July 8, 1908, the body of Executive Members was dissolved. On May 22, 1909, notice of an amended by-law was published entitled, "No Interference," Article XXIII, Section 10. This by-law provided for the complete democratization of branch churches and shed light on the abolishment of Executive Members. It reads:

A member of The Mother Church may be a member of one branch Church of Christ, Scientist, or of one Christian Science society holding public services, but he shall not be a member of both a branch church and a society; neither shall he exercise supervision or control over any other church. In Christian Science each branch church shall be distinctly democratic in its government, and no individual, and no other church shall interfere with its affairs.

On June 21, 1908, the Committee on Publication issued this notice from Mrs. Eddy:[1]

The house of The Mother Church seats only five thousand people, and its membership includes forty-eight thousand communicants, hence the following:

The branch churches continue their communion seasons, but there shall be no more communion season in The Mother Church that has blossomed into spiritual beauty, communion universal and divine. "For who hath known the mind of the Lord, that he may instruct him? But we have the mind of Christ." (I Corinthians 2:16.)

On the same date the following letter was written which appeared in the *Sentinel* for June 27, 1908:[2]

BELOVED CHRISTIAN SCIENTISTS:—Take courage. God is leading you onward and upward. Relinquishing a material form of communion advances it spiritually. The material form is a "Suffer it to be so now" and is abandoned so soon as God's Way-shower, Christ, points the advanced step. This instructs us how to be abased and how to abound. Dropping the communion of The Mother Church does not prevent its distant members from occasionally attending this church.

(Signed)   MARY BAKER EDDY

The above provision was embodied in the Manual under Article XVIII. It has been shown in a previous chapter how the Founder of Christian Science solved the difficult problem of organization, and in these important amendments of the Manual is shown her wise provision for the harmonious government of the church, and the removal of a motive for religious pilgrimages to The Mother Church by advancing its

[1] Miscellany, p. 141.   [2] See also Miscellany, p. 140.

form of Communion to the spiritual understanding of its gracious compact with the branch churches of the entire world.

It had been said to the author of this book by one of Mrs. Eddy's very oldest loyal students, that the Leader would stand by her post until her work was done, that the world's criticisms, the lawsuits of enemies, the burden of years, would not affect her to drive her from the post of duty until her plans and purposes for the church in the world were accomplished. On September 28, 1910, Mrs. Eddy sent the following notice to the Christian Science periodicals:[1]

I hereby announce to the Christian Science field that all inquiries or information relating to Christian Science practice, to publication committee work, reading-room work, or to Mother Church membership, should be sent to the Christian Science Board of Directors of The Mother Church; and I have requested my secretary not to make inquiries on these subjects, nor to reply to any received, but to leave these duties to the Clerk of The Mother Church, to whom they belong.

MARY BAKER EDDY

During the year 1909 Mrs. Eddy's labors for the *Monitor* and her attention to a heavy correspondence which she had not as yet laid down combined to fill her days with as much activity as a man in his prime would care to assume. It was therefore of especial significance that to her should have come at this time news of the dedication of a splendid church edifice in the largest city of the world, First Church of Christ, Scientist, London, England.

[1] See Miscellany, p. 242.

Two letters came to Mrs. Eddy from the board of directors of this church, one in May explaining the steps which had been taken to make possible the dedication, and another in June to say the dedication was solemnized June 13. In the letter of particulars these interesting facts were printed in the *Sentinel*, July 3, 1909:

The whole of our liabilities, amounting to upward of eighty thousand pounds (approximately four hundred thousand dollars), have been met, and the church stands on its own freehold site in one of the most convenient positions in London. Our aim throughout has been to keep to the key-note of simplicity and dignity, to accommodate as many as possible within the limits of our space, and to arrange that all should be able to see and hear to the best advantage. All the Christian Science churches in London, and other Christian Science churches in the United Kingdom, have generously contributed to our building fund. The meeting on April 26 had been called for the purpose of taking up a collection to enable us to pay off the sum still remaining as a liability on the land, but at the commencement of the meeting the treasurer was able to announce that the sum was already in hand, and that he had that day paid off the last installment. The members then decided that a practical expression of our thankfulness to God could take no better form than in a gift to the publishing house, so a collection amounting to £1417-13-4 (approximately seven thousand dollars) was taken at the meeting, and it was also resolved that the collection at the dedication service should be devoted to the same purpose.

Mrs. Eddy sent to this church a letter of sympathetic rejoicing as she was also enabled to do in November of the same year to First Church of Christ, Scientist, Edinburgh, who had announced to her that they were ready to begin their structure in the land of her forefathers.

In the month of November, 1909, the Leader's heart was gladdened by the reassurance of First Church of Christ, Scientist, New York City, of its support of the Board of Directors of The Mother Church, Boston.[1] This took place after a patient and thorough examination into methods and practises of certain members of that church which had been complained of for a period of years. The directorate of The Mother Church, after patient remonstrance with the chief offenders of the New York congregation, acted for The Mother Church by removing the names of the persistent offenders from the roster of its membership. It did not interfere, however, with the local government of First Church, New York City, but left that church to the democratic dealing with its own affairs which has ever been the policy of the Christian Science organization. The church responded loyally to the Leader's appeal, and at a meeting held in November reorganized its own board of trustees and accepted gratefully and lovingly the correction of error among its members.

Following this episode of church history Mrs. Eddy gave to the field valuable doctrinal instruction on two specific points, reprinting[2] the gist of an address to the members of the Christian Scientist Association delivered in July, 1895, and also by replying to a letter of inquiry raised by a student in the West. The exposition of her address, reprinted November 13, 1909, is as follows:

---

[1] See *Christian Science Sentinel*, November 27, 1909.

[2] *The Christian Science Journal*, July, 1895; also Miscellany, p. 363.

My address before the Christian Scientist Association has been misrepresented and evidently misunderstood by some students. The gist of the whole subject was not to malpractise unwittingly. In order to be sure that one is not doing this, he must avoid naming, in his mental treatment, any other individual but the patient whom he is treating, and practise only to heal. Any deviation from this direct rule is more or less dangerous. No mortal is infallible, — hence the Scripture, "Judge no man." . . . The rule of mental practice in Christian Science is strictly to handle no other mentality but the mind of your patient, and treat this mind to be Christly. Any departure from this golden rule is inadmissible. This mental practice includes and inculcates the commandment, "Thou shalt have no other gods before me." Animal magnetism, hypnotism, etc., are disarmed by the practitioner who excludes from his own consciousness, and that of his patients, all sense of the realism of any other cause or effect save that which cometh from God. And he should teach his students to defend themselves from all evil, and to heal the sick, by recognizing the supremacy and allness of good. This epitomizes what heals all manner of sickness and disease, moral or physical.

The instruction to the student in the West came almost a year later, being printed in the *Sentinel* September 3, 1910. It embodied the right standpoint of the Christian Scientist in the world to-day, and had an especial value in that it was almost the last word of the Leader to her church. The question and Mrs. Eddy's reply were as follows:[1]

Last evening I was catechized by a Christian Science practitioner because I referred to myself as an immortal idea of the one divine Mind. The practitioner said that my statement was wrong, because I still lived in my flesh. I re-

1 Miscellany, pp. 241, 242.

plied that I did not live in my flesh, that my flesh lived or died according to the beliefs I entertained about it; but that, after coming to the light of Truth, I had found that I lived and moved and had my being in God, and to obey Christ was not to know as real the beliefs of an earthly mortal. Please give the truth in the *Sentinel*, so that all may know it.

Mrs. Eddy's reply. — You are scientifically correct in your statement about yourself. You can never demonstrate spirituality until you declare yourself to be immortal and understand that you are so. Christian Science is absolute; it is neither behind the point of perfection nor advancing toward it; it is at this point and must be practised therefrom. Unless you fully perceive that you are the child of God, hence perfect, you have no Principle to demonstrate and no rule for its demonstration. By this I do not mean that mortals are the children of God, — far from it. In practising Christian Science you must state its Principle correctly, or you forfeit your ability to demonstrate it.

(Signed) MARY BAKER EDDY

Mrs. Eddy's rejoicing over the healthy state of the church was further augmented in the month of November, 1909, by a letter received from the Associate Manager of the Committees on Publication, Willard S. Mattox, which was published in the *Sentinel* with these words from Mrs. Eddy:

Hear, O Israel. The following letter from Mr. Willard Mattox tends to comfort, reconcile, and elevate the waiting hearts of all Christian Scientists:

I have just returned from a six-weeks trip to the Northwest and to the Pacific coast, where I attended meetings of the state committee on publication and assistants. It may interest you to hear briefly of the nature of these meet-

ings and of some of the conditions prevailing in the field.
The energy and vigor of our great western country and of
the Pacific coast are proverbial, and I found that this
typical western alertness was characteristic of the Christian Scientists and of their work.

The meetings were everywhere well attended, and the
Scientists seemed eager to get any message that would improve the quality of their service and make them more
intelligent and more effective workers in our great Cause.
I was most hospitably received, and it made me especially
happy to notice everywhere a hearty and generous desire
to support the Directors and all of the activities at headquarters. There were many expressions of grateful appreciation of the Directors and others connected with The
Mother Church. One man, who came to the meeting at
Portland, Ore., traveled ninety miles over the mountains
in a stage-coach before he reached the railroad line. This
shows how keen the Scientists are for anything that will be
a benefit to them.

What impressed me most and what pleased me most,
were the evidences of the loving regard in which you are
held by Christian Scientists everywhere. Your wise leadership is recognized, and the genuine love for you which is
being constantly expressed, is so substantial and so potent
a force for good that I feel sure it must encourage and sustain you. One gentleman, at the meeting at Los Angeles,
said that he did not want the meeting to close without expressing his thanks for what he had got out of it, that the
point which had impressed him most was the necessity for
shielding and protecting our Leader. He said he could see,
as never before, that this was one of the practical ways in
which we could prove our gratitude and affection.

The subject-matter of the meetings seemed to be interesting and helpful to those who attended, and I sincerely
hope, and have every reason to believe, that much good
will result from this series of conferences. If the churches
and societies of each state are brought into closer fellow-

ship, if the ties are strengthened which unite in a common cause The Mother Church and the branch churches, if individual thought is aroused to more scientific and more consecrated activity, the purposes of the meetings will have been achieved.

And this month of November, 1909, which had witnessed the subsidence of controversy in New York, the founding of a beautiful outpost of the faith in the great city of London, and the arousing to a closer, vital relationship with The Mother Church of the whole Pacific coast, gave Mrs. Eddy also the comfort of being able to reconcile her son, George Glover, to her wise plans for him. The consummation of an agreement took place and was signed on November 10, 1909, between Mrs. Eddy and her son and her adopted son, by which settlement she transferred to George W. Glover and his family the sum of $245,000 and to Ebenezer J. Foster-Eddy the sum of $45,000. The sum given to her son, George Glover, was inclusive of the trust fund previously created by which she had conveyed securities valued at $125,000 to the guardianship of her counsel for his benefit, but which he had previously rejected, and also funds already paid for the benefit of himself and family. Her son and adopted son professed themselves satisfied with this settlement and executed deeds relinquishing all their present and prospective rights or expectant interests in their mother's estate, either as heirs-at-law or legatees under any previously made will of Mrs. Eddy. They severally acknowledged that full particulars of her estate had been made known to them. The settlement was brought about through a series of

conferences held between General F. S. Streeter, Mrs.
Eddy's counsel, the Honorable Henry M. Baker,
Mrs. Eddy's trustee, and former United States Senator William E. Chandler, counsel for the sons. On
July 16, 1910, two younger grandsons arrived at her
home at Chestnut Hill, they having come East to visit
her on her eighty-ninth birthday.

It seems proper to state here that Mrs. Eddy
throughout her life yearned with the natural solicitation of a mother over her son and grandchildren; she
made various and repeated efforts to guide and direct
them, to see that they were comfortably situated, and
that her grandchildren were being properly educated
and reared. She did not believe, however, that they
required vast sums of money or great luxury to ensure
their happiness, for she herself lived simply, never indulging in luxury. But she had given nearly fifty
years of arduous labor to promulgate the doctrine of
Christian Science and to establish the Christian
Science Church as the guardian in the world of this
truth. She had accumulated a fortune which has been
conservatively estimated at $2,000,000 at the time of
her leaving this world. This had been largely the result of the sale of her writings, though some of it had
been earned by the investment of the money from her
books in securities. It is proper to say that the church
which grew up on the basis of her doctrine, the church
which so widely bought and read her books, had contributed largely to this fund. It was therefore eminently just, and revealed Mrs. Eddy's sincerity of motive and dearest purpose, that she should have left in
her last will this sum to The Mother Church of Boston

for the carrying out of a specific plan, to advance the cause of Christian Science.

After the demise of Mrs. Eddy the details of her will greatly interested the world. This was largely because her sons endeavored to have its provisions set aside. Mrs. Eddy's will gave $10,000 to each of her four grandchildren in addition to the previous settlement with her sons; it gave bequests to her secretary, Calvin A. Frye, and her companion, Mrs. Laura E. Sargent, long faithful in her service, as household stewards. It provided for the lifting of the debt of Second Church of Christ, Scientist, New York City, and the sum of $100,000 to be set aside for a trust fund to educate Christian Science practitioners. The residue was left to The Mother Church as above set forth. The will was probated in Concord, New Hampshire, January 17, 1911, by Mrs. Eddy's executor, one of the former trustees of her estate and her cousin, Honorable Henry M. Baker.

CHAPTER XXIII

LIFT UP THY GATES

O F Mrs. Eddy's daily life it is no longer possible to speak in the present tense as it was happily one's privilege to do at the time of writing the chapter of this book, "The Leader in Retirement." Mrs. Eddy has since then passed beyond the veil which an all-wise Providence wraps around our period of mortal living, sheltering His children from the burden of a too great knowledge and the splendor of a too glorious vision. Her acts are no longer subject to mortal inspection. But of the time intervening between January 26, 1908, when she took up her residence at Chestnut Hill, and that evening of December 3, 1910, when she gently and silently withdrew from the theater of the world's activity, a period of nearly three years, it is possible to speak briefly and simply.

Her suite of rooms at Chestnut Hill had been arranged almost exactly like the rooms she used at Pleasant View, save for the fact that in this larger house she retained for herself a private sitting-room beside her study. The suite was in the southeast corner of the mansion and was therefore sunny, and commanded a view of Brookline reservoir, adjacent well-kept estates on the Old Orchard Road, and a distant view of the Blue Hills. The house being in the midst of twelve acres was secluded; the landscape architecture of Brookline is world famous and Chestnut Hill towered above a vista which fell away from the rear of the mansion in beautiful gradations. The bay window of Mrs. Eddy's study was encircled by a balcony which extended under the windows of her bedroom. Access to this was had through French windows opening like doors and here Mrs. Eddy was accustomed to walk to refresh herself for the renewal of her work. In summer her own grounds and the adjacent estates became a veritable paradise of lawn and shrubbery, of flowers, birds, and bees. Mrs. Eddy's grounds were like an Italian garden falling in terraces to the beautiful flower court.

The interior of her study and bedroom were kept much as at Pleasant View. The bedroom was most simple, having a three-quarter bed of walnut and a bureau and dressing-table of the same wood. In the study her flat-topped desk stood in front of the bay window, her easy chair behind it. She could turn in this chair to a small bookcase which held the books most often required, she could look out over the hills, or, turning in the opposite direction she could command a view of the driveway and the gates which opened on Beacon Street. It became more and more her habit to sit here looking out at those gates. After coming to Boston she took her usual daily drive around the reservoir and through the charming country roads and boulevards. At Chestnut Hill she resisted the idea that she must drive or be reported ill, and claimed for herself the privilege of respecting her business claims or considering the welfare of her horses in inclement weather. Nevertheless her drives were an almost invariable custom with her for an hour after luncheon. On these outings she was usually accompanied by Mrs. Sargent, who has said that she was pleased at the sight of little children in the care of their nurses whom they often passed, and would kiss her hand to them and smile at their return of her salute. She regarded them, trooping along under the care of their nurse-maids, as her little colony of neighbors whose innocent looks and ways made the roads and gardens populous with tender ideas.

Mrs. Eddy's daily routine continued about the same at Chestnut Hill as it had been at Concord. Her household was increased by several members, which the larger house gave opportunity for accommodating and the larger needs of her affairs made necessary. Adam H. Dickey was now her secretary, and the assisting secretaries were Irving C. Tomlinson and William R. Rathvon. Mr. Frye remained in the capacity in which he had been so long employed, and Mrs. Rathvon assisted Mrs. Sargent. Various members of the household were summoned from time to time to Mrs. Eddy's study for conversation, and these hours with their Leader became sacred opportunities to each one, as day after day melted into eternity. Also at regular intervals she received members of her larger household, the officers of The Mother Church, who waited upon her for that loving advice which should hold their course true in the voyage of experience which devolved upon each.

It was in the days toward the end of her earthly pilgrimage that Mrs. Eddy grew accustomed to sit after her evening meal with chair turned toward the vista before her home. She looked long at the drive,

watching for the light to come in the electric globes
on either side of the iron gates. She would sit here far
into the twilight and evening until the stars twinkled
in the night sky above the lights at the gate. So she
would often in silence commune with the thoughts
which filled her consciousness, sometimes reaching
out her hand to the tiny electric light which rested on
her desk and pressing its button illuminate a page of
her Bible or Science and Health.

On the first day of December she declared her
wish to take her usual drive, and this proved to be her
last drive. This was Thursday, a pleasant day, and all
the bright, frosty beauty of early winter lay over the
wooded country, the balsam of the evergreens faintly
perfuming the air. Mr. Frye and Mrs. Sargent accompanied Mrs. Eddy on the drive, and were observant of
the heavenly smile with which she surveyed the distant hills before stepping into the carriage. On the
drive she passed her little neighbors as usual, lifting
her hand slightly to them as she passed each merry
group, the smile deepening in her eyes and settling
faintly about her lips. When she had reached home
she rested for a while in her study and then asked a
student to bring her pencil and tablet. On the tablet
she wrote:

"God is my life."

Her message seemed written for the world, for
though she spoke to her family after that, these were
her last written words.

It was apparent to those who were used to her
habits of living that she was withdrawing from them
minute by minute after this drive. On Thursday eve-

ning she had her supper in her bed-chamber. On Friday she arose and was dressed, and remained for almost the usual hours in her study, but did no writing. She retired to her bed that night not to rise again in this world. Members of her household watched with her and she spoke with them, assuring them she felt no pain. She was conscious that her students were opening their minds to the realization of Life; this conscious thought was, as it had been for fifty years, her great and only physician. As one falling asleep, at a quarter before eleven o'clock, Saturday night, she ceased to breathe, passing out of earth consciousness.

In compliance with laws of Massachusetts which require that a medical examiner shall issue a death certificate where there has been no physician in charge at the hour of physical dissolution, Dr. George L. West of Newton Center, medical examiner for the district, was summoned early Sunday morning. Dr. West, after the usual investigation, pronounced death due to natural causes and issued the customary certificate.

In the New York *Herald* for December 5, the unusual experience of the medical examiner is described in these words:

The request to Dr. West that he go to the magnificent home of Mrs. Eddy in Chestnut Hill and view the body with the idea of granting a certificate of death was received about nine o'clock in the morning from Edward F. Woods, an alderman of Newton Centre, and Dr. West departed at once for the house in Brookline. On reaching there Dr. West was ushered at once into an upper front room in which on the bed, and clad in a heavy white robe, was the body of the Leader of the Christian Science cult. There were several persons in the room at the time, and several others were observed moving about other parts of the house by Dr. West as he entered and as he left. They were members of the Christian Science faith.

"To me it merely was the performance of a perfunctory duty," said Dr. West in comment. "Although, had I realized at the moment that I was in the presence of the body of a woman who had ruled thousands for many years, I might have been impressed with the importance of the official service I was performing. What struck me most as I looked into the dead face was its extraordinary beauty. She must have been a beautiful child, a beautiful maiden, and extraordinarily beautiful when in the full flower of womanhood. There still were substantial traces of beauty left in the white face reposing on the pillow. Time indeed had laid its hand lightly on her all through the years. Wrinkles there were, of course, but they were not the wrinkles that come with age, after a life fraught with the cares of a home, of the bringing up of children, or of a thousand and one things that arise in the life of the ordinary woman to furrow her brow. The wrinkles that she bore looked more as if some one had been playing a little prank, and as if they might be brushed away with the gentle smoothing of a hand. They did not seem to belong amid those features. The entire countenance bore a placid, serene expression, which could not have been sweeter had the woman fallen away in sleep in the midst of pleasant thoughts. I do not recall ever seeing in death before a face which bore such a beautifully tranquil expression."

The news of the passing from earth life of their Leader was given to the congregation of The Mother Church a little before twelve o'clock on Sunday, December 4, and at about the same hour telegrams were sent to the Christian Science publication committees (see note p. 340) throughout the world and a statement was given to newspapers through the Associated Press and local press representatives. Calvin Frye sent a personal telegram Sunday morning to George W. Glover, Lead, South Dakota, as follows:

I regret to inform you that your mother passed quietly away late Saturday night after a few days' illness. Funeral arrangements will be delayed until we are advised whether you or any of your family will be present and when we may expect you.

By reason of the lateness of the hour on Saturday when the great change transpired it was not necessary, indeed not possible, to give the information to the press before it was given to the Church. Christian Scientists, therefore, all over the world received the news from their readers' lips. The attendants at The Mother Church were informed at the morning service, elsewhere the news was given out at afternoon or evening services. In Boston the morning services were conducted as usual. There is seldom any break in the formality of the Sunday worship, and on the morning of December 4, 1910, there was none until just before the pronunciation of the benediction. Then the first reader, Judge Clifford P. Smith, paused impressively after reciting "the scientific statement of being," [1] and the reading of its correlative Scripture, I John, Chapter III, verses 1, 2, and 3, which are:

Behold, what manner of love the Father hath bestowed upon us, that we should be called the sons of God: therefore the world knoweth us not, because it knew him not.

Beloved, now are we the sons of God, and it doth not yet appear what we shall be: but we know that, when he

1 Science and Health, p. 468.

shall appear, we shall be like him; for we shall see him as he is.

And every man that hath this hope in him purifieth himself, even as he is pure.

Those who had already bowed their heads for the benediction lifted them as the reader, refraining from pronouncing it, began to deliver his message, and they received it in calmness to the close, after which there was no display of emotion beyond the fact that many eyes filled with tears. The message was given in these words:

I shall now read part of a letter written by our revered Leader and reprinted on page 135 of "Miscellaneous Writings":

"MY BELOVED STUDENTS:—You may be looking to see me in my accustomed place with you, but this you must no longer expect. When I retired from the field of labor, it was a departure, socially, publicly, and finally, from the routine of such material modes as society and our societies demand. Rumors are rumors,—nothing more. I am still with you on the field of battle, taking forward marches, broader and higher views, and with the hope that you will follow. . . . All our thoughts should be given to the absolute demonstration of Christian Science. You can well afford to give me up, since you have in my last revised edition of Science and Health your teacher and guide."

Although these lines were written years ago, they are true to-day, and will continue to be true. But it has now become my duty to announce that Mrs. Eddy passed from our sight last night at 10.45 o'clock, at her home in Chestnut Hill.

After the pronunciation of the benediction the congregation seemed held in an awesome spell, as the top crest of a wave seems to hang before it breaks. A flood of music from the great organ, at whose desk sat Albert Conant, seemed to release the suspension, the recessional being a Toccata of Bach's which filled the church with radiant tone color, like a burst of triumphant celestial voices. The solo had been the comforting Twenty-fourth Psalm, phrases of which seemed yet to circle under the vast dome, or sink into the hearts of the devotional hearers:

> Lift up your heads, O ye gates;
> And be ye lift up, ye everlasting doors.
> Who shall ascend into the hill of the Lord?
> Or who shall stand in his holy place?
> He that hath clean hands, and a pure heart.
> Lift up your heads, O ye gates!

On Thursday morning, December 8, services of interment were held at Chestnut Hill. All the world seemed covered with white snow. It was a bright, cold day and the sun gave to the snow a brilliance which made it appear a sacred, radiant carpet. More than one hundred guests, among whom were members of Mrs. Eddy's family, her personal students of Boston, the members of her household, and the officers of The Mother Church, also a few distinguished jurists and statesmen, assembled in the parlors of the house. They sat in silence from about a quarter before eleven until the hour struck, after which Judge Smith read the Ninety-first Psalm, and portions of St. John, thirteenth and fourteenth chapters, also passages from Science and Health. Mrs. Carol Hoyt Powers, the second reader of The Mother Church, read Mrs. Eddy's poem, "Mother's Evening Prayer," and Our

Lord's Prayer was recited by all. A procession then
formed to pass the bier, a ceremony which was performed with deliberation and consideration for the
earnest desire of each one present to gaze upon the
features of the departed Leader.

Sunshine filtered through the partly drawn white
shades and rose-colored draperies of the drawing-
room, especially in the southeast corner of the second
drawing-room where in the bay window on a cata-
falque stood the bronze casket, a sheaf of pink roses
across its foot. Enshrined therein was a pallid,
waxen figure, like a perfect model or masque of life,
the gray hair brushed from the white brow whereon
seemed written in memorable expressiveness the
word "Principle." The figure was clothed in a simple white silk gown over which was wrapped a shawl
of white lace, stretching from throat to feet, as
though loving hands had wound this mortal clay
with yards of filmy, fine-spun fabric as a last tribute
of tenderness.

When all had passed in slow defile, the bearers
closed the casket and lifted it to their shoulders. They
bore it out through the wide hall, walking after a
group of distinguished men who had been especially
singled out for the honorary escort. These loving students, some elderly and white-haired, some in the full
prime of stalwart manhood, walked proudly with their
burden, tears unheeded bathing their faces. At the
sight of these men escorting the bearers, a white-
haired jurist, a former governor of the Commonwealth, one of the foremost journalists of the United
States, and of these gifted men of the Church from

London, New York, Chicago, with that body lifted high among them, the wonder of the life which had animated that clay irresistibly swept the consciousness of all. That life, lived for forty years in the mountains of New Hampshire, which had come out of its hill refuge with God to a strenuous active life in the world for half a century, and but yesterday laid down its burden at ninety years, had well demonstrated that its Principle was Life and Love.

The casket was placed in a tomb of steel and cement at Mount Auburn, near Boston, where it was sealed, and guarded until the seal was inviolable. Here rest the ashes of the mortal garment of Mary Baker Eddy, near the shores of Lake Halcyon, tall English poplars rearing their plumy heads above it, and here is raised a memorial which shall mark an epoch in the progress of the world.

But it is well to be reminded that in Mount Auburn does not rest the real life and being of this great Leader. From the Atlantic to the Pacific the press of the great cities of America lifted the voice of tribute to her influence and work in the uplifting of the human race. No newspaper of importance in the civilized world failed to pay editorial homage.

As there was, following the interment of Mrs. Eddy, a widespread query as to whether Christian Scientists believed that Mrs. Eddy would return to this world, and whether there was some mystic doctrine involved in the placing of a guard at her tomb, it is well to record here the statement which Alfred Farlow gave to the world, and which was entirely based on Mrs. Eddy's own words. Mr. Farlow said:

There was no mysticism or supernaturalism in the minds of the persons who placed the guards at the entrance of Mrs. Eddy's tomb. It was done for the usual reasons. Many years ago Mrs. Eddy caused to be published the following statement: [1]

"A despatch is given me, calling for an interview to answer for myself, 'Am I the second Christ?'

"Even the question shocks me. What I am is for God to declare in His infinite mercy. As it is, I claim nothing more than what I am, the Discoverer and Founder of Christian Science, and the blessing it has been to mankind which eternity enfolds. . . .

"My books and teachings maintain but one conclusion and statement of the Christ and the deification of mortals. . . . There was, is, and never can be but one God, one Christ, one Jesus of Nazareth. Whoever in any age expresses most of the spirit of Truth and Love, the Principle of God's idea, has most of the spirit of Christ. . . .

"If Christian Scientists find in my writings, teachings, and example a greater degree of this spirit than in others, they can justly declare it. But to think or speak of me in any manner as a Christ, is sacrilegious. Such a statement would not only be false, but the absolute antipode of Christian Science, and would savor more of heathenism than of my doctrines."

Mr. Farlow continues:

While absolute Christian Science teaches that all is Spirit and Spirit's manifestation it does not ignore the relative fact — the temporal and false appearance — that in our present immature condition we have more or less of a misconception of creation which will improve and eventually disappear as we advance spiritually and that eventually we will be able to see all things as God sees them in all their spirituality and perfection.

[1] New York *Herald*, February 6, 1895; "Pulpit and Press," pp. 74, 75.

While Christian Scientists believe the Scriptural teaching that the time will come when there will be no more death, they take the common-sense view that centuries may pass meanwhile before this exalted spiritual estate is reached.

Christian Scientists believe the Scriptural teaching concerning the resurrection, that it means a putting off of mortality and a putting on of immortality. In other words a gradual spiritual growth wherein the individual makes a transition from a material condition to a spiritual condition.

They believe that the resurrection begins in this life and continues here or hereafter until perfection is attained. This is the belief that they entertain concerning Mrs. Eddy. They do not look for her return to this world.

Mrs. Eddy taught immortality of the individual consciousness, and immortality is everywhere the underlying spiritual significance of her writings. Before her individual form fades from our vision in the lovelier realms of a more etherealized condition, it may be well to fix her thought of the future life in her own words. She has said:

"Truth demonstrated is eternal life." [1]

[1] Science and Health, p. 289.

INDEX

INDEX